Life

in the

Spirit

World

*What Near-Death Experiences May
Teach Us About Life on the Other Side.*

Chas Hathaway

Table of Contents

Introduction...4
Near-death Disclaimers...7
The Near-Death Experience...13
    Leaving the Body..17
    The Void..22
    The Tunnel...28
    The Light..35
    The Life Review...37
    Meeting Loved Ones...66
    Meeting God or Jesus Christ..................................68
    Hell...80
Different Levels..98
Travel...105
Time and Space..111
Communication...129
Oneness and Unity...132
Landscapes and Cities..138
Bodies, Food, etc..165
Homes...187
Work and Technology...191
House of Learning..203
Abilities and Knowledge..217
Clothing...244
Music..248
Relationships..252
Goals, Dreams, and Ambitions..264
Beings, Animals, and Plants...270
Symbolism and Metaphor...287
Conclusion..292
Appendix..296
    Spirit World Evidence...296
    Explanations for Reincarnation..............................307
Glossary...330
Index..331

Introduction

When I set out on this journey, it was basically out
of curiosity. I simply wanted to know if I could glean from
studying near-death experiences any information about
the smaller details of the spirit world. I was raised in a
deeply religious home, and I have always been a faithful,
devoted member of The Church of Jesus Christ of Latter-
day Saints. And I wasn't just a follower of the faith—I
have spent much of my life studying the scriptures and the
words of church leaders. I had a deep conviction that there
was life after death. I knew that God is our Father, and
Jesus Christ is my Savior, and I knew that they loved us
intimately and *infinitely*. I firmly believed in life before life,
as well. I knew that we'd lived with God as spirits before
we came to this life, and that we would someday return. I
knew that families could be together forever, and that it
was intended that this blessing would be available to all of
us.

What I didn't know was the details. If a spirit doesn't have a body, what was experience in the spirit like? What did it *feel* like to be a spirit. And even beyond the essential, what is day-to-day life for a spirit? Does a spirit eat? Sleep? Does a spirit have a house, yard, or pets?

I knew there was a spirit world, and I knew it was good, but what was that world like? Is there a sunrise? Do they have work, hobbies, and recreation? Obviously, and I emphasize this, these minor details *don't matter*. They're not what we're here on earth to learn. There's obviously a reason for us to not remember our spirit home.

But if it's not *essential* that we learn the details of spirit life, then why am I writing this book on its details? Why publish something that is neither important to our salvation nor known for certainty to even be true? After all, the veil over our memories was brilliantly, even divinely designed. So why this book?

To be honest, the only certain answer I can give is, like I said, curiosity. Even at the beginning, I struggled and wrestled with the question of whether it was even appropriate to read the records of people's near-death experiences. After all, what if near-death experiences turn out to be something totally different than we think?

I can only answer that by telling you the deeper reason I wrote this book. The subject has changed my life. It's made me want to be more kind and loving than ever before. I always felt the necessity, but I think this subject has refined my understanding of the reasons for the necessity. More than anything, studying near-death experiences has given me a deeper love for my infinite spiritual family.

I set out to discover any details I might find about the spirit world, but what I found in the process was that God is in every detail of both the mortal *and* the spirit world.

And though I have to be so careful about how I say this, I can honestly say that I am seriously giddily excited to die—not that I plan to yet, of course, because I have a *lot* to do here before I go, and it would be a tragedy and a massive disappointment to try to jump the gun and hurry that process along (I'm here for a purpose, and it's not my place to know when my time is up), but when my time to die comes, I'm so ready!

Why? Because from what I've come to believe, the spirit world (spoiler alert) is absolutely *amazing*!

Near-death Disclaimers

I'm sure you knew this was coming. We don't know how much of what people say about their near-death experiences is true. There are liars out there (shame on them), and there are exaggerators (though in my experience, around this subject, there are far more under-exaggerators), and there are those who are misguided or deceived. There are those who are hallucinating from meds, drugs, or physical trauma. But a careful reading of near-death experiences leads one to be able to fairly discern who is being dishonest, who is mistaken, and who are having an honest spiritual experience. For the record, I have only shared the experiences of those who, in my judgement, fit into the latest category.

Since the individual sharing an experience is the only one who experienced their particular personal experience, every near-death experiences shared is (by definition) subjective and anecdotal. So how do we approach learning from these people? Well, it helps to keep a few points in mind, and as we progress through this book, we'll expound further on these. These are a few points to keep in mind as disclaimers as you read any near-death experience:

1. Background: The spirit world is full of people from all backgrounds, Christian, Buddhist, Atheist, or no belief system at all. In every background, there are both good and not-so-good spirits.

2. Not all spirits are fully an influence for good or evil. Just as on earth, they are at multiple levels of good and bad. A well-meaning good spirit can share something to a person that is either incorrect or easily misunderstood.

3. Though spirits are in a world where knowledge is abundant, there are still varying levels of knowledge and understanding in the spirit world. Even a well-meaning spirit can lack particular knowledge on a subject. In other words, while an honest, loving spirit may say something to an experiencer, the words may or may not actually be true.

4. (Extending from the previous points) A good spirit can still be incorrect in their *understanding* of the full truth.

5. (This may be obvious, but the point ought to be made) Spirits on the other side of the veil, from whatever background, probably understand more than we do about what spirits and the spirit world are like than mortals do.

6. A person who experiences the spirit world and then returns to tell about it has to come up with their own interpretation of their experience, and though they're experience may have been genuine, they may not be interpreting it correctly. In other words, believe their experience, but don't assume they're correct in their interpretation of the experience.

7. A person may gain incredible insight in their near death experience, but can only communicate it through the filter of the limited, broken, ego-centric mortal body to which they have returned. Basically, we're getting the experience filtered through their mortal person, not unfiltered from their immortal spirit.

8. People returning from the spirit world are often made to forget details of events and/or words from a near-death experience. It's possible that some of the details they don't remember would make the details the do remember make a lot more sense.

9. The veil is strong, and can mask anything from memory to intelligence capacity, and it is impossible to know from an account how much

else was masked from an experiencer at their
return.

10. We are mortal, and can therefore not fully
comprehend spirit nor the spirit world.

Now, some of these points may seem confusing,
others may seem redundant or obvious, but I hope they'll
make more sense as we go along. I make these points
because these are the things I had to continually remind
myself of during my study. Sometimes an experience
would be so far into left field that I'd have to put it away
and say, "Yeah, I'll shelf that until I get more information,"
and other times things would be so familiar and ordinary
that I'd wonder if the person actually just had a dream.

The fact is we can't always tell. The point is to take
everything you read with a grain of salt and let each piece
act as a puzzle piece in a stack of pieces that may or may
not belong to the puzzle we are trying to solve.

I may refer to these disclaimers throughout the
book, so you might want to dog-ear this page or
something. But don't let the disclaimers frighten you away
from reading about near-death experiences. If you keep
these points in mind, you may find that a study of near-
death experiences can completely change your life, your
mind, and your heart, in remarkably beautiful ways. What
I'm sharing in this book is my take on all of this.

To get the bigger picture, you'll want to study the
experiences yourself. If you want to study the hundreds or

thousands of near-death accounts yourself, a good place to start is to Google, "The International Association for Near Death Studies," or IANDS. Another fantastic one (and probably more comprehensive one, as far as the number of accounts is concerned) is the Near-Death Experience Research Foundation, or NDERF. There are other organizations that study this topic, but these seem to be the biggest and most comprehensive I've discovered so far. Their goal is not to steer you toward particular conclusions about the afterlife, but rather to provide enough recorded near-death accounts for people to be able to study, explore, and learn for themselves what, if anything, is going on as far as near-death experiences are concerned. From written to audio to video accounts, you can find plenty to study.

I've also included references to the experiences from which the samples I share are taken so you can go and read the rest of the experience.

And then of course there are books, websites, and scads of individual Youtube videos of people sharing their experiences. Not to mention, you probably know at least a few people personally who have had some kind of near-death experience. The secret is to start asking around. Don't be invasive, but be supportive and curious, and you'll discover that this isn't a rare phenomenon. It's actually extremely common, but because it's also very counter to modern culture and expectation, most such experiences are hushed or ignored. Many even feel that their experience is too sacred to share, and if they do feel that way, it's probably because they were told so during their experience. Never push someone to share when they express this idea.

Others are commissioned during their experience to share their experience upon their return in order to bless the lives of those around them. There is no one rule that fits all as far as sharing is concerned.

Another reason I'm writing this book is to unload a bit. I've learned so much that I feel like I'm going to pop if I don't write much of it down. And my ultimate hope is that it will do for my children, my family and friends, and of course all of you, what it did for me—that is, it has given me a new appreciation for both life, death, and our beautiful eternal relationship with our Father in Heaven and Jesus Christ.

The Near-Death Experience

In order to understand the context of the information given in the rest of this book regarding the spirit world, you'll want to know something about the near-death experience itself. After all, most of the details about the spirit world given in this book come from those who have experienced a near-death experience (NDE).

There are a few elements that are commonly found in near-death experiences that I will share. And while there does seem to be some level of sequence about the events discussed, no NDE can truly be called typical, since every individual has a unique experience. The elements I will introduce show up in varying degrees in people's near-death experiences. And while one experiencer may experience many or even all of these elements, another may only experience one or two. And they don't always happen in any particular order. We will discuss these elements after a discussion of the experience of death itself.

The Dying Process

First off, what does dying feel like? Obviously this varies based on the way a person dies, and anyone who has approached death can attest to the various levels of suffering or pain associated with the moments just prior to actual death. But what about that moment of death itself? What's it like?

Mohammed describes his death in these words:

"I was not anesthetized and didn't go into a coma. I remember a young woman around 22 years old entered the room. She seemed to be inexperienced and rather new to the hospital. She seemed beautiful and I wished I was not in this mess so I could talk to her and befriend her. But once again, I was distracted by unbearable pain and all the angry thoughts that were playing in my head. My attention was constantly shifting from my pain, to my angry thoughts, to this young lady; back and forth, and round and round.

"Suddenly, I felt that everything shifted. I felt a deep calm and peace engulfing me. This feeling was totally opposite to what I was feeling a few minutes ago. I was not angry anymore and I was seeing perfection in everything in the world and around me. Now I was feeling that everything is exactly the way it should be. Whenever I focused my attention to any object or subject, I could get deep and complete insights into that matter. I could even understand the chemical compositions of objects I looked at and all its physical and mathematical properties. I shifted my attention to that young woman again. She seemed a little different than a few minutes ago. I noticed that I am seeing her like 360 degrees around her, like I have totally engulfed her. I could see her thoughts and feelings as well. In fact, I felt that I am present in the entire hospital. I could see that she had a lot of sadness and worry about what she was seeing. She was thinking that it was so sad that this young man is dying like this. I tried to soothe her and tell her that I am alright and that nothing is wrong with me. In fact, I've never felt so good in my life. But she kept ignoring me, like she does not see or hear me.

"I noticed that she was staring towards a fixed point. I followed the direction she was looking and noticed that she is looking at the body of a young man who is lying on a bed. I was shocked because this man had striking similarities with me. I wondered who he was and why does he look so much like me? I even thought that maybe I have a twin brother I didn't know about who happens to be in the same hospital. I tried to tap on the shoulder of the young woman to get her attention but my hand simply went through her body without any resistance. I was so puzzled. I looked at myself and saw that I have a transparent and illuminated body. I was so confused and bewildered. I started to think to myself, *Am I dead? Is this my body on the bed? My mom would be so devastated. She is expecting me back home tomorrow.*

"As soon as I thought about my mom, I immediately found myself in front of her in our house in Isfahan. It is hard to explain, but strangely I was still in the hospital too. I was aware and seeing everything there as well, without any difficulty and confusion. My presence at home did not decrease my awareness and presence in the hospital at all. It was like I had split into two pieces with equal awareness. My mom was sitting on the patio and preparing some vegetables for the dinner. I went behind her to hug her from behind, in order to surprise her. Again to my surprise, my hands went right through her body. I tried to talk to her but she did not pay any attention to me.

"During this period as I thought about various friends and relatives, I instantly went to them while still present in previous places of the hospital, home, etc. For example when I thought about one of my teachers who I loved so much back in the days of high school. Suddenly I was beside him, while still in the hospital and also in my house in Isfahan beside my mom. I could immediately see all his thoughts, feelings, and all the things that were going on for him in life such as his thoughts, concerns, financial status, and health. I saw that I am no longer in his thoughts and heart. I could see that at that moment he was worried about his son. So I lost interest in him and left that scene. I thought about a few other relatives and friends and similarly I visited them as well. In every case I tried to communicate to the person I was visiting and make them aware of myself, to no avail. I realized that there is no use trying to communicate with people. Nobody could hear or see me." [1]

This account is so typical of NDEs that I think it's fair to say that the precise moment of death is usually quite peaceful, comfortable, and even enjoyable.

So with that, let's discuss the most basic elements common to the near-death experience.

Leaving the Body

Many people, at the moment of death, find themselves standing over their body, surrounded by doctors, family, or whoever is in the room. In that spirit form, many report having an expanded awareness of their surroundings, as well as a clear understanding of the thoughts, feelings, and even history of other people in the room.

Spencer records the following experience while standing over his body in the doctor's office as medical staff worked to return his body to life:

"Immediately people assembled to try to revive me. A doctor I had not seen before ran into the room, and for some reason, I immediately knew that he was having an affair with the nurse who started the IV. It came as a complete surprise to me that I knew this. I found my mind full of new information that was coming at me more

---

1   http://www.nderf.org/NDERF/NDE_Experiences/mohammad_z_nde.htm

from my heart than from my usual senses. I also knew that this nurse was recently divorced. I knew how much she valued and also feared this relationship with the doctor who was now working beside her to save me. I knew how hard she struggled to be good at her profession and still be a good mom to her two sons at home. I knew she had terrible financial problems. I knew everything about her, actually every detail of her life, and every decision, fear, hope, and action that had created her life. I could hear her mind screaming in fear. She was praying for help, trying to take control of her fear and remember her training. She desperately did not want me to die.

"I looked at the other people in the room and was astonished that I could hear their thoughts and know the details about their lives just as vividly as the nurse.

"There is a heightened spiritual sensitivity that comes from being dead that I had never anticipated or heard of before. I knew what everyone was thinking. Actually, it was greater than just knowing what they were thinking. I also knew every detail of their lives. I knew if they were good people or bad, if they were honest or corrupt, and I knew every act that had brought them to that state. It wasn't something I felt or could see, it was just knowledge that was in me.

"What was even more interesting to me was that I felt no judgment of them. I simply knew these things. It was like knowing a rose is red; it isn't something to judge, it is just the way that flower is.

"What I did feel, which was totally new to me, was a

rich compassion for them and their circumstances. Since I knew so much about them, I also knew their pains and their motivation for everything they had done that had taken them to this moment in time. I also felt their fear of losing me." [2]

Many, in this disembodied state, seek to communicate with the mortal people around them, especially loved ones. Spencer, after spending several moments next to his body, and finding an expanded ability to "read" the thoughts and feelings of the doctors and nurses at his bedside, set out to find his wife, who waited anxiously in the waiting room, unaware of Spencer's predicament, in hopes of receiving communication that he was okay. He floated out to her in the waiting room.

"I found myself standing right next to her. I could tell everything about her. I knew exactly what she was feeling and thinking. I knew what she had been reading in the magazine she had just placed on her lap. She was concerned and wishing someone would come tell her that I was okay, that I was not the one having the cardiac arrest.

"I thought, 'Here I am. I'm dead and out of my body, and I can't even communicate with you.' I felt empathetic for her fear and pain, but it struck me as a dilemma, even a bit funny. I could see her and hear her thoughts, but I couldn't talk to her in a way she could understand.

"I remember thinking, How am I going to let you

---

2   Pontius, John M, *Visions of Glory*, (Cedar Fort, Inc., Springville, UT, 2012), pp.5-6

know that I am all right even though I am no longer living?

"I began to wonder if she would be able to sense me, or hear me perhaps, if I moved through her. I asked her in my mind if I could have her permission to move through her. Even though she was not aware of me, her spirit answered, 'Yes.' I instinctively knew I had to have her permission to do this. I understood this, but I'm not sure why or how. It wasn't until later that I began to understand that entering another person's body is very invasive, and a righteous spirit always seeks permission if it is ever necessary. Evil spirits wait for opportunities when we are spiritually weak or after we have rendered ourselves vulnerable by disobedience to God's laws, and they enter into us in an act of spiritual violence.

"After her spirit responded that I could, I moved through her, and I immediately understood the difference between her physical body and her spiritual body. Her physical self had no realization that I was interacting with her. Her spiritual self, however, was fully aware of me and what I was trying to do and say. The problem was that like most mortals, she was only aware of her physical body—captive to it, so to speak—and not in tune with her spirit at that time in her life.

"I realized that moving through her was of no advantage to my trying to communicate with her. As I passed through her, I learned many things about what her experience in mortality had been like, what it felt like to be a woman, to be loved, to be protected, and now to be fearful for her protector. I understood her completely, including what it was like to have our sons and daughters, and how hard it was to live with my illnesses and struggles." [3]

Sometimes when people first leave their body, they don't realize they're dead.

Pegi Robinson, at the moment of drowning in a pond, says,

"I started choking, my throat—it felt like it could burst, and I thought about my mom and my sister up at the house. And as I thought about them, I saw them. I saw them in the kitchen getting stuff to bring down. I felt their emotions, just calmly and lazily getting things, taking their time.

"Then it felt like I went to sleep and woke up, because all of a sudden I felt different. I wasn't choking, and in pain, and scared anymore. Suddenly it was like I had just woke up—that relaxed feeling you have when you just woke up.

"It wasn't muddy water anymore. The water was now a real pretty, light, transparent green. So I wasn't scared, because it wasn't dark, I wasn't having any trouble breathing. And my first thought as a five-year old child was, *My parents lied to me! They said, 'be careful, don't go in too deep or you'll drown!' And I didn't drown, because apparently I'm breathing because I feel just fine!*" [4]

---

3   Pontius, John M, Visions of Glory, Springville, UT, Cedar Fort, Inc., 2012, pp.19-20

4   Pegi Robinson, from a podcast interview, https://neardeathexperiencepodcast.org/pegi-robinsons-near-death-experiences/

The Void

The void is something that many people experience when they first get to the other side. It's a complete, utter darkness, but not necessarily frightening or negative at all. For most, the void is comfortable, thoughtful, and anticipatory.

Bettie J. Eadie describes,

"I saw my body still lying on the bed about two and a half feet below me and slightly to my left. My three friends were still there, waiting for me. Again I felt their love and the joy they felt in helping me.

"As I was filled with their love, somehow I knew that it was time for me to move on. I also knew my dear friends, the monks, would not be going with me.

"I began to hear a rushing sound.

"When you are in the presence of enormous energy, you know it. I knew it now. A deep rumbling, rushing sound began to fill the room. I sensed the power behind it, a movement that seemed unrelenting. But although the sound and power were awesome, I was filled again with a very pleasant feeling — almost hypnotic. I heard chimes, or distant bells, tinkling in the background – a beautiful sound I'll never forget. Darkness began to surround my being. The bed, the light by the door, the entire room seemed to dim, and immediately I was gently drawn up and into a great, whirling, black mass.

"I felt as if I had been swallowed up by an enormous

tornado. I could see nothing but the intense, almost tangible darkness. The darkness was more than a lack of light; it was a dense blackness unlike anything I had known before. Common sense told me that I should have been terrified, that all of the fears of my youth should have risen up, but within this black mass I felt a profoundly pleasant sense of well being and calmness. I felt myself moving forward through it, and the whirling sound became fainter. I was in a reclining position, moving feet first, head slightly raised. The speed became so incredible that I felt that light years could not measure it. But the peace and tranquility also increased, and I felt that I could have stayed in this wonderful state forever, and knew that if I wanted to, I could.

"I became aware of other people as well as animals traveling with me, but at a distance. I could not see them, but I sensed that their experience was the same as mine. I felt no personal connection to them and knew that they represented no threat to me, so I soon lost awareness of them. I did sense, however, that there were some who were not moving forward as I, but were lingering in this wonderful blackness. They either didn't have the desire, or simply didn't know how to proceed. But there was no fear.

"I felt a process of healing take place. Love filled this whirling, moving mass, and I sank more deeply into its warmth and blackness and rejoiced in my security and peace. I thought, *This must be where the valley of the shadow of death is.*

"I had never felt greater tranquility in my life." [5]

While the description of a void may sound somewhat troubling, only occasionally does the experiencer have negative emotions during their brief stay in the void.

One such fearful individual was George Rodonaia, who, as an atheist, was shocked to find that he still had conscious, clear thought.

"The first thing I remember about my near-death experience is that I discovered myself in a realm of total darkness. I had no physical pain, I was still somehow aware of my existence as George, and all about me there was darkness, utter and complete darkness—the greatest darkness ever, darker than any dark, blacker than any black. This was what surrounded me and pressed upon me. I was horrified. I wasn't prepared for this at all. I was shocked to find that I still existed, but I didn't know where I was. The one thought that kept rolling through my mind was, 'How can I be when I'm not?' That is what troubled me.

"Slowly I got a grip on myself and began to think about what had happened, what was going on. But nothing refreshing or relaxing came to me. *Why am I in this darkness? What am I to do?* Then I remembered Descartes' famous line: 'I think, therefore I am.' And that took a huge burden off me, for it was then I knew for certain I was still alive, although obviously in a very different dimension. Then I thought, *If I am, why shouldn't I be positive? That is what came to me. I am George and I'm in darkness, but I know I am. I am what I am. I must not be negative.*

"Then I thought, *How can I define what is positive in darkness? Well, positive is light.* Then, suddenly, I was in light; bright white, shiny and strong; a very bright light. I was like the flash of a camera, but not flickering—that bright. Constant brightness. At first I found the brilliance of the light painful, I couldn't look directly at it. But little by little I began to relax. I began to feel warm, comforted, and everything suddenly seemed fine." [6]

Linda Stewart experienced a similar darkness, and though it seemed to her all-encompassing, it didn't frighten or worry her.

"Although I knew I was not in the lifeless body lying on my bed, and that the eyes and brain I had previously identified as mine, were in that inanimate object with which I no longer identified, I was still aware of sight and thoughts and sensations. I observed my new reality with tranquility. Slowly I looked around and below me I saw a vast, endless blackness. Like a void or black hole, I was irresistibly drawn toward the darkness. Gradually, I felt myself sinking toward it. I thought, without fear or any emotional reaction, *Isn't that strange?* I had been so afraid I was going to be judged and sent to either heaven or hell. But it appeared I would simply disappear into the dark

---

6   George Rodonaia, https://www.near-death.com/science/evidence/some-people-were-dead-for-several-days.html

nothingness. As even my new awareness waned, I yielded to the heaviness overtaking me as darkness filled my mind. My vision became obscured as I began to merge into the blackness.

"Offering no resistance, I released my hold on any remaining shred of consciousness and personal identity. At the very moment I felt the last of me disappearing into nothingness, I was suddenly buffeted by a powerful, energetic force that swooped beneath and lifted me, carrying me upward.

"Barely conscious, my only awareness was a sensation of rising. I seemed to be traveling upward at an unimaginable speed. A clean sensation of wind rushed over my face and body with tremendous force and yet there was no discomfort. Vast distances seemed to fly by me and the higher I rose, the more my head cleared. I became aware of a deep sense of peace and warmth that permeated my senses. Confused, because the energy that had enveloped me had a definite presence, I tried to see what was happening and who was carrying me; who or what cared so deeply for me? I felt peaceful and loved immeasurably. I knew I was in the arms of a being who cherished me with perfect love and carried me from the dark void into a new reality." [7]

Sharon describes encountering such a void during her near-death experience.

"I wrapped or cocooned within what felt like a warm, soft, thick, black, velvet blanket. I could see myself in this

---

7   Linda Stewart, https://www.near-death.com/experiences/notable/linda-stewart.html

cozy blanket as well as outside of myself. And I felt so warm, and safe, and protected. You know how on a cold night, when you're really tired, and you climb in bed and you just wrap yourself up in a blanket and go to sleep, and you feel so comfy? That's what it felt like.

"I knew there was a presence with me, and all around me, and I couldn't see the presence with my eyes, but I knew that it was God.

"I didn't have any worry, or fear, or anything, but I called up in a fetal position inside this beautiful velvet blanket. I could see through it, and I could see stars and planets. It was almost as if I was a baby again, and I looked at those things with amusement. You know, *Oh, okay, that's cool!* But I felt more comfortable inside this black encasement, or whatever it was—this blanket.

"There was no sense of time. It seemed like I was there for a long time, and I just kind of hung there, suspended among the stars, wrapped in this black thing.

"I heard a conversation—and I don't know if it was God talking to someone else, or God talking to my soul.

"I had to make a decision at that point whether I was going to stay, or if I was going to go. And I think God held me suspended there for awhile because *I* would have made a hasty decision." [8]

---

8   Sharon Milliman, from a podcast interview, https://neardeathexperiencepodcast.org/sharon-millimans-near-death-experiences

The Tunnel

Many people, either at the moment of death, after finding themselves out of their body, or after spending an indeterminate amount of time in the void, discover a tunnel, conduit, or hallway of some sort, and find themselves drawn into it. As they enter the tunnel, they tend to speed up until they reach a remarkable speed, which many intuitively feel to be much faster than the speed of light.

This tunnel is described in many ways, and while many travel this tunnel alone, others sense or see others around them.

While having an emergency surgery, Rachel says,

"My body succumbed to the anesthetic, but I was quite aware still—very disinterested in what they were doing down there on me (my body), and started ascending. It seemed to be the most natural thing to ascend. I was in a tunnel and it seemed things were soaring by me.

"I knew there were two male entities along side of me as I sped in this tunnel. They were Angelic Beings. I knew that and they were like escorting me up. (At least it seemed up. I don't know.) Then all of a sudden, I saw my paternal Grandmother, just radiant and glowing with light coming to me with elation on her face and her hand outstretched toward me. She was smiling. She was like in a mist or cloud? Her hand was trying to reach mine for an embrace. I could somehow sense there were other people with her like a welcome wagon party or something and I had extended my hand to grab hers. I somehow was so surprised and said, 'Grandma what are you doing here?' She'd been dead many years." [9]

During a cardiac stress test, Sammy walked on a treadmill, and explains the following:

"During the first stage of my test, I felt a crushing pain in my chest. It was as if someone had placed a giant vice on my chest. I remember the doctor asking me if I was okay and beginning to fall, but I don't remember landing on the treadmill or floor.

"After that, my memories are bits and pieces of images and feelings. I remember going through a tunnel or tubular passage with a loud rushing noise in the background. I do not remember entering or exiting the tube.

"The next thing I remember was being drawn toward a magnificent light of immeasurable brilliance. As I moved toward the light, my first [deceased] wife intercepted me. She was happy to see me but concerned because it was not time for me to be there. I knew she was happy and contented in her present form. I don't remember her telling me any of that. I just knew it." [10]

One woman, who died after complications following giving birth, relates,

---

9   Rachel, http://www.nderf.org/Experiences/1rachel_probable_nde.html
10   Sammy, http://www.nderf.org/Experiences/1sammy_nde.html

"Once again, traveling with the speed of thought, I found myself approaching what looked like a tunnel. Naturally curious and also quite cautious, I stepped up to the ribbed opening. The tunnel was tall enough to walk into, but it appeared to narrow as it progressed. It was a dark color, brownish, grayish, pinkish, and felt soft, like velvet. As I investigated, I was drawn to look to the far end, towards the brightest light I had ever seen. The light was alive. Imagine a powder snow that falls off an evergreen tree into the wind, and the sun catches it falling, each flake is a translucent rainbow sparkling in the wind. That is what it was like, only more magical, because it was alive. I decided I had to go and see it no matter what the cost.

"As I arrived at the end of the tunnel and stepped into the light, I noticed golden egg-like shapes of light moving. I can't exactly say how I realized this, but within each golden shape there was a recognizable person." [11]

Though many describe this tunnel through which they pass in their journey toward the light, it is described in many ways (such as a cave, a tube, the center of a tornado, a vortex, a wormhole, a hallway, a shaft, a corridor, or road) with such a variety of details that one is led to think that perhaps the tunnel itself is unique to each person, and perhaps even unique to each experience.

Pam Reynolds describes:

---

[11] IANDS, *It is Here in Our Bodies that the Lessons of Love are Manifest*, 17 February 2017, https://iands.org/research/nde-research/nde-archives31/newest-accounts/1198-it-is-here-in-our-bodies-that-the-lessons-of-love-are-made-manifest.html

"There was a sensation like being pulled, but not against your will. I was going on my own accord because I wanted to go. I have different metaphors to try to explain this. It was like the Wizard of Oz—being taken up in a tornado vortex, only you're not spinning around like you've got vertigo. You're very focused and you have a place to go. The feeling was like going up in an elevator real fast. And there was a sensation, but it wasn't a bodily, physical sensation. It was like a tunnel but it wasn't a tunnel.

"At some point very early in the tunnel vortex I became aware of my grandmother calling me. But I didn't hear her call me with my ears... It was a clearer hearing than with my ears. I trust that sense more than I trust my own ears.

"The feeling was that she wanted me to come to her, so I continued with no fear down the shaft. It's a dark shaft that I went through, and at the very end there was this very little tiny pinpoint of light that kept getting bigger and bigger and bigger.

"The light was incredibly bright, like sitting in the middle of a light bulb. It was so bright that I put my hands in front of my face fully expecting to see them and I could not. But I knew they were there. Not from a sense of touch. Again, it's terribly hard to explain, but I knew they were there." [12]

After a horrendous car accident, in which she and

---

12   Pam Reynolds, https://www.near-death.com/science/evidence/people-have-ndes-while-brain-dead.html

her son were killed, one mother found herself with her son in a tunnel:

> "I remember one of the EMTs saying, 'We just lost the Mother too.'

> "Then my son and I were walking hand in hand through a dark tunnel. After we came to the end of the tunnel, loved ones and friends who had died were waiting for us. Then Jesus walked over to me and said that I had a choice; I could stay in Heaven or go back to Earth. He said that he would show me what would happen in my life if I was to go back to Earth but I was not going to remember any of it. I remember that my life was going to be hard and full of pain. I looked at my son and told him that I loved him very much; I then took his hand and placed it in my Uncle's hand.

> "I then told Jesus and my son that I had to go back to Earth because my daughter had nobody but me to care for her. In a blink of an eye, I was back in my body and still in the ambulance." [13]

Grace Bubulka-Hatmaker also experienced a tunnel:

> "While I was at the hospital room ceiling I was somewhat stationary. Now I was in motion. I was proceeding slowly in an upward and outward direction, slightly angled to the left. I was aware of being surrounded but I didn't know by what or by whom. At first it just seemed like a foggy grayness about me. As the speed of my upward and outward movement increased,

---

the enclosing fog seemed to have a bright ending at the distance. I remember at the early moments of moving ahead through this enclosure a brightness to my left where I could see through the cloud-like tunnel. Beyond the walls of my tunnel was a shimmering, glowing light. The light contained an infinite number of specks within it. The specks were moving about. Some specks were going fast, some slow. They were all going in different directions yet none ever touched or impacted with each other. The only comparison I can draw with what I saw was what a person can see if you look into a sunbeam. It looked like the dust particles that ride within a sunbeam. I remember smiling to myself (or at least having a happy, knowing feeling) that I was akin to these specks and they were journeying as I was between realities.

"I was also very aware of being helped through this transition. I was in the company of an innumerable amount of others who were just like me. It was as though they were family... that I didn't know or I had forgotten. They knew all about me and were there to celebrate, comfort, ease and move me ahead. There was no sense of recognition but I knew they were there to help.

"My tunnel structure thinned along the sides but the light ahead was beckoning me. I was intensely attracted to reaching the light. As the sides of the tunnel became clearer, the light ahead became brighter and closer as my speed increased.

"The level of joyous anticipation I was feeling was indescribable. At this point I had no insight into what any

of this was about. I did not think I was dead. I knew I felt
like a spirit or a disembodied person. I knew that the real
'I' continued to exist in the absence of my earthly body. I
had a sense of heightened knowing, of peace and of
assured expectancy.

"As I neared the warm, glowing radiance ahead of me,
I felt pure ecstasy. I was in the beginning of the light. I
was part of the light. The light was part of me... but the
light was more." [14]

Diane Goble described her tunnel as a vortex:

"Suddenly, I was whisked away and found myself
traveling rapidly through a vortex toward a beautiful
white light in the far, far distance. I continued to
experience an overwhelming feeling of love within me
and around me. There was no fear, no anxiety, and no
worry. I even felt as if I'd done this before and was
remembering that I was going home. I was filled with joy.
I had no sense of a body, no feeling of limitations or
boundaries. Yet, I was still me and aware that I was
having this experience." [15]

Jack's discription of the tunnel is interesting—
unique, with more detail than is often given, yet fitting of
other descriptions.

"After a few moments, I blacked out. The next thing I
knew I was watching a kind of movie of my life. Not a
whole life story as some people experience but only some

14   Grace-Bubulka-Hatmaker, https://www.near-death.com/experiences/notable/grace-bubulka.html
15   Diane Goble, http://www.nderf.org/Experiences/1diane_g_nde.html

great and happy childhood memories. I don't know how
long this lasted but after this I was in a tunnel and out of
body. I realized that my body was behind me but I was
afraid to turn around and look. But then, being of a
nature that is very analytical, I began taking an interest in
the tunnel itself. There was an array of colors—not bright
like psychedelic colors but rather pastel and soothing.
They rotated with the entire tunnel. In a way like colors
move in a kaleidoscope.

"I can remember vividly being extremely aware of
moving further and further into this tunnel and being
fully aware of having all the natural feelings of having a
body but not being able to see it. For example, I would
move my fingers and all the sensations were there without
a physical form to identify them with.

"I never saw a bright light before me or any god figures
or anyone. I just continued deeper and deeper into the
tunnel and I was having a great time of it." [16]

The Light

One of, if not *the* most common element of the near-death
experience is experiencing what is often referred to as *the
light*. This is a light that seems to go far beyond any
experience with light we can have on earth. Not only is it
brighter than any earthy or cosmic light, but it is
completely, utterly, and unquenchably filled with love.

Ned Dougherty had a heart attack and died, and

---

16   Jack, http://www.nderf.org/Experiences/rjack_m_nde.html

after passing through a remarkable tunnel, describes,

"Suddenly, I was enveloped in this brilliant golden light. The light was more brilliant than the light emanating from the sun, many times more powerful and radiant than the sun itself. Yet, I was not blinded by it nor was I burned by it. Instead, the light was a source of energy that embraced my being.

"I was alone in the glow of this light and suspended before a magnificent presence. I immediately believed that I was in the presence of God, my Creator. I felt that God was embracing me, and he had love for me, a love greater than any love I had ever known on Earth. I realized that God was bestowing his light of love on me, as his light transformed from a brilliant golden light to a pure white light. As I became more accepting of God's love, the light of God became brighter, of a pure whiteness beyond description. When I sensed that my spiritual being had received God's love to the point of overflowing, I became aware that God was stabilizing and energizing my being in preparation for my mission. I realized that I would be returning to earthly life and that God was preparing and orienting me for that return.

"God began to imbue me with universal knowledge. I realized that I had always thirsted for this knowledge and I wanted to absorb as much as I could. As I remained suspended in God's light, I felt this knowledge penetrate and absorbed by my spiritual being. This knowledge was flowing through me in the same manner as God's love, pulsating through my being.

"As I became more receptive to the idea that I was in God's presence, He became more available to me. He was infinitely wise and knew everything about me. He knew that I wanted to know where I had gone wrong, and He showed me. He showed me that I had stopped searching for universal knowledge, and that I had blinded myself to my origin and to the meaning of existence." [17]

In Betty J. Eadie's book, Embraced by the Light, she describes a light penetrating the darkness:

"I saw a pinpoint of light in the distance. The black mass around me began to take on more of the shape of a tunnel, and I felt myself traveling through it at an even greater speed, rushing toward the light. I was instinctively attracted to it, although again, I felt that others might not be. As I approached it, I noticed the figure of a man standing in it, with the light radiating all around him. As I got closer the light became brilliant—brilliant beyond any description, far more brilliant than the sun—and I knew that no earthly eyes in their natural state could look upon this light without being destroyed. Only spiritual eyes could endure it—and appreciate it. As I drew closer I began to stand upright." [18]

The Life Review

One of the most profound elements of the near-death experience is what many have come to refer to as the life

---

17   Ned Dougherty, *Fast Lane to Heaven*, Hampton Roads Publishing; Revised edition (September 1, 2002)

18   Betty J. Eadie, Embraced by the Light, (Gold Leaf Press: Carson City, Nevada, 1992), 40

review. This is more than just your life flashing before your eyes. Sharon describes from her NDE:

> "By this time, I was given the information that I had died and was entering Heaven. It was like an infused knowledge. It was given as a simple fact. There was no feeling of fear or shock. I felt like I was floating. It felt good, so I didn't fight it. Then, as people gathered around me for support, I was given my life review. I was shown my life; everything I had ever said and done was shown to me. It was like watching a black and white movie on a reel. There was no feeling and no judgment at all. It was right then that I learned that God does not judge us. We judge ourselves, standing there before Him in all of His glory and perfection while we watch our lives pass in front of us.

> "For me, all He did was love me throughout the review of my life. Not a word was said, and it was over in a blink of an eye. It was after the life review that I heard a male voice say, 'What you put out into the universe will come back to you.'" [19]

In experiencing a life review, there are certain aspects of the experiencer's life that seem to get more emphasis than others. There are some things that are gloriously "applauded" and others that are viewed with compassion and empathy. Among the elements given great emphasis, love for all forms of life seems to be a priority. Mohammed Z shares the following from his near-

---

19 http://www.nderf.org/NDERF/NDE_Experiences/sharon_m_nde.htm

death experience:

"One example of my life review was when I was a little kid. We were traveling by car and stopped somewhere along the way. There was a river not far from the road and I was asked to go and bring some water in a bucket from that river. I went to fill up the bucket but on my way back, I felt that the bucket was way too heavy for me. I decided to empty some of the water to make the bucket lighter. Instead of emptying the water right there, I noticed a tree that was alone by itself in a dry patch of land. I took the effort to go out of my way to that tree and emptied some of the water at the tree base. I even waited there a few seconds to make sure the water is soaked in the soil and is absorbed. In my life review, I received such an applaud and joy for this simple act that it is unbelievable. It was like all the spirits in the Universe were filled with joy from this simple act and were telling me, 'We are proud of you.'

"That simple act seemed to be one of the best things I had ever done in my life! This was strange to me, because I didn't think this little act was a big deal and thought I had done much more important and bigger things. However, it was shown to me that what I had done was extremely valuable because I had done it purely from the heart, with absolutely no expectation for my own gain.

"Another example of my life review was when I was a 10 years old boy. I had bullied and mercilessly beaten another boy who was also around my age. He felt tortured and deeply hurt. In my life review, I saw that scene again. The boy was crying in physical and deep emotional pain. As he was walking in the street crying and going back home, he radiated negative energy which affected everything around him and on the path. People and even birds, trees, and flies received this negative energy from him, which kept propagating throughout the Universe. Even rocks on the side of the street were affected by his pain. I saw that everything is alive and our way of grouping things in categories of 'alive' and 'not alive' is only from our limited physical point of view. In reality everything is alive. I felt all of the pain and hurt that I had inflicted upon him inside of myself. When this boy went home to his parents, I saw the impact that seeing him in that state had on his parents. I felt the feeling and pain it created in them and how it affected their behavior from that point forward. I saw that as a result of this action, his parents would be always more worried when their son was out of home or if he was a few minutes late." [20]

From his near-death experience, Leonard describes his life review as follows:

"Suddenly, there was a vision in front of us that played like a movie of my life. We could see moments that I had actually lived on earth with my living family. Not only was I viewing those moments, but I was feeling them happen again as if I were there. I was very much loved by the living family members who played with me, and I was blessed with a large family that enjoyed spending time

---

20   Mohammed Z, Near Death Experience,
      http://www.nderf.org/NDERF/NDE_Experiences/mohammad_z_nde.htm

together. Mother and I could select any part of time in my
life that we wished. I know that I witnessed my birth
again. Nothing was said or explained about my birth, but
I remember seeing something about it that stuck in my
mind. More detail will be explained by me later in this
story. I could feel myself being pulled out into the world,
and I did not like the way the doctor handled me.

"One of my favorite visions came at a time when I
recognized living members of my family sitting around
the kitchen table in my parent's home. I cried out with joy
when I saw my mom's parents, Steve and Bess L. There
were other relatives there as well, but grandpa Steve
stood out the most as he played a game with me. I was
sitting safe and comfortable in my mother's arms. I
reached my hand out toward grandpa, and he playfully
made a face like he was going to gobble down my fingers.
He did it in a funny and animated way that made me
squeal with delight. I pulled my arm back to hug mom in
safety. Then I turned around to stick my arm out again,
and grandpa acted like he didn't see me, but suddenly my
fingers were in his mouth, and he pretended to munch on
my hand in a silly way. Once again I squealed with delight
before retreating to mom. The whole family was
laughing, and it was very pleasant to experience it again.
Grandpa Steve truly loved to play with his grandchildren,
and we all loved him very much. He could get a baby to
laugh and play like nobody I have witnessed before, and
there were many babies for him to play with because he
had eleven children of his own. One of my aunts is only a
few years older than me.

"Mother and I held each other many times as we
watched the different episodes of my short life. Then she
came to one incident that was pointed out as important
because I had done something that she wanted to correct.
I lost my temper with my older brother, Steve. I
remembered it happening because the high level of anger
I felt toward him made it easy to lash out. I hit him on the
head with a toy baseball bat. It was made of wood, and it
hurt him more than I knew at the time. Mother pointed
out that losing one's temper to the point of hurting
another is wrong, and I should never do it again. I
understood completely, and I have never hit or injured
another human being since. Not on purpose anyway." [21]

While some re-experience their life in full (in a few
moments' time), others see it in either a holographic or
movie-like manner.

"Then after a space of time the length of which I could
not determine, a bright light began to glow in the room.
Brighter and brighter it became! It was somewhat above
me and in front of me. I tried to look but was almost
blinded from it! I held my hands up in front of me and
could make out the appearance of a figure setting on
some type of seat.

"Then without warning it happened.

"'What have you done with your life?'

"The voice penetrated my very being. I had no answer.

"Then to my right I saw what seemed to be like a

21   Leonard K. http://www.nderf.org/Experiences/1leonard_k_nde.html

movie, and I was in it. I saw my mother giving me birth, my childhood and friends. I saw everything from my youth up. I saw everything I had ever done before my eyes!

"As my life played out before my very eyes I tried to think of good things I had done. I was raised in church and had been very active in church functions.

"Yet as I pondered on this, I saw a man in his car that had ran out of gas. I had stopped and given him a lift to a local store about a year ago. I had bought him some gas as he had no money and helped him get on his way. I thought to my self, *why am I seeing this?* The voice was loud and clear.

"'You took no thought to help this soul and asked nothing in return. These actions are the essence of good.'

"I saw all the people I had hurt as well and was shown how my actions had set in motion the actions of others. I was stunned! I had never thought of my life having an effect on the actions that friends, family, and others I had met would take. I saw the results of all I had done. I was not pleased at all.

"I looked on until the events came to an end. Indeed I had done so little with my life. I had been selfish and cruel in so many ways. I was truly sorry I had done so little. Then again loud and clear I heard the voice speak again, 'You must return.'

"I did not want to return though. I was content to stay and longed to stay even after the things I had seen and heard.

"'I have so many questions,' I replied, 'things I need to know and don't understand.'

"'You must return and help others to change by changing your life. Physicians will want to perform surgery on you. Do not let this happen. If you do you will never walk again. You will be visited by one who will bring you answers to the questions you have. When I call you will come again. You will recover from all that has happened if you do these things.'" [22]

Many experience not only their own life review *and* the perspective of those around them throughout their life, but they experience those perspectives from multiple angles and viewpoints. Thomas Saywer shares the following account:

"I know that I experienced a total life review, but I have never been able to fit it properly into any of that basic chronology. It had to have happened from the center of the tunnel or the movement within the tunnel, prior to what I call the confrontation with the light. And the best way to describe it is to give you an example.

"When I was around eight years old my father told me to mow the law and cut the weeds in the yard. We had a cottage in the back and a double house in the front. Aunt Gay, my mother's sister, lived in the cottage out back. Aunt Gay is a very delightful person; she's a friend of mine as well as my aunt. Aunt Gay was very clever, as was

---

22   Ricky Randolph, https://www.near-death.com/experiences/notable/ricky-randolph.html

my mother I'm sure it's a genealogical trait! Everybody
liked Aunt Gay. She was always fun to be with. Certainly
all the kids thought she was a cool person to know. She
had described to me her plans for some wild flowers that
grew on little vines in the backyard.

"'Leave them alone now, Tom,' she said, 'and as soon
as they blossom we'll make tiaras for all the girls, and
flower necklaces for some of the guys.'

"And then everybody could pitch in and she'd teach
them how to weave such things. That was typical of her.
We were looking forward to that.

"However, my father told me to mow the lawn and cut
the weeds. Now, I had several choices. I could explain to
my father that Aunt Gay wanted the weeds left to grow in
this particular area. If he said to cut them all, I could have
explained to Aunt Gay that father had just told me to
mow the lawn and said to cut that patch of weeds. I could
ask if she wanted to make her request to my father. Or, I
could methodically and deliberately go ahead and mow
the yard and cut the weeds. I did that. Well, worse that
that, I even came up with a name for the job. I called it
'Operation Chop-Chop.' I deliberately decided to be bad,
to be malicious.

"And I went ahead, feeling the authority that my
father gave me when he told me to cut the grass and the
weeds.

"I thought, "Wow, I got away with it. I did it. And if
Aunt Gay ever says anything I'll just tell her father told

me to do it. Or if father asks me I'll say, well that's what you told me to do."

"And I would be vindicated. It would be okay; it would be a perfect Operation Chop-Chop. End of story. My Aunt Gay never said a word to me. Nothing was every mentioned. I got away with it totally.

"Guess what? I not only relived it in my life review, but I relived every exact thought and attitude; even the air temperature and things that I couldn't have possibly measured when I was eight years old. For example, I wasn't aware of how many mosquitoes were in the area. In the life review, I could have counted the mosquitoes. Everything was more accurate than could possibly be perceived in the reality of the original event.

"I not only re-experienced my eight-year-old attitude and the kind of excitement and joy of getting away with something, but I was also observing this entire event as a thirty-three-year-old adult; with the wisdom and philosophy I was able to attain by that time. But it was more than that.

"I also experienced it exactly as though I was Aunt Gay, several days later after the weeds had been cut, when she walked out the back door. I knew the series of thoughts that bounced back and forth in her mind.

"*Oh my goodness, what has happened? Oh well, he must have forgotten. But he couldn't have forgotten, everyone was looking forward to Oh no, knock it off. Tommy is he's He's never done anything like that. I love him so Oh, come on, cut it out.*

Gee, it was so important. He had to know... he couldn't have known.

"Back and forth, back and forth, between thinking of the possibility, and saying to herself:

"Well, it is possible. No, Tommy isn't like that. It doesn't matter anyway, I love him. I'll never mention it. God forbid, if he did forget and I remind him, that will hurt his feelings. But I think that he did, though. Should I confront him with it and just ask him?

"Thought-pattern after thought-pattern. What I'm telling you is, I was in my Aunt Gay's body, I was in her eyes, I was in her emotions, I was in her unanswered questions. I experienced the disappointment, the humiliation. It was very devastating to me. It changed my attitude quite a bit as I experienced it.

"I experienced things that cannot be perceived. I watched me mowing the lawn from straight above, anywhere from several hundred to a couple of thousand feet, as though I were a camera. I watched all of that. I was able to perceive and feel and know everything about my Aunt Gay regarding our relationship in that general time frame and regarding Operation Chop-Chop.

"In addition to this, and what is probably more important, spiritually speaking, I was able to observe the scene, absolutely, positively, unconditionally. In other words, not with the horrendous emotional ill-feelings that my Aunt Gay experienced not knowing for sure, and yet being afraid to question for fear that she would inflict some kind of dis-ease, or ill feelings on my part. Heaven forbid, if I did it by accident and her reminder would hurt my feelings. And yet she experienced hurt in losing the flowering weeds, not being able to do the things for all the children she had promised, and constantly questioning whether I could have done it on purpose. I did experience that in this unconditional way, with this unconditional love that is only God's eyes, or the eyes of Jesus Christ, or the light of Jesus, or the light of Buddha enlightened, the spiritual entity.

"It is that combination that is God unconditionally, not 'Boy, Tom, you sure did a good rip-off,' or 'There, Tom, now do you feel bad enough?' Or, 'You sure were bad.'

None of that, only, as in the eyes of God, simple, pure, scientific observation, complete, totally, non-attachment. No judgmental aspect whatever. This is simultaneous with the total devastation of what I created in my aunt's life. And the arrogance, the snide little thoughts, the bad feelings, and the excitement of what I created in my own life at that young age, that was one event." [23]

This ability spirits have to relive their lives in their entirety doesn't seem to be limited to the self. Some spirits share their own life review with other spirits—essentially allowing them to share the experience of the other's life.

During his near-death experience, Spencer saw the events preceding his own life, including the lives of his mortal parents, with all their thoughts, fears, and motivations.

"When I saw my biological father's perspective on these events, and his leaving and divorcing my mother, I learned that it was not all selfishness, not all narcissism, as I had supposed all of my life. When he realized my mom was pregnant, he knew, or thought he knew, that I would be better off without him. That may not have been true, but that was his perception. He knew his life choices would only damage me. He did not leave me because of selfishness or because of alcoholism alone, as I had been taught. He truly thought that I would be better off without him.

"I understood his pain, his childhood, his conflicts with his parents, and his relationship with his father. I understood those things perfectly, which no mortal can understand while yet mortal; not even my father understood it this way. I understood for the first time that my father actually loved my mother very much. His weakness and history handicapped his ability to let love triumph in his decisions. I also saw Christ's love and Heavenly Father's love for him, no matter what mistakes he had made.

"This served to completely change my judgment of my mother and father and my assumptions of why they had done what they had done. This new perspective created great conflict in me because it changed almost every judgment and conclusion I had made during my life. It was all swept away a split second in this non-mortal time frame. I had seen things which now forced me to abandon my anger and resentment. It has literally taken me decades since then to reconcile what I was taught as a child with what I had seen really happen. At times my emotions and old thinking have taken up a bitter conflict within my mind and soul. This is the conflict that took so long to resolve because I knew the truth now, but my natural man fought against the spiritual insights gained through this non-earthly experience." [24]

Sara Menet describes a painful experience from her life-review during her near-death experience:

"Because I had lived in foster homes, I was called a rag doll and white trash most of my life, and kids making fun of me, and I had very low self-esteem. I went into a foster home... They lived in a beautiful home—it was the first time I'd ever been in a home that was lovely like that. The mother cooked health foods, and Joanne (my foster sister) was gorgeous. She had all these beautiful clothes, and she was so generous. She said, 'Anything you want to wear of mine (I came with two cotton dresses and a pair of tennis shoes), you can wear anything that I have.' And I was just like, 'Wow!'

"So coming from a life where people made fun of me, called me a rag doll and everything else—here I lived in this beautiful home as a foster teen, with this beautiful foster sister and her beautiful clothes. And we were kind of in the 'in' crowd. I was accepted because I was Joanne's foster sister.

---

24   Pontius, John M, Visions of Glory, Springville, UT, Cedar Fort, Inc., 2012, pp.11-12

"And there was this girl that kind was in our school, and the kids all made fun of her. And she kind of had facial hair. And the kids would in front of her go, 'Rachel, zzzzzzt!' like, 'You need to shave!'

"And Joanne and I would do it behind her back. We never did it to her face, but the terrible part was *I* was able to feel what Rachel was feeling. We would plan these parties and invite all the 'in' kids, and she would be there, and we'd never ask her if she wanted to come.

"I was able to feel Rachel's pain as though I were Rachel. It was so hurtful to me to see what we had done to her, and that I didn't help her!

"They talk about all these kids bullying in school today—they have *no idea* what they're doing! My pain was so great from that, I wanted to take it back, I couldn't change it. And the pain was so great! Just over something like that. Can you imagine people who really hurt people? After trying to find her for 30-40 years, I can't find her. She may have already crossed over. Then she'll know how sorry I am!

"Please don't hurt each other!" [25]

Spencer also went on to see his life as a young boy, being beat up by a school bully. Of the experience, Spencer says,

"I was frightened in my young life of the bullies in the school, especially of Jake. He was a year older, bigger, and

25   Sarah Menet, Iands Utah Meeting, September 2017,
      https://iandsutah.files.wordpress.com/2013/02/iands-11-09-sept-2011-sara-menet.mp3

just plain mean. He seemed to delight in terrifying me. At least once a week, Jake hit me or did something aggressive and mean to me. I went home with many bruises and black eyes because of him. Those were the days when adults figured it was best for boys to work out their problems and learn to stand up for themselves, so my mother and grandparents urged me to learn to defend myself rather than interfering in my life. I finally got up the courage in fifth grade to fight back. In my life rehearsal, I watched that day. I also saw my newfound courage from his perspective, which included the horrible abuse that he was receiving from his father.

"When I stood up to Jake and hit him back, it totally changed his thinking about his world. I saw that he felt powerless and victimized himself. My little act of courage showed him that he was not. He never bullied me or anyone else again. He was changed by that experience. He became my friend because I had unknowingly given him the key to his own freedom from tyranny. Our new friendship allowed Jake to resolve his own relationship struggles with his father. He was emboldened to stand up to his father because of my action. Just as Jake stopped bullying me, his father stopped abusing him when Jake refused to submit, and his dad actually left shortly after that.

"Seeing the impact that my friendship had upon him was a revelation to me. I had never suspected that there was any motivation for his bullying except meanness. After the vision, I understood why he had taken his frustration out on me and others.

"From my life rehearsal I learned that this was all divinely engineered, that we both needed this close relationship, and it had to start with his bullying me in order to heal him. I saw that I had agreed to all of this prior to our birth. Our divinely ordained friendship had a lasting impact in his healing and his relationship with his family, and upon me. I could not have learned these things without him.

"What I learned by seeing all of this was that our relationship was engineered by God and had a significant impact upon both of us. We both changed. I quit being afraid of bullies and of life in general. Not only did my actions begin the healing of his abuse, but his part in my life began my healing as well. I realized that fear was not necessary and that I could stand up for myself and actually make friends because of my courage. That realization still influences me today. Our relationship was ordained and engineered by God to save us both. In my thinking today, it was well worth the few bruises it cost me." [26]

Some who experience the life review even see future events that haven't taken place yet. Lisa, who died at the age of five, but then revived, explained

"The being of light knew everything about me. It knew all I had ever thought, said or done, and it showed me my whole life in a flash of an instant. I was shown all of the details in my life, the one I'd already lived, and all that was to come if I returned to earth. It was all there at

---

26   Pontius, John M, Visions of Glory, Springville, UT, Cedar Fort, Inc., 2012, pp.14-15

the same time, all the details of all the cause and effect relations in my life, all that was good or negative, all of the effects my life on earth had had on others, and all of the effects the lives of others that had touched me had had on me. Every single thought and feeling was there, nothing was missing. And I could experience the feelings and thoughts of all the other people involved myself, almost become them, which gave me pure experiential understanding of what brought other people pain, or joy, the positive or negative experiences and effects of my own actions.

"The being was not judging me in any way during the life review, even though I saw a lot of shortcomings in my life. It simply showed my life the way it had been to me, loved me unconditionally, which gave me the strength I needed to see it all the way it was without any blinders, and let me decide for myself what was positive, negative, and what I needed to do about that. I don't remember any details of the events that were shown to me, neither past nor future, but I remember what was most important.

"The being of light showed me that all that was really important in life was the love we felt, the loving acts we preformed, the loving words we spoke, the loving thoughts we held. All that was made, said, done, or even thought without love was undone. It didn't matter. It simply did no longer exist. Love was all that was really important, only love was real. Everything we did lovingly was as is was supposed to be. It was okay. It was good.

"And the love we'd felt during our lives was all that

was left when everything else, everything perishable in life, had vanished." [27]

Howard Storm talks about his life review, and says,

"I got to go through all those kinds of experiences in the company of these magnificent beings.

"When I was a teenager my father's career put him into a high-stress, twelve-hour-a-day job. Out of my resentment because of his neglect of me, when he came home from work, I would be cold and indifferent toward him. This made him angry, and it gave me further excuse to feel hatred toward him. He and I fought, and my mother would get upset. Most of my life I had felt that my father was the villain and I was the victim. When we reviewed my life I got to see how I had precipitated so much of that myself. Instead of greeting him happily at the end of a day, I was continually putting thorns in him in order to justify my hurt.

"I got to see when my sister had a bad night one night, how I went into her bedroom and put my arms around her. Not saying anything, I just lay there with my arms around her. As it turned out that experience was one of the biggest triumphs of my life...

"Every time I got a little upset they turned the life's review off for awhile, and they just loved me. Their love was tangible. You could feel it on your body, you could feel it inside you; their love went right through you. I wish I could explain it to you, but I can't...

---

27   Lisa, http://www.nderf.org/Experiences/1lisa_m_nde.html

"My friends explained, quite clearly, that all it takes to make a change was one person. One person, trying, and then because of that, another person changing for the better. They said that the only way to change the world was to begin with one person. One will become two, which will become three, and so on. That's the only way to affect a major change." [28]

In Renelle Wallace's near-death experience, she experienced both the incredible thoroughness of the life review, as well as insight into the few things that she *didn't* have to see or relive.

"Then I heard voices. It seemed people were traveling beside me somehow, although there was no room for them. I became aware of one person near me who was alone and not speaking. I couldn't see anyone; I just knew the person was there.

"The voices stopped and a brief scene flashed before me. A series of pictures, words, ideas, understanding. It was a scene from my life. It flashed before me with incredible rapidity, and I understood it completely and learned from it. Another scene came, and another, and another, and I was seeing my entire life, every second of it. And I didn't just understand the events; I relived them. I was that person again, doing those things to my mother, or saying those words to my father or brothers or sisters, and I knew why, for the first time, I had done them or said them. Entirety does not describe the fullness of this review. It included knowledge about myself, that all the

---

28   Howard Storm, https://www.near-death.com/experiences/notable/howard-storm.html

books in the world couldn't contain. I understood every reason for everything I did in my life. And I also understood the impact I had on others.

"A part of me began to anticipate certain events, things in my life I would dread seeing again. But most of them didn't show up, and I understood that I had taken responsibility for these actions and had repented of them. I saw myself repenting of them, sincerely wanting God to remove the weight and guilt of those terrible actions. And He had. I marveled at His sublime love and that my misdeeds could be forgiven and removed so easily. But then I saw other scenes that I hadn't anticipated, things that were just as awful. I saw them in horrible detail and watched the impact they had on others. I saw that I had let many people down in my life. I had made commitments to friends and family that I had just let ride until they were irreversibly unfulfilled. People had depended on me, and I had said, I'm too busy or it's not my problem, and just let it go. My cavalier attitude had caused real pain and heartache in others, pain I had never known about.

"I was shown a friend who I knew had suffered terribly in her life. She lived in a beautiful, spiritual world before she came to this life, and she had been confused and hesitant about coming here at all. But she was given the promise of good parents, family members, and friends, and she agreed to come for the experience and growth this life would afford her. I was shown that I was one of the key friends who had been given to her as a guide and help. Then I saw my own personal follies and uncaring attitudes. I saw how these had combined to mislead my friend and propel her into new mistakes and grief.

"I had messed up my own life, not really caring about the consequences, and in so doing had hurt her as well. If I had followed through on my obligations to myself and others, she would have lived an easier and more productive life. Until that moment I had never realized that ignoring responsibilities was a sin.

"What was happening? Why was I seeing all this? My mind spun with questions.

"Next, I saw a woman whom I had been asked by our local church leader to visit periodically. I was just to check up on her and see if she needed any help. I knew the woman quite well but was afraid of her constant pessimism and negativity. She was locally renowned for her bitterness. I didn't think I could handle the depressing influence she would have on me, so I never went to see her. Not once. I saw now that the opportunity to visit her had been orchestrated by Higher Powers, that I had been just the person she needed at that time. She didn't know it, and I didn't know it, but I had let her down. Now I lived her sadness and felt her disappointment and knew I was a cause of it. I had fallen through on a special mission to her, a responsibility that would have strengthened me over time. I had retreated from an opportunity for growth, both for me and for her, because I was not caring enough to fight through my petty fears and laziness. But the reasons didn't matter; I could see that, even now, she was living in sadness and bitterness, living through it just as I now experienced it, and there was nothing I could do to go back and help.

"I re-experienced myself doing good things, but they were fewer and less significant than I had thought. Most of the great things I thought I had done were almost irrelevant. I had done them for myself. I had served people when it served me to do so. I had founded my charity on conditions of repayment, even if the repayment was merely a stroke to my ego. Some people had been helped, however, by my small acts of kindness, a smile, a kind word, little things I had long since forgotten. I saw that people were happier because of my actions and in turn were kinder to others. I saw that I had sent out waves of goodness and hope and love when I had only meant to smile or to help in a small way. But I was disappointed at how few of these incidents there were. I had not helped as many people as I thought."[29]

It appears that some people are even shown the different choices they *could have* made. Yet along the way, we have more help than we often realize. One woman who died, upon finding herself out of her body and after flying high into space, shares:

"Then, wondering what to do in this new situation, I began to see my life played before me, like a holographic movie. What I mean by that is that I watched it in three dimensions, with all my senses employed; I was a witness to my own life, an objective witness. I say objective because I felt the feelings of everyone involved and saw

29   Wallace, Ranelle, *The Burning Within*, (Carson City, NV: Gold Leaf Press, 1994), pg. 91-94

each person's point of view, not just my own selfish perspective.

"The first scene that I saw was when I was about 2 yrs old, and I pushed my neighbor off my swing, sending him home crying; and I felt good because it was MY swing.

"In another there was a young man in college who fell in love with me quickly because he knew I was 'The One for him.' His passion and intensity frightened me, so I ran away without an explanation. I felt his pain. I'd broken his heart.

"During this review of my life I saw another theme. By not telling the truth when I was clear about how I felt, I kidded myself about sparing the other person or I avoided a confrontation by pretending confusion. I was shown how damaging this was. It is like a stone dropped into the middle of a still pond. The ripples go on till they meet the shore, then bounce and travel some more, acting and inter-acting. The consequences are felt in ways we can't even imagine.

"When it was over I felt confused. I said to myself, wait a minute, I didn't see any of my good deeds, not one time I gave or received love. And a voice said to me, 'The love you give and the love you receive are yours for all eternity; you only answer for your incompletions—all the things not said or done.'

"What I had seen made sense; I saw all my incompletions. Why hadn't someone told me? I could have done it differently.

"I also realized I was being shown all the paths not taken in my life. There were many paths available, paths seemingly effortless, virtual super highways, straight and well-lit with no speed limit, like the Autobahn in Germany. There were also twisting, wooded paths with rest-stops, like the beckoning roads through the country side, mysterious and dark, alluring because I couldn't imagine where the path might end or what adventures might await.

"We often choose this winding path because it is the model which has been set for us by our families. We don't believe we deserve the clear, effortless path, or it will be boring and uneventful, or it might be too visible, or not challenging or too adventurous. Also we are afraid that if we take the direct path, we will arrive at God too quickly and our lives will be over. Which, I might add, shows us how little we trust the Almighty. This is one way we perpetuate suffering.

"Then I was shown the times in my life where angels had been there to directly help me. They wore many disguises and I was appalled at my lack of recognition, and lack of gratitude, stunned at how loved and protected I had been in my relatively short life.

"At fifteen, I was in the hospital to have a cyst the size of a grapefruit removed from an ovary. The operation had gone wrong, and... an infection set in. As I lay in bed, I wanted to die. It seemed my life was only full of pain.

"A presence appeared at the side of my bed in the dark and kept vigil. As the sun rose in the morning and the rays shone in on my face, this presence said, 'Have heart, the best is yet to come...' Then he disappeared. I began recovering.

"In another instance while in college, I had been away out of state for a homecoming weekend and had to make it back to my dorm before curfew. There had been a comedy of errors during my attempts to return: I misplaced my ticket; the plane was late, etc. I had a one hundred and three degree temperature from strep throat, and no money. I got into Port Authority in NYC and realized I needed nineteen dollars and change to get a bus back to my college. I was sick and desperate when a man walked out of the crowd, handed me a twenty-dollar bill and said, 'Get back safely.' He was gone before I could say thank you. He was an angel.

"I was shown others and that these examples were just a few of many incidents. It took me awhile to absorb all that I was being shown. It felt like I was being broken open." [30]

In short, the life review appears to be one of the most powerful aspects of the near-death experience, because it is when you will see your life for what it *really* was, stripped of all the blindspots, excuses, and false assumptions. You might even say it's the moment you will see your life the way God sees it. And though the thought of this causes some to experience great anxiety, there

30   IANDS, *It is Here in Our Bodies that the Lessons of Love are Manifest, 17 February 2017,*
https://iands.org/research/nde-research/nde-archives31/newest-accounts/1198-it-is-here-in-our-
bodies-that-the-lessons-of-love-are-made-manifest.html

seems to be many things we can do to prepare for it.

First, we can strive to live loving, kind lives. That seems to be a really, *really* big one.

Second, we can pray and sincerely repent of things we've done that we know weren't right. We can strive to learn the lessons from those experiences now so that we don't have to be reminded of the lesson later. It appears from several near-death experiences that the experiencer doesn't have to relive the events that he/she sincerely repented of.

And even those who do relive those experiences are also accompanied by loving, warm, compassionate companions to help the person get through the experience.

The thing that really impresses me about the life review is the fact that the greatest praise seems to come for the simple acts of sincere, selfless love.

This concept of the life review, along with ability to experience others' life reviews may be an explanation for other aspects of near-death experiences that many religious people may struggle with. For example, the subject of reincarnation comes up occasionally in NDEs. Some are given a life review that was *not* the life they were leaving. When they return and tell others of the experience, they sometimes conclude that they have lived more than one mortal life. In fact, some suggest that they lived thousands of lives, either as a human, or as any number of other life forms.

But taking into consideration the ability to share or experience others' life reviews opens the possibility to the concept that while each person only comes here once, they may be able to "experience" the lives of untold numbers of others.

In order to be able to accept this theory, we have to keep in mind that even long-past spirits who have evolved in remarkable spiritual progress are still learning, and though a family member, temporarily returned home, may encounter said spirit, that spirit may be inaccurate in their suggestion that reincarnation is actually what is taking place. Even in that state, they may believe it to be so, as their perfect memories can experience the lives of others in their entirety.

Of course, this is speculation: a conjuring of possibilities based on what very little we know about spirits and the spirit world. Actually, my personal suspicion is that the ideas of reincarnation *and* shared life reviews are only wiry inaccurate skeletons of the true nature of what's really happening in both this world and that one. A further discussion on some alternative views to reincarnation can be found in the appendix of this book.

It's okay that we don't understand how this all fits, but being aware of the ideas gives us a frame to think on them. And the aggregate of all the ideas we learn may open our minds to new and fresh possibilities that will take much longer than this life to fully comprehend. As Henry shared from his near-death experience:

"I became aware of other voices, the orbs or other souls around me I could hear them communicating to each other. There seemed to be cliques of orbs that were together. They spoke to one another about their lives on Earth and all they had perceived and felt. They shared not only in words, but in sharing the experience. If one orb couldn't understand, it disappeared and then reappeared. The orb somehow went back to Earth and experienced that 'life' to further understand. I understood that here time did not exist and these beings could manifest themselves at any time on Earth they desired. These orbs, or rather 'souls,' would leave this realm, detach themselves with this universe, and return to the universe of our Earth. There they would live and die, then return and share the experience with all the other souls. A soul that could not understand the experience could go and live that life also to experience that life. I learned we have many lives, past, present and future.

"These souls, our souls, cannot experience certain things like pain, sorrow, hatred, and anger. Though these are negative things, it was important for them to understand and experience them. Perhaps to understand the motivations of human beings, or (and I believe this in my heart) to eventually evolve into a being like God—all knowing and understanding." [31]

Meeting Loved Ones

Duane shares his encounter with loved ones as he crossed the veil in this way:

> "On the distant horizon, silhouetted against the light, I saw what, at first, looked like an uneven line across the night-sky. As I drew closer, it grew into a line of people that spanned the horizon. As they came out to greet me, backlit against the light, I knew them all. Some of them were from my life on earth; others were not. There was my grandfather Amos, along with my favorite dog, Butch, his tail wagging in greeting. Both were central characters in the idealistic part of my childhood. There also was my wise-old-granddad Frank with his wry, bemused grin. Included in this welcoming was my sweet Aunt Eleanor and my favorite uncle, Sidney. There was even a man who lived on a ranch up the river from us, who always had been nice to me. He gave me a job, even when he really didn't need the help. I saw my favorite schoolteacher and various other people who had played a part in my life on earth but had gone on ahead. As wonderful as it was to see those whom I loved in my current life incarnation, there were others. There were also entities I had known and loved from other times and other places not of this incarnation." [32]

---

31   Henry W, https://www.nderf.org/Experiences/1henry_w_probable_nde.html

32   https://www.nderf.org/Experiences/1duane_s_nde.html

Ned Dougherty describes from his experience:

"I turned to my right, realizing that a group of spiritual beings had joined us on the celestial field. This event was indeed a homecoming for me. Among the group of spiritual beings, I recognized deceased friends and relatives from my life. I also recognized other friends from my spiritual life prior to my birth on Earth. I was filled with joy when I recognized my grandparents, aunts, and uncles who had died during my life. However, I was disappointed because I did not see my Dad among the group. I then recognized other friends from my life, including a girl from high school. I did not know she had died. The feelings of love and joy that I shared with these relatives and friends were far beyond the emotions I had shared with them during my life. As the child of an alcoholic and broken home, I did not communicate feelings to relatives or friends very well. In fact, I wasn't aware that I had many feelings. Most of my feelings were hidden inside.

"Now that I was at my homecoming as a spiritual being, the greetings were the kind that I had imagined took place in a healthy family. It seemed as if we were celebrating every major holiday, every birth and birthday, every wonderful event in all of our lives in a manner that we could never celebrate as mortal human beings. I wanted this celebration and homecoming to continue forever" [33]

Since the major focus of this book is about life in the

---

[33]   https://www.near-death.com/experiences/notable/ned-dougherty.html

spirit world, and much of that life includes experiences with family, friends, and loved ones, there will be more discussion about these in future chapters. But it's worth pointing out here, because the meeting of loved ones at the time of death itself is so very common. Not everyone meets loved ones immediately, but many (possibly the majority) do.

Meeting God or Jesus Christ

From our mortal perspective, the idea of meeting Jesus Christ or God may sound a little overwhelming, and some hesitate to suggest that they would want to do so. The opportunity is rare in this life, and if it happens, it is extremely sacred. We're taught to love, serve, and obey Him, but we're given the impression that we're likely never to see Him in this life. That may indeed be so for those who don't have a near-death experience. But to those who do, the opportunity is not only possible, but rather common—which suggests that for anyone who dies (which we all will), it will also be common.

From her near-death experience, Sylib describes,

"I stood there and suddenly I saw Jesus. It was quite an awesome shock to be standing in His presence. I was in such awe. I could not speak. My eyes were fixed upon Him. His hair was white like wool and hung down to His shoulders. His skin was like brass without one wrinkle. His eyes were like flames of fire and when He spoke, it was with great authority. Yet when He spoke it was kind and gentle and loving. When He spoke, it sounded like thunder rolling across the North Carolina skies but much louder than any I had ever heard. You would think I would have been afraid but I was not. Quite the contrary. I felt happy! I felt so happy, a feeling like none other I had ever felt.

"Then He told me to look and I saw a white cloud like form. Inside the white background, I was shown my life from beginning to end but only the painful parts. As He unfolded my life before me, He told me the reason all these bad things had happened and I understood every one of them. The unusual thing was, His lips never moved. It was as if His thoughts were sent directly to my mind and I saw and understood everything He told me. Then He said. 'All the bad things are gone. No more bad things are going to happen but you must go back because your work is not finished!'" [34]

Betty Eadie also met Jesus, and shares,

"I saw that the light immediately around him was golden, as if his whole body had a golden halo around it, and I could see that the golden halo burst out from around him and spread into a brilliant, magnificent whiteness that extended out for some distance. I felt his light blending into mine, literally, and I felt my light being drawn to his. It was as if there were two lamps in a room, both shining, their light merging together. It's hard to tell where one light ends and the other begins; they just

---

34   Sylib, https://www.nderf.org/Experiences/1sybil_s_nde.html

become one light. Although his light was much brighter than my own, I was aware that my light, too, illuminated us. And as our lights merged, I felt as if I had stepped into his countenance, and I felt an utter explosion of love.

"It was the most unconditional love I have ever felt, and as I saw his arms open to receive me I went to him and received his complete embrace and said over and over, 'I'm home. I'm home. I'm finally home.'

"I felt his enormous spirit and knew that I had always been a part of him, that in reality I had never been away from him. And I knew that I was worthy to be with him, to embrace him. I knew that he was aware of all my sins and faults, but that they didn't matter right now. He just wanted to hold me and share his love with me, and I wanted to share mine with him.

"There was no questioning who he was. I knew that he was my Savior, and friend, and God. He was Jesus Christ, who had always loved me, even when I thought he hated me. He was life itself, love itself, and his love gave me a fullness of joy, even to overflowing. I knew that I had known him from the beginning, from long before my earth life, because my spirit remembered him."[35]

After sharing an account of her near-death experience, in which she met Jesus Christ and God the Father, Lucinda Pottle was asked *how* she knew God was God, and how Jesus was Jesus. She replied, "You *know*. It isn't a guessing game up there. You *know!*" [36]

---

35   *Bettie Eadie, Embraced by the Light, (Gold Leaf Press: Carson City, Nevada, 1992),*

36   Lucinda Pottle, Iands group meeting audio recording, May 2012,

During her near-death experience Sharon Milliman saw many things and visited various areas. As part of this experience, she says,

"When I looked up, I saw a man sitting on the other end of the log next to me. The air was cool and comfortable and I could hear the birds singing their sweet songs. I knew the man was God. He had shoulder length dark, curly hair, a neatly cut beard, beautiful blue eyes, and a happy smile. He was about 6 foot tall and He wore a white robe and sandals. We sat there on the log together for the longest time just talking. He had a wonderful laugh and such sparkling happy eyes. He became silent for a moment. Then He turned and faced me. He looked into my eyes and in a quiet, gentle voice, He asked me 'What would you do if it were just me and you?'

"I looked at Him and asked, 'What do you mean?'

"He smiled and was so patient, like a father with a young child. He asked me again, 'What would you do if it were just me and you?'

"I looked down at my hands in my lap and I thought for a minute and then looked at Him again and said, 'I don't know what you mean.'

"He was still smiling and He very patiently explained, 'No parents, no children, no husband, no friends. Just me and you, no one else.' Looking into His beautiful face, I shook my head and kind of stuttered, feeling a bit intimidated and unworthy all of a sudden. I said, 'No, I

---

https://iandsutah.files.wordpress.com/2013/02/iands-11-05-may-2011-lucinda-pottle.mp3

would drive you crazy after the first ten minutes with all my questions and chatter and then you would not like me very much, if it was just me and you.'

"He just smiled at me. He was so patient and so loving. So gentle, in fact, that those feelings of inadequacy had began to disappear. He then got up and motioned for me to follow. We walked a short distance. Then, He showed me the whole universe with no one in it. There were no people, no buildings, no cars, no animals, and no trees. There was nothing but swirling, rainbow-colored gases, sparkling diamond stars, and spinning planets. It was breathtakingly beautiful, but it seemed so huge. I never realized how big the universe really was. It seemed like within a second we were back again sitting on the log by the stream and He asked me once again, 'What would you do if it were just me and you?'

"I was at a loss for the right words to properly answer His question. He waited.

"I found myself looking at a very large oak tree that was in front of me. I saw the details of the trunk and the little life-giving veins in the tender leaves and the roots beneath the ground. What I saw was not just a tree, but the individual parts that made up the whole tree. And I saw how important all these parts were to the life of the tree and how important the tree was to the environment around the tree and then I could see how all things are connected to each other and that every part was important in its own way. I studied this for a few minutes, feeling that my noticing this was exactly what God had planned and that this was a very big part of understanding what God was trying to teach me. Then, I answered Him.

"Now, I have no idea why I would have answered Him in this manner since I have never read the Quran in my life, I have never even seen the book nor do I know anything about the Islam faith, but I said, 'God, your hundredth name in the book of the Quran is *God is everywhere, God is nowhere and God is in me.*'

"He said, 'Yes, that is right, that it is, And…?'

"I looked at the tree again then back at Him and said, 'God, You made this tree, you are in this tree, so when I look at this tree I see you.'

"He looked at me, smiling that beautiful smile and He said 'Yes, and…'

"Then I began thinking about my parents and I said 'God, You made my parents, you are in my parents, so when I see my parents I see you.'

"Again, He said 'Yes, and…'

"He was trying to get me to think further. So I began thinking that there are people in this world who are cruel to others and there are those who have hurt me. I don't particularly care for these people so I said, 'God, There are some people who I don't really care for because they hurt others, but you made these people, you are in these people, so when I see these people, I see you'.

"He again smiled at me and He said, 'Yes, that is right.

Now, I have a question for you. When you look in the
mirror, what do you see?'

"I looked down again at my hands and I thought for a
moment, my normal response would have been
something like, 'I see me; No one special. Just me.' But
then I looked into His beautiful eyes and those feelings
melted away because of the deep love I saw there. Then, I
said, 'God, You made me, you are in me, so when I look in
the mirror, I see you'

"He said, 'Yes, that is right.' He seemed so happy and
He was smiling from ear to ear. And I could feel His joy
and His deep love surrounding me. I was completely
immersed in His love as He looked at me. To me, this was
so big. I could feel the hugeness of this revelation; I could
feel it just spinning in my heart and mind.

"I can see the beauty of God so easily in others all
around me, but it is much more difficult to see God's
beauty in myself. I find, even now, I have to remind
myself that I am special and that I am beautiful. Each and
every one of us is special to God. He made us; He is in us.
He doesn't make mistakes and he doesn't make junk. To
Him we are all important, we are all beautiful. He sees us
with perfect love. We are imperfect beings who He loves
perfectly. Perfect love makes our souls shine so
beautifully. What I had to learn was that real beauty
shines from deep within the soul. External beauty fades
with time, but real beauty comes from inside and never
fades because it is internal and eternal. I had to learn that
my worth as a human being isn't dependent on what

others think of me or whether they were happy with me or not. I also needed to learn that happiness doesn't come from an external source. In order to be truly happy, it has to come from inside my own heart. To God, I am me; that's all, just me. In His eyes, I am a perfect being 'just me'. My worth is in being who God made me to be. I don't have to make everyone else happy. What God wanted me to know was that He is always happy with me. What I have to do is be happy with myself and find Joy in my life. I have to stop worrying about what everyone else thinks. I need to see His beauty in myself.

"We finished our conversation and then we got up. We started walking through the forest and were met by two beautiful, ornately-gowned women who led me to a calm, serene lake at the end of the wooded area." [37]

Carol Vengroff had a direct encounter with Jesus Christ, and she was deeply touched by the experience:

"I had a most amazing communion with Christ... The Christ I met on the other side is nothing—*nothing* like the Christ I was taught about as a Presbyterian, and a Baptist, and a Catholic—I was raised in all the faiths. And He was just... the Man... the Spirit, the essence! There's the basic Christ that we all know, and that's who I saw, but it wasn't like we're taught down here, totally.

"And after I met Christ, I did understand there were other masters or other entities that are wise and Christlike, like Buddha, Krishna. I understood that Christ isn't necessarily the only great person to have come to earth. There were others, also. And I got to experience them, too, but my focus was Christ. That was the highlight of my experience...

"I recognized Him instantly... It was a reunion for us to be together again, so I recognized Him immediately... there was information that He shared with me. When I came back and my Sunday School teachers started saying He said this or that, I would just shoot up and say, 'No, He didn't mean it that way!' and I'd be so upset that I had to calm down because I remember what He meant—from Him...

"And He was beautiful! Oh my gosh, He was just so amazing." [38]

When Suzanne Freeman died during childbirth, she knew what was happening, and worried about her children. She tried to return to her body, but then Jesus appeared, and asked her to come with Him. She says,

"Have any of you ever wondered if when you saw the Savior, you would know who He was? I used to wonder that...

"When I saw Him, *it was Jesus!* He stopped me [from going back into my body], and when I looked up and saw Him, it scared me. I thought in my head, when someone dies, and Jesus gets you, it's your time. And in my head, I was thinking mortally (just because your spirit leaves your body, you still think mortally—there's like this

---

change that has to occur, I think—it did me, anyway). So I look up, and thought, *Oh, that's Jesus! It's my turn to die, and I'm NOT going to let that happen.* So I started squirming. I said, 'I need to go back!'

"He's like, 'Come with me.'

"I said, 'No, I have to go back!' And I started really kicking! Kicking and almost screaming.

"And I could feel his energy. He's like, *Okay, this isn't how it usually is.* He didn't say it, but I could feel it.

"I saw His deep, deep blue eyes, and I saw His hair. I didn't care—I was going to go back and be with my children. I had seven at the time.

"Anyway, He says, 'Come with me.'

"I said, 'No! I have to go back.' And then I started kicking and squirming even more...

"I almost got away!

"He says (out of pure frustration), 'But there's people who want to meet you!'

"And with that, I turned to Him and I said, 'Well then, you'll have to bring them to me because I'm not going with you.'

"And with that, He bust a gut laughing. All of a sudden, He just laughed, and I look up, and I thought, *Oh! That's the most beautiful* (And I can't describe it any better) *man laugh I've ever heard.*

"I used to say the most beautiful sexy man laugh, but I didn't figure that was a good thing to say to describe the Lord! But He has a perfect laugh. And it is forever etched in my mind. It's just this perfect, perfect laugh. They always say the Savior is perfect, but He has the perfect laugh, He sings perfectly, He has the most perfect blue, *deep* blue eyes I've ever seen.

"He was laughing for a little while. He really was. He had to get His composure back, and still giggling He says, 'I promise, you can come back!'"

Later in the description of her near-death experience, Suzanne again describes Jesus Christ.

"I wish you all could feel the love the Savior has for us. It is deep, and pure, and never-ending. I miss the piercing blue eyes. And there's times when I see people with blue eyes that are the Savior's...

"The Savior's color of hair—He had curly locks, about down past His shoulders—very thick. You could tell it was kind of course. And it had auburn highlights and blond highlights. It was a brown color, but it had auburn and blond highlights.

"My granddaughter has these auburn highlights in her hair, and she's twenty-two months, and she has so much hair, it's so thick. You could just put it in a pony tail and it's just so thick. I look at her and I think, *oh!* Jesus brings down little bits of Him in people, and I am just in awe of someone that has blue eyes and auburn colored hair. He looks like the pictures I saw. I just remember how much

He always wanted to touch me. I had my little space—I like to hug people, but I have my space. I just remember Him peering down at me and I could just feel how much He loved me.

"There was a point, when I was on the other side... I was allowed to feel His handprints, and His feet prints, and I could touch His side and feel a hole. I just knew what He did for us was perfect love. He didn't care about the pain. He cared about us. And I *felt it*. I felt the depth of it. I don't know how to describe it, but—the depth of what He's done for us all is—I just wish you could all feel what I felt." [39]

The Return to the Body

The most painful part by far, in nearly every example I can find of the near-death experience, is the return to mortal life. This is the unfortunate part of dying that most of us (hopefully) will never experience. But for those who do, the experience is enlightening because of all it can teach us about mortality, the body, and physical suffering.

Pam Reynolds, during her near-death experience, knew she would need to return to her body, and agreed to do so. After discussing a visit with her grandmother and other family and friends on the other side, she says,

"My grandmother didn't take me back through the tunnel, or even send me back or ask me to go. She just

---

39   Suzanne Freeman, from a Utah IANDS conference, 10 October 2011,
      https://iandsutah.files.wordpress.com/2012/12/iands-11-10-oct-2011-susan-freeman.mp3

looked up at me. I expected to go with her, but it was communicated to me that she just didn't think she would do that. My uncle said he would do it. He's the one who took me back through the end of the tunnel. Everything was fine. I did want to go.

"But then I got to the end of it and saw the thing, my body. I didn't want to get into it... It looked terrible, like a train wreck. It looked like what it was: dead. I believe it was covered. It scared me and I didn't want to look at it.

"It was communicated to me that it was like jumping into a swimming pool. No problem, just jump right into the swimming pool. I didn't want to, but I guess I was late or something because he [the uncle] pushed me. I felt a definite repelling and at the same time a pulling from the body. The body was pulling and the tunnel was pushing... It was like diving into a pool of ice water... It hurt!

"When I came back, they were playing Hotel California and the line was 'You can check out anytime you like, but you can never leave.' I mentioned [later] to Dr. Brown that that was incredibly insensitive and he told me that I needed to sleep more. [laughter]" [40]

Hell

I don't want to go into too much detail on this subject, because it can get fairly gruesome, but it is important to understand that some people experience what is often called *distressing near-death experiences*. These are

---

40   Pam Reynolds, https://www.near-death.com/science/evidence/people-have-ndes-while-brain-dead.html

experiences when people get to the other side and come across people, entities, creatures, and places that are at some level hellish in their content.

And while only a few experience truly frightening things during their near-death experience, I have yet to meet one that stayed long and didn't find their way out of a dark place or situation we might call hell. And almost always, the way out has come by calling upon God or Jesus Christ for deliverance.

Some experienced this hellish realm firsthand, while others see or are made aware of it from something of a distance.

Bonnie Burrows saw such a place, but never went there.

"The one place that I could not go was a very dark place. It was gray, and the spirits were gray. It wasn't like my concept of Hell or anything I have thought of or ever read about—even since then. It wasn't like these spirits were being punished. It was like they were punishing themselves, to a *great* degree. Just like I had great sorrow in my life review for anything that I caused pain. They were experiencing the pain that they had caused, and they were filled with sorrow. And it's like they were just shattering. But it wasn't like they were being judged. It was like they were judging themselves.

"And the angels were there to help them pull the pieces of themselves back. And I knew that was a *huge* process. And maybe a forever process, I don't know." [41]

Speaking of some of the people of this gray place, Lisa explains,

"When I saw the unborn spirits... there were burdened spirits teaching them. And when I asked about that, I was told that these were souls that had lived on this earth who had cause great pain, who had taught their children, and now they were trying to teach the children [soon to be born] in their line that were going to be born to resist and overcome and change what *they* had done."[42]

In other words, Lisa saw that many *post*-mortal perpetrators of abuse, alcoholism, or other spiritually damaging habits were sent to teach their soon-to-be-born descendants how to overcome the problems they had perpetuated in their own lifetimes.

While traveling through the tunnel toward the light, another woman named Sarah saw doorways out from the tunnel, and became curious about some.

"Looking back into the tunnel, I noticed there were doorways in both sides of the structure... I floated along and up observing that some 'door-ways' were open while others seemed to have been shut. The first doorway I peered into resembled a classic Hell. There was the sound of shrieking and agonizing screams. Naked human beings

41   Bonni Burrows, IANDS Utah meeting audio recording, April 2013,
      https://iandsutah.files.wordpress.com/2013/05/iands-april-2013-bonni-burrows.mp3

42   Bonni Burrows, IANDS Utah meeting audio recording, April 2013, https://iandsutah.org/archive-
      2013/

were strewn about a blasted landscape with pools of bubbling excrement and jagged boulders. Devils and other animals were torturing people in all imaginable ways; and people were also torturing each other.

"As I neared the doorway to this sinister scene, I felt a sucking sensation drawing me in like a whirlpool, and I found myself 'flying' above the miserable landscape. The smell was putrid and the heat was almost unbearable but a part of me was fascinated by the seemingly infinite varieties of pain and anguish that was being inflicted on the inhabitants of this realm. Most of me wanted to leave so I had no difficulty and my feeling was that anyone could leave if they wished. I felt that no one or nothing had put those people in captivity except their belief in the agony they continued to suffer. I 'flew' back to the doorway which was clearly visible from everywhere in the 'Hell.' I left with nothing but joy, but I still had a sense of myself as apart from that joy.

"The next doorway in the tunnel wasn't much better. As far as the eye could see people walked on barren yellow ground with their heads down, completely engrossed in their own depressed self- pitying thoughts, unaware that anyone else was around them. A great feeling of loneliness and isolation emanated from the scene, and I shied away from getting too close, although no sucking sensation was felt near this opening in the cloud tunnel."[43]

Angie Fenimore, after committing suicide, found

---

43   Sarah, http://www.nderf.org/Experiences/1sarah_nde.html

herself in a place that she considered to be hell.

"I look around, and all these people are just talking to themselves—mumbling to themselves. Very much like being at a party or movie theater where you hear the din of people talking. They're *not* communicating with each other—none of them. They're all just talking about themselves, like what it was they were stuck on in life.

"There was this one woman in particular. She had a beehive hairdo, and she was wailing. She was louder than some of the others, and she was saying, 'If only you had listened to me! If only...'"

"That is just the gravity of the place."

"With every moment that I'm there, I can feel this darkness sucking the life out of me, becoming me. And I can just feel its presence just killing life, and shutting down everything that we know as human beings that connects us: love and contribution...

"All of a sudden, I hear a voice, and it's out in the distance, but it's booming like the entire universe can hear it, but it's not loud. And this voice says, 'Is this what you really want?'"[44]

Howard Storm also had a distressing near-death experience in which he was brutally attacked by what he thought were other humans, but upon really calling out to God for help, was delivered.

---

44   Angie Fenimore, https://iandsutah.files.wordpress.com/2013/02/iands-11-07-july-2011-angie-fenimore.mp3

"Fighting well and hard for a long time, ultimately I was spent. Lying there exhausted amongst them, they began to calm down since I was no longer the amusement that I had been. Most of the beings gave up in disappointment because I was no longer amusing, but a few still picked and gnawed at me and ridiculed me for no longer being any fun. By this time I had been pretty much taken apart. People were still picking at me, occasionally, and I just lay there all torn up, unable to resist.

"Exactly what happened was (and I'm not going to try and explain this), from inside of me I felt a voice, my voice, say, 'Pray to God.'

"My mind responded to that, 'I don't pray. I don't know how to pray.' This is a guy lying on the ground in the darkness surrounded by what appeared to be dozens if not hundreds and hundreds of vicious creatures who had just torn him up. The situation seemed utterly hopeless, and I seemed beyond any possible help whether I believed in God or not.

"The voice again told me to pray to God. It was a dilemma since I didn't know how. The voice told me a third time to pray to God.

"I started saying things like, 'The Lord is my shepherd, I shall not want...' 'God bless America' and anything else that seemed to have a religious connotation.

"And these people went into a frenzy, as if I had thrown boiling oil all over them. They began yelling and screaming at me, telling me to quit, that there was no

God, and no one could hear me. While they screamed and yelled obscenities, they also began backing away from me as if I were poison. As they were retreating, they became more rabid, cursing and screaming that what I was saying was worthless and that I was a coward.

"I screamed back at them, 'Our Father who art in heaven,' and similar ideas.

"This continued for some time until, suddenly, I was aware that they had left. It was dark, and I was alone yelling things that sounded churchy. It was pleasing to me that these churchy sayings had such an effect on those awful beings.

"Lying there for a long time, I was in such a state of hopelessness, and blackness, and despair, that I had no way of measuring how long it was. I was just lying there in an unknown place all torn and ripped. And I had no strength; it was all gone. It seemed as if I were sort of fading out, that any effort on my part would expend the last energy I had. My conscious sense was that I was perishing, or just sinking into the darkness.

"Now I didn't know if I was even in the world. But I did know that I was here. I was real, all my senses worked too painfully well. I didn't know how I had arrived here. There was no direction to follow even if I had been physically able to move. The agony that I had suffered during the day was nothing compared to what I was feeling now. I knew then that this was the absolute end of my existence, and it was more horrible than anything I could possibly have imagined.

"Then a most unusual thing happened. I heard very clearly, once again in my own voice, something that I had learned in nursery Sunday School. It was the little song, 'Jesus loves me, yes I know...' and it kept repeating.

"I don't know why, but all of a sudden I wanted to believe that. Not having anything left, I wanted to cling to that thought. And I, inside, screamed, 'Jesus, please save me.' That thought was screamed with every ounce of strength and feeling left in me.

"When I did that, I saw, off in the darkness somewhere, the tiniest little star. Not knowing what it was, I presumed it must be a comet or a meteor, because it was moving rapidly. Then I realized it was coming toward me. It was getting very bright, rapidly. When the light came near, its radiance spilled over me, and I just rose up —not with my effort—I just lifted up. Then I saw (and I saw this very plainly) I saw all my wounds, all my tears, all my brokenness, melt away. And I became whole in this radiance. What I did was to cry uncontrollably. I was crying, not out of sadness, but because I was feeling things that I had never felt before in my life. Another thing happened. Suddenly I knew a whole bunch of things. I knew things... I knew that this light, this radiance, knew me. I don't know how to explain to you that I knew it knew me, I just did. As a matter of fact, I understood that it knew me better than my mother or father did. The luminous entity that embraced me knew me intimately and began to communicate a tremendous sense of knowledge. I knew that he knew everything about me and I was being unconditionally loved and accepted."[45]

Howard's account demonstrates what I have found over and over in my studies—that when a person calls upon God in the spirit world, they are delivered from misery. At times, they see the pinpoint of light and are invited into the tunnel, and at other times, God Himself of Jesus Christ appear and deliver the individual. But however the deliverance takes place, it seems always to come to those who call out to God for it.

This is especially good to know, since these kinds of distressing near-death experiences don't only come to those who have lived particularly *bad* or faithless lives. On rare occasions, they even come to the faithful, God-fearing individual. But the distress rarely lasts long for such people, since they are generally rather quick to call out to God for deliverance. In fact, often when a person finds themselves in the void, with no positive or negative feelings, they call out to God for deliverance, and the rescue comes. Whether they would have had a distressing near-death experience, we'll probably never know, since they seem to have prevented the opportunity.

Even in situations where a person simply finds themselves in the presence of a potentially malevolent being, again the answer seems to be to cry out to God for deliverance. Karen says,

---

45   Howard Storm, https://www.near-death.com/experiences/notable/howard-storm.html

"Then I felt like I was just in the dark somewhere. I must have really been struggling. I remember a male being. I remember him talking or mentally communicating with me. He kept telling me that it was ok to die, to quit fighting so hard and to just give up. He was there for a long time.

"All of a sudden it was like he slipped up somehow. I felt that he was evil and trying in my mind to get me to commit suicide by giving up. I remember asking God to help me and the evil being was gone.

"Then I remember being in a very brightly lighted place. It was like being in the air or a cloud but I knew at the time that it wasn't a cloud. It was wonderful. The light seemed to hold me, like someone carrying or cuddling me. The only way I can describe it is feeling like I was part of the universe. I remember not feeling surprised, as if I knew all along that I would soon be there, as if I had been there before. I was more at ease than I could ever imagine in life. I sincerely felt like I was back where I came from and knew it." [46]

Suicide

Suicide comes up often in questions about near-death experiences. What happens to those who commit suicide? Do they go to hell? From my studies, it has become plain that suicide is not a shortcut to the joyful afterlife. And while it's not a doom to everlasting and

---

46   Karen D, https://www.nderf.org/Experiences/tkaren_d_nde.html

endless torment, it does seem to have to be dealt with in some way. During Mandy's near-death experience, she was visiting many loved ones and family members, and then saw her nephew, who had committed suicide.

"I spoke with each and every one of them briefly, but had a longer discussion with my Uncle Donald. Donald is my Dad's brother who drowned June 30, 1989 (I may not be correct on the year). He was about 60 years old. I spoke with him and he told me to give his brother Joe a message. He told me what I was to tell his brother for him.

"As I was getting ready to ask him another question, I looked up and saw my nephew floating above the others. He was not on the right or left—he was just floating around. I asked him, 'Richard what are you doing up there?'

"He answered, 'It was not my time. I have to stay here until it is my time.'

"My nephew Richard committed suicide in September, 1989. I felt the hurt in my heart to know he was not able to be at peace." [47]

One man described the events following his suicide, where he drifted from his body, and looked back to see it.

"My mind felt cleared and my thoughts seemed quick and decisive. I felt a great sense of freedom and was quite content to be rid of my body. I felt a connection with everything around me in a way that I cannot describe. I

---

[47]   Mandy, https://www.nderf.org/Experiences/1mandy_j_nde.html

felt as if I was thinking faster or that time had slowed down considerably.

"I then felt a sensation of warmth behind me and simultaneously could see the room was getting brighter. I turned to see a small pinpoint of light above me floating further away than was possible considering the physical dimensions of the room. I felt drawn to the light and could not look away. As I stared at the point of light it gradually grew brighter and brighter. It filled the entire room with light so bright it filled every corner and nook until the room just faded away. I felt as if I was rushing towards a giant, intensely bright, round sphere and was overcome with a feeling of deep happiness and contentment. It felt warm, though not in a temperature sort of way that I was accustomed to feeling with my skin, but rather warmth that permeated me to the core of my perceived 'self'. It was unlike anything I have ever felt before or since, but it was definitely a feeling of love. Not love in the sexual or intimate sense, but a love filled with understanding, acceptance and happiness.

"The sensation was as if the most intense feeling of joy I had ever experienced had been amplified infinitely and was now a tangible thing that I was immersed in. It was so intense that the worry of the pain I knew my loved ones would feel over my departure was completely stripped away. I understood that mortal life was such a temporary and brief experience that all the pain I had ever experienced seemed so innocuous and benign, it was as if it had not ever mattered at all. The love and warmth felt so natural I felt as if I had always felt this way and it had been taken away from me while I was alive. It was if I had returned to the familiar after a long journey and was finally home at long last. Truly back home in that I knew deeply that I originated from there, I belonged there and my time on Earth suddenly felt so foreign and brief. My physical life felt like it was so long ago. I felt as if I was being showed what awaited me. I knew that it was only available to me if I was worthy and that the circumstances of my passing did not warrant it. I knew then what mattered most in my life. The love I shared, the compassion I had for others, the kindness I displayed to everyone and ultimately how much of myself I gave to those I crossed paths with in my prior life.

"Instantly I was in my room staring up from my bed. I felt intense pain." [48]

Sometimes when the suicide is of a materialistic or prideful nature, souls find themselves wandering the earth, not returning to the light—which they could do if they chose to. Sometimes it's the pain they now see that they've caused their loved ones that keeps them from moving on.

When a man named Mohammad died, he saw some of these individuals.

"I got the understanding that everybody who dies has a guide. But some humans are so attached to their physical and material world that they are still worry about their money, possessions. or power even after death. They

---

48   Mr. W, https://www.nderf.org/Experiences/rmr.w.nde.html

don't notice their guide and might not even notice that they are dead! Their soul can stay earth-bound for a long time after their death. For example, my guide showed me a man who apparently used to be in a position of authority and power back on the earth. After this man's death, he still went to the office he used to work in, trying to sit at the same chair and sign documents. He was oblivious to the fact that his signature does not leave any marks and he has no power and effect in the physical world. He kept going to that office trying to sign things and act as he was still working there, not realizing that he is dead. I got this understanding that any strong earthbound attachment can keep our souls from soaring.

"I saw people who had committed suicide and they seemed to have the worse situation among all these earthbound souls. They were completely trapped and had no way of communicating to anyone. Sometimes these souls would follow their loved ones on earth like a shadow for many years, begging for forgiveness for the hurt and pain they had caused them by their suicide. But it was no use and they wouldn't be heard. My guide showed me these scenes." [49]

Though suicide is a touchy topic, and can fill many with anxiety, it's an important topic when people are suffering from sever depression, trauma, anxiety, or fear.

One of the messages that seems to ring through near-death experiences is the importance of developing a sense of purpose—which is the *choice* to do something

---

worthwhile. It's not an easy message to accept when a person feels like a real victim, but it may be the key to getting through what they're suffering.

Linda died from suicide, and though the suicide itself was not addressed directly in her NDE, she is told that her life has a purpose. She says,

"I heard the nurse yelling that I was going into cardiac and respiratory arrest. I then found myself falling in this dark tunnel. It was pitch dark and I couldn't see anything. All of a sudden, I saw a bright lizard-like snake jump out at me and I became terrified. The next thing I knew there were these snake-like creatures all around me. They were lunging out at me as I kept falling. I was petrified beyond what I could ever express. I really felt that I was headed for some sort of hell and so I started thinking that there really must be some sort of a God.

"Then for some strange reason, I started thinking of a prayer my grandmother use to say with me when I was a little child, which I had totally forgotten about until now. It went, 'I pray to the Lord to forgive my wrongs. If I should die before I wake. I pray the Lord my soul to take.' I started praying this over and over. The next thing I knew, I saw my sister who had just recently been hit and killed by a drunk driver. She had a light glowing around her and there was a peace about her that was indescribable. She started to guide me and the next thing I knew I was in another tunnel to the right that was going upwards. This tunnel was very bright with many indescribable colors and tons of little white lights. I was moving extremely fast and there was a big white illuminating light at the end.

"I felt more serenity, peace and love than I could ever express in words. I felt totally mesmerized and in complete awe. I was very much drawn to this light and wanted to keep going toward it, but when I started getting close, I heard a male voice tell me I had to go back. It was not yet my time. This voice continued to tell me that I was going to help educate and teach many people.

"I then became aware of being back in my body" [50]

Jane similarly learned the value of purpose after her suicide and resuscitation.

"I heard a loud bang as if heavy doors were slamming shut behind me and I felt such a great sense of relief. Then I felt I was bubbles, popping like effervescence in lemonade, and I was stretching for millions of miles. The further I stretched, the less bubbling I felt. I went on forever. I would compare it to being like I was a raindrop returning to and becoming conscious of the fullness and expanse of the ocean only on a much larger scale. Love was all around, peace, and blissful-joy. I felt myself moving forward and after traveling faster than light. I thought, 'This is further than our galaxy!' I questioned, 'How come I don't feel afraid?' I went to look at my stomach where I expected to feel fear but I saw nothing and it didn't matter. I continued to move forward, in this amazing peace, joy and love at increasing speed.

---

50   Linda S, https://www.nderf.org/Experiences/1linda.s.nde.html

"Then suddenly in my mind and every single cell in my being, I went through this explosive... glorious intelligence and power. It was astounding; words cannot describe the beauty, glory and power of that intelligence, energy and bliss. Moving through that into a place where the love was so magnified was awesome. I heard the sound of singing. It was unimaginably beautiful. There were no words or voices, but musical tones that sounded like angels singing. I moved past crowds of beings so fast, I couldn't see anyone clearly. I just heard the sound of moving past assemblies of energy people. Then there was a flash of quiet space, more crowds of people, then quiet again. This happened rapidly and repeatedly. I was whizzing by so fast that all I could hear was what sounded like low, mumbled voices.

"In a split second I came to a place where there were lots of rainbows. I saw an energy-person express shock as it realize I was arriving. Then it was as if I was in a spiral or vortex, twisting downwards for 3 turns. I heard a deep, prolonged voice say, 'TEACH' only it sounded like 't-e-e-e-a-a-a-c-c-c-h-h-h...'.

"A week later, I awoke in hospital. I believe I was shown my true identity in Spirit, moving through perfect love to go through Divine and Holy intelligence and power. I had no fear. It is our brain that engenders fear through our thoughts, like we are biological computers. Heaven is real. The things that are eternal are the only real things; like love, peace, and joy. It was an awesome experience. I was returned to my body with a divine purpose 'to teach'. Sixteen years later with my three

autistic sons and my marriage braking up, I studied to
become a teacher and have never looked back! My 3 sons'
behavior was crazy and they each spent a lot of times in
juvenile detention centers. They are still abusive towards
me but I distance myself from them. I have had some
amazing adventures teaching." [51]

While suicide is never the answer, I should say that
most of the near-death experiences I've read involving
suicide attempts (and there are many) contain the same
elements as other types of NDEs. The same tunnel, light,
love, etc. Of course, every NDE is unique, but suicide does
not seem to be a separate category, except that in my
observation there is a higher percentage of distressing
near-death experiences among suicide attempters than
among others. Is this a "consequence" of the suicide itself
or is it a reflection of the state of mind they are in at the
time of death? The answer isn't clear.

The thing that does prove clear is that (as I've
already said) suicide is not an answer to problems. It isn't
an answer to helplessness. It isn't an answer to physical or
mental illness or injury. You might say it isn't an answer at
all. And it's consequences (whether in the next life *or* by
those left behind on earth) are tragic.

51   Jayne S. https://www.ndertf.org/Experiences/1jayne.s.nde.html

Different Levels

While there are these darker realms, as mentioned, there also appears to be many, *many* levels of paradise on the other side. What feels like paradise for one individual may seem dim and unloving to another. And while there is some crossover between the realms, there also seems to be barriers that separate different levels based on the kind of life a person lived.

Ranelle Wallace, who died in a plane crash and visited the spirit world before being resuscitated, experienced meeting a friend who was in a different level of the Spirit world. While being guided by her grandma, she asked about this friend.

"'Come on,' and she reached out for my hand, 'You have a lot to see.'

"But I thought, 'Wait, what about Jim?'

"Jim was a friend who had been killed in an automobile accident several months earlier. If Grandma was here, maybe she could tell me what happened to him. 'What about Jim?' I said again, and then I saw him in the distance, walking toward us.

"Instantly I wanted to run and embrace him, but my grandmother put out her arm and said, 'No, you cannot.' I was startled. There was a power in her words, and I knew I couldn't oppose them. 'Why not?' I asked.

"'Because of the way he lived his life,' she said.

"He had come closer now and had stopped ten or twelve feet away. He was dressed in jeans and a blue shirt that was unbuttoned to mid-chest. This was how he normally wore his shirts on Earth, but I thought, *my goodness, that's risqué. Do they let you dress like that in heaven?*

"He smiled, and I could feel his happiness. Although he didn't possess the same kind of light or power that my grandmother did, he seemed content. He gave me a message to give to his mother, asking that I tell her to stop grieving over his death, to let her know that he was happy and progressing.

"He explained that he had made certain decisions in life that had hindered his growth on Earth. He had made the decisions knowing they were wrong, and now he was willing to accept their consequences. When he was thrown from the van that he and his wife and a friend had been in, his head had hit a rock, and he had been killed instantly. When he got to the other side, he was given a choice to stay in the spirit or return to Earth. He could see that his growth on Earth had come to a stop and that if he returned he might lose even that light which he had gained. So he chose to stay.

"He asked me to explain this to his mother, and I said I would, not knowing how I would accomplish it since I had no thought of going back myself. Then he said that he had a lot of work waiting for him, and he turned and left. I could tell that he was very busy, very engaged in matters that were vital to him, that would help him, though I didn't know what they were. I looked at my grandmother and asked why she had prevented me from embracing him. She explained that this was a part his of 'damnation'.

"'The powers we are given,' she explained, 'are self-given. We grow by the force of our desires to learn, to love, to accept things by faith that we cannot prove. Our ability to accept truth, to live by it, governs our progress in the spirit, and it determines the degree of light we possess. Nobody forces light and truth upon us, and nobody takes it away unless we let them. We are self-governed and self-judged. We have total agency. Jim decided to limit his growth on Earth by rejecting things he knew were true. He hurt himself and others by using and selling drugs. Some of the people were hurt severely. He had various reasons for turning to drugs but the fact remains that he knew these things were wrong. He chose darkness over light often enough that he would not choose light again. And, now, to the degree that he became spiritually dark, he is consigned to a similar degree of darkness—or lack of light —here in the spirit. Yet he still has agency. He can grow. He can still find all the joy he is willing to accept, all that he is capable of receiving. But he knows that he does not have the same powers to progress and achieve joy that others with more light have. This is a part of damnation, because his progress is limited. But he is choosing to grow. And he is happy.'

"'The Lord never gives more challenges in life than can be handled," she continued, 'Rather than jeopardize someone's spiritual progression or cause more suffering than can be endured, he will bring that spirit home, where he or she can continue progressing.'"[52]

During her near-death experience, Natalie Sudman experienced several different realms (seemingly at once, but it was like she would find herself in the one where she put her focus), each of which seemed to have a different important purpose. One such realm was a restful environment, where Natalie was able to think about different aspects of her life on earth, what she'd learned, and what she still needed to do.

"It was almost like folding completely into myself, and by going totally in, I was in an infinite space. And this infinite space was just really, *really* comfortable. It's where I was resting, I was recuperating, I was kind of poking though things that had happened in my life, and saying,

---

52   Wallace, Ranelle, *The Burning Within*, (Carson City, NV: Gold Leaf Press, 1994), pg. 97-99

'Oh, yeah. That worked out great!', 'Cool, I want to do that again,' or whatever. And there was another being there that was sort of doing mechanical tinkering, but not interacting with me, really, just sort of like taking the car to the mechanic.

"Just a lot of deep, deep breaths. It' really just a beautiful, *beautiful* environment."[53]

One woman tells of the experience of her husband, who had a stroke, and he told her that he almost went to heaven.

"He went through a tunnel and to a light so bright that he needed shades, but the light did not hurt his eyes. Things were shiny and glistening. God talked to him. His voice was loud like thunder. He was huge and behind a cloud. He said he learned that God was the universe. He is love and never ending. He is in every blade of grass. It was calm and peaceful.

"He told my husband that he had to go back; his work wasn't finished. He was told God sends us people to help us get to heaven, a handle to God. He told me there were several levels; he was on the brightest level. Below are darker and darker levels. He told me he was in an in between place, 'the other side,' and people were around him in white gowns, like sitting on a train. He saw his brother-in-law that passed away about a year before." [54]

Some people give specific numbers of the different

---

53   Natalie Sudman, from an interview with Bob Olsen on Afterlife TV,
      https://www.youtube.com/watch?v=NVzWcDK9qRs

54   IANDS, NDE Accounts, https://iands.org/ndes/nde-stories/484--almost-went-to-heaven.html

levels in the spirit world. Linda also speaks of different levels in the spirit world:

> "I was taken to many different levels by this friend and learned that anything is possible in this place. I can't remember most of the levels as each one seemed more complex than the last, but I do remember the lower levels so to speak. I'm sure I was taken to higher places, but I am not to remember these places as my life here would be affected. I think there maybe about seven or possibly more but I have a basic memory of about three or four." [55]

Others say that the number of levels on the other side is limitless. Wayne says,

> "I had a strong desire now to join the river of life and felt this was home, where I came from. Touching the river gave me insight into realms beyond realms, universes beyond universes, dimensions beyond dimensions; I experienced infinity. I was shown a long line of experiences in other realms of realities and on other worlds...

> "There were beings and objects unlike anything I had ever seen or heard of, even in the imaginings of science fiction writers I had read. I was made to know there were an infinite number of realms of existence and all were part of the One, the Source. The stream had distinct layers or levels that were not divided by any kind of barrier but each seemed to be of a different density. The one I experienced was the highest level. Where I first

---

came after death was into the lowest level; I call it the 'between place' or 'lowest level of transition.'" [56]

To sum it up, it appears there are different realms in the spirit world—different levels of existence, some of which are affected by the kind of life a person lived here, and others simply have different purposes. The lowest spiritual levels include unpleasant beings of a very low "vibration," of lower energy—of lower light or glory. At the lowest of these levels, the beings and people seem to have no other interest than the suffering of themselves and others. But at higher levels, the amount of love, acceptance, joy, and fulfillment go way beyond anything conceivable here.

And even within these higher levels, it appears that there are realms of peace and healing, realms of work and play, realms of light and glory, and levels of nature and beauty.

---

56   Wayne H. https://www.nderf.org/Experiences/1wayne_h_nde.html

Travel

As we have discussed briefly, and will discuss further in a later chapter, time and space have little meaning in terms of traveling time and distance. But according to most near-death experiencers, travel does still take place, and though the details of travel can be confusing to study, it is a curious study indeed.

Jennifer W. said,

"The next moment, I traveled to space. My spirit was taken in an instant to outer space and exploded into pure consciousness! I was acutely aware in my mind that I was traveling and had become an astral (spiritual) being. I was taken into the sky and into space. I was above the beach and to the right of the almost full moon. I was completely conscious of being alive without a body! As I began to comprehend where I found myself, my mental dialogue was the same as when I was in the physical realm. I noticed my mind was still thinking, hearing, and seeing. I tried to figure out where I had been taken. My spirit eyes felt the same as seeing through my body's eyes. My mind told me I was in a holy place. I was a visitor in a house of God.[57]

Brigham Young gave this description of travel in the spirit world:

"When you are in the spirit world, everything there will appear as natural as things now do. Spirits will be familiar with spirits in the spirit world—will converse, behold, and exercise every variety of communication with one another as familiarly and naturally as while here in tabernacles. There, as here, all things will be natural, and you will understand them as you now understand natural things. You will there see that those spirits we are speaking of are active; they sleep not. And you will learn that they are striving with all their might—laboring and toiling diligently as any individual would to accomplish an act in this world (DBY, 380)...

"I can say with regard to parting with our friends, and going ourselves, that I have been near enough to understand eternity so that I have had to exercise a great deal more faith to desire to live than I ever exercised in my whole life to live. The brightness and glory of the next apartment is inexpressible. It is not encumbered so that when we advance in years we have to be stubbing along and be careful lest we fall down. We see our youth, even, frequently stubbing their toes and falling down. But yonder, how different! They move with ease and like lightning. If we want to visit Jerusalem, or this, that, or

---

the other place—and I presume we will be permitted if we desire—there we are, looking at its streets. If we want to behold Jerusalem as it was in the days of the Savior; or if we want to see the Garden of Eden as it was when created, there we are, and we see it as it existed spiritually, for it was created first spiritually and then temporally, and spiritually it still remains. And when there we may behold the earth as at the dawn of creation, or we may visit any city we please that exists upon its surface. If we wish to understand how they are living here on these western islands, or in China, we are there; in fact, we are like the light of the morning... God has revealed some little things, with regard to his movements and power, and the operation and motion of the lightning furnish a fine illustration of the ability of the Almighty (DBY, 380).

"When we pass into the spirit world we shall possess a measure of his power. Here, we are continually troubled with ills and ailments of various kinds. In the spirit world we are free from all this and enjoy life, glory, and intelligence; and we have the Father to speak to us, Jesus to speak to us, and angels to speak to us, and we shall enjoy the society of the just and the pure who are in the spirit world until the resurrection (DBY, 380–81)."[58]

This description fits the experience of Barry, who, upon finding himself out of his body, did some wandering.

"My own identity appeared to also be composed of light, I noticed that my light had the ability to reach anywhere I wanted, and whatever beam of light

---

58   Teachings of Presidents of the Church: Brigham Young, (1997), 279–84,
       https://www.lds.org/manual/teachings-brigham-young/chapter-38?lang=eng

consciousness I chose to direct my attention to, I could instantly travel down. I did this and found myself in a floral shop. What I found extremely fascinating was that I was able to experience all of the flowers simultaneously, and that no matter where I went, I was always at the center of everything!"[59]

In one sense, it appears that to a spirit, the universe is all available for the exploring, without the constraints of gravity, travel-time, and distance.

Sara Menet describes from her near-death experience:

"I was starting to learn things about the spirit body. Number one, your eyes—your spiritual eyes—can see for *long* distances. It can move faster than the speed of light. You just have to think you want to be there, and there you are. I didn't have to walk or glide, I was just there."[60]

During her near-death experience, Bonni Burrows wanted to visit other worlds in the universe besides earth. She says,

"I wanted to know about other worlds. I was kind of a science fiction buff as a teenager. I wanted to know, were there other worlds? Were there other people? How did that all work?

"I got to visit some of those other worlds. The... one that I can even give you a concept of is one that in my mind I call Harmony. And that's because everything was

---

59   Barry W, https://www.nderf.org/Experiences/1barry_w_nde.html
60   Sarah Menet, Iands Utah Meeting, September 2017,
      https://iandsutah.files.wordpress.com/2013/02/iands-11-09-sept-2011-sara-menet.mp3

different than here. There was no conflict. There was no competition. The best concept I can give you is, if you want to accomplish something, everyone around you wants to help you do that. And there's no one who will feel good about your failing. No one will feel good if you aren't doing it the very best. And so there's a joy in your success.

"And it seems like you wouldn't have individuality, but they were more individual than we are here. They were more whole.

"They didn't have any basketball, so if you like basketball, you'd probably better stay here! Because there was no competition. But there were things that were greater than all the competition. They were successful. There was success, but the success belonged to everyone. Yet everyone was more individual...

"But it wasn't just a different planet. It wasn't just someplace else in the universe... It's more than just getting in a rocket-ship and traveling to that place. It's a consciousness, also."[61]

One woman discovered the beautiful simplicity of travel after leaving her body when she died shortly after childbirth:

"Then I heard her yell, 'Code Blue, this woman has no pulse...'

"In what I am sure was just seconds, I popped out of

61   Bonni Burrows, IANDS Utah meeting audio recording, April 2013, https://iandsutah.org/archive-2013/

the crown of my head. 'Popped' is a good description, because there was an internally audible pop as I left my body through the spot in my skull that in infants is called the soft spot, or fontanel.

"The panic was over almost instantly, and I was floating around the ceiling of the hospital room looking down on a body I realized was me. I felt no attachment to the body, just curiosity...

"As nurses and doctors ran into the room I realized I didn't want to be there anymore, so I traveled up and out of the building into the night sky. I felt free and unencumbered, and was drawn toward the stars. I realized I could just float over the treetops and go home to visit my family. But the call of the night sky was stronger. I wanted to soar into space and be free.

"I realized I was traveling at the speed of thought. All I had to do was think upward and I would be moving until I changed my thought, or altered it. That was amazing, and it took some getting used to. I felt the way my old belief systems severely limited me. I realized my thoughts were instantly creating my reality, so I'd better be clear.

"I turned, looked back and saw Earth. She was a jewel suspended in space, so beautiful! I loved Earth; in fact, I was more attached to it than I had been to my own body. I felt bereft to be leaving Her, and I now understood what was meant by the saying, 'The Earth is our Mother. She is a living organism.' I had been too self-absorbed to notice." [62]

---

62   IANDS, *It is Here in Our Bodies that the Lessons of Love are Manifest*, 17 February 2017,

Time and Space

It appears from *many* accounts that time has little meaning in the spirit world. In the time it takes to resuscitate a person, that person may experience what feels like months, or even years of time. Consequently, concerns around the passage of time don't exist. Duane shares the following:

"Even though I had people there (on earth), whom in earthly terms, I had loved as dearly as earthly conditions allowed, I had no desire to return once I had seen the alternative. From that vantage point, I could see how trivial the world I had left was. Here, on the other side, I would always be with souls who had loved me from the beginning of time, and will continue to do so forever. Plus, I now knew that the loved ones who lagged behind on earth would join us momentarily. It might be years to them, but it would only be moments to us. Time is funny

https://iands.org/research/nde-research/nde-archives21/newest-accounts/1198-it-is-here-in-our-bodies-that-the-lessons-of-love-are-made-manifest.html that way from a celestial view." [63]

Anna A, during her near-death experience, says, "Time and space had no physicality, no validity."[64]

During Anthony's near-death experience, time seemed to pass like normal, but the time he spent there was only about eight minutes in mortal earth time.

"Everything in this other world was made of what I can only describe as liquid light. Everything was alive, the ground, the mountains even the sky. The voice was still with me and during this experience never left me. It told me that where I was the 'real' world and that I had a job to do whilst I was there. I alighted on the side of a bare earth mountain; there were no trees grass or rivers etc. There was light everywhere but no sun, the light seemed to come within everything, even the air.

"On this mountain about halfway up was a large boulder. On the boulder was a glowing golden brick (I know how this must sound). The voice told me that I was to build a garden on the mountain and that every year a brick would appear on the top of the boulder and with the bricks, I was meant to build a path up the mountain from the base to the boulder. I was told to plant trees that appeared as acorns etc. at the top of the mountain.

"I was there for a *very* long time, in which time the voice was always present, I never felt alone and I never questioned why I was there, I was totally at peace, and

63   Duane S. https://www.nderf.org/Experiences/1duane_s.nde.html

64   Anna A, http://www.nderf.org/Experiences/1anna_a.nde.html

feelings of absolute joy and unconditional love pervaded me the entire time. I knew that the voice was the most trustworthy person/thing in the universe. As the years passed I watched the trees grow, the flowers and grass I planted also grew, the color of the flowers weren't of any color I have ever seen, like there was twenty different colors in the rainbow there, I couldn't describe them as there's just no frame of reference to what they looked like.

"I was taught a lot of things, and was able to, for want of a better phrase, 'see into people's souls' and understood in an instant all the ramifications of all our actions on each other, that anger is borne of pain or fear, and many other teachings about what I now think of as the human condition. Then I saw everyone on the planet interconnected on these lines, and a feeling of such overwhelming love and empathy went through me I felt like my heart was going to explode.

"The last brick appeared on the boulder some two thousand and five hundred years after I had first arrived. I was aware of every year, this was not dreamlike, it was 'real time' if that makes any sense. The path now stretched form the base to the boulder but over the years, the boulder had gradually changed shape and now looked square like some sort of alter. The trees I had initially planted had grown, the bows and branches had arched, and the trunks thicken to form what I can only describe as a temple at the top of the mountain. The voice told me that the first part of my job was finished and I now had to set foot upon the path. I went to the bottom of the mountain and put a foot onto the path.

"At this point, the most searing, unbearable pain tore through me but the voice told me not to step off the path. I asked what the pain was as it wasn't physical, it felt like (and this again sounds bizarre) but it felt like a spiritual pain. The voice told me that it was the pain of the least sin I would commit against my own soul. It was conveyed to me that this didn't mean sin in any religious sense, but specifically it was the pain of the wound to my own soul that I myself would commit in my lifetime. I continued up the path and each time I stepped onto another brick, the pain was worse than the one before until nearing the top I told the voice I couldn't finish.

"The voice was kind and patient and said that it was with me and that I would finish but I needed to learn the lessons it was teaching. I got extremely angry at this point and asked why I had been brought here for all this time in order to experience such terrible pain. I continued to the end of the path with the encouragement and presence of what was now I understood to be some higher spiritual being. I reached the entrance to the tree temple, went inside, and saw the only other being I saw the entire time I was there. It had its back to me and was kneeling as though in prayer.

"I was angry again and I rushed up to this figure saying that I now knew that everything was real so why did I have to experience all the pain. The figure stood up and turned around, and it was indescribable, a being of perfection and what I can only be described as made out of pure love. I knew that this was the source of the voice. I was dumbstruck after all that had happened and could only say, 'I can see you.' The being touched me on my cheek gently, and said simply, 'And now you know. It is time to go back now.' I was also told that the garden I had created would exist there forever, and I would return there one day.

"As I walked with the being back out of the tree temple I saw for the first time other people coming to the garden and sitting on the grass, looking at the flowers, talking and laughing. The being smiled and said, 'See what you've accomplished here.' I felt completely overwhelmed, but I was then immediately transported back into my body, which I immediately felt as being incredibly heavy and cloying and almost unnatural. The asthma attack had totally passed, and I checked the clock, which said 9:23 pm. The entire experience had taken about eight minutes from my initial attack to being 'back'." [65]

Twenty-five hundred years! All of which took place in a matter of eight minutes earth-time. Clearly there's no obvious conversion table that converts so-many minutes earth time to so-many minutes heaven time. This demonstrates again that when it comes to spiritual things, time really isn't a factor.

Grace Bubulka-Hatmaker also experienced time as being meaningless:

---

[65]   Anthony, https://www.nderf.org/Experiences/1anthony_n_nde.html

"During this experience, time had no meaning. Time was an irrelevant notion. It felt like eternity. I felt like I was there an eternity. No remnants of the tunnel remained. There was no cloud or fog. The light was pure and all-good. I needed nothing, I wanted nothing. I was in communion with all the light around me. The specks, the others and I were all part of the light that existed forever. I felt I had an infinite sense of knowing, of understanding it all. I was completely at ease."[66]

While Sharon Milliman experienced a definite sequence of the events in her near-death experience, the time spent in heaven far surpassed the time she was dead on earth.

"There was a sequence to the events. It seemed like *this* happened, and then *this* happened, and then next *this* happened. And it felt very planned, and organized. But yet, I was probably only there just minutes, but it seemed like I was there for weeks and weeks. So much happened.

"You know, I had no sense of time—there was no sense of time. I was just taking in every detail—the feel of the grass on my feet, the sweetness of the air, talking with people, Jesus, God and the angels—just, everything. There was so much, it was almost overload. I was overloaded!"[67]

While there seems to be no hard and fast rule for the measurement of the difference between the passage of

---

66   Grace-Bubulka-Hatmaker, https://www.near-death.com/experiences/notable/grace-bubulka.html
67   Sharon Milliman, from a podcast interview, https://neardeathexperiencepodcast.org/sharon-millimans-near-death-experiences

time in the spirit world vs. earthly time, or even than the
passage of time of someone outside of the body vs. those
in the body, that difference can manifest itself in very
interesting ways. When Janet's heart stopped, apparently
time did, too.

> "Suddenly my heart started to do what I can only
> describe as a *shudder*. I started to call out to my daughter
> when my heart stopped. I suddenly realized that
> *everything* had stopped. There was no sound, no
> movement, nothing. I was standing there taking in this
> fact, when I looked down and saw my body on the bed. I
> thought, *Oh, I'm dead*, like it was a completely ordinary
> thing.

> "Then I remember thinking, *I wonder if the rain stopped
> too...* So I went through the wall and looked around
> outside. The rain had not just stopped; the raindrops
> were suspended in mid-air. It was the most awesome sight
> I'd ever seen. I remember moving around looking at
> different drops and I found one that was quite large, so I
> was looking at it closely and was about to touch it when it
> started to fall.

> "At that same instant, I was back on the bed. My heart
> was beating again and I felt so happy, and realized I was
> grinning from ear to ear."[68]

It appears also that the passage of time in the spirit
world isn't strictly one direction as it is here. It may be
possible to step back and see an event from the recent

---

68   Janet, https://www.nderf.org/Experiences/1janet_s_nde.html

past. At least that seems to be the implication from Cristine's experience. Cristine found herself exploring a beautiful garden, and upon discovering a little boy and girl, followed them around, experiencing what they were experiencing. Says she,

"I was having such a great time that I would have been content to stay and explore more but then I felt 'him'. I flew above and watched as the boy entered the garden path.

"The boy appeared to be around 14 years of age. He walked along a stone path which went through the center of the large flower garden and ended at the front door to the house. He wore a high collar blue-gray jacket that looked like velvet, with shiny buttons down the front. I could see white ruffles of his shirt sticking out the jacket sleeves. His pants matched the jacket and were cuffed around his knees. He wore long pale stockings and dark brown leather shoes which appeared well worn. The shoes had brass buckles and the sunlight bounced off of them as he walked. His longish brown curls moved gently and framed his smiling and radiant face. He carried a bouquet of flowers that he picked from a garden elsewhere. Despite his age, he had a confidence and sureness about him. The boy was happy and humming a song that sounded old and silly. The faster he walked the faster he hummed and it made me smile. He did not seem to notice me flying about him (or the other me watching it all from another place). As he entered the garden, the flowers were taller than he and they were very excited by his presence... they truly loved this boy. I followed him closely and realized I could feel his joy. As we came closer to the front door I noticed I became an invisible nothingness that could go through walls and even the boy. I felt incredibly light and every thought I had was good and beautiful. There wasn't the ticking of time passing and it would slow down or go backwards so that I could take every detail in.

"The girl lived in a charming country home, that looked like it belonged in Europe, perhaps France. The house looked like light colored stone bleached by the sun. The door was centered with a large window on both sides. The walls were very thick and windows set deep, the second floor windows were much smaller and I noticed wooden shutters, aged a beautiful bronze. The front door was a thing of beauty, with it's solid craftsmanship and it's layers of pale paint, I noticed a delicate webbing and texture that I had to fly up close to study it.

"The door reminded me of seashells as well. Adorning the door was an oval brass door knocker where I saw the boy's reflection in it as he went to use it. Time could go backwards so I could watch the boy approach the garden and feel the wonderful feelings all over again. We again got to the door, knocked and we waited excitedly for it to open. The boy went in through the door but I followed through the wall. The inside of the house was filled with sunlight and colors much like the garden. I noticed several vases of fresh cut flowers throughout the large room. The furniture was beautifully crafted and covered in materials of floral designs and cheery colors. My eyes then looked towards the back, right side of the room at the bottom of the stairs and I saw the girl.

"She was small and petite, looked about thirteen or fourteen. She looked so lovely in her long, pale yellow satin dress fitted to her tiny waist. A matching colored ribbon was tied around her head where long ringlets of light brown jumped around her shoulders. Her face really glowed and seemed transparent like the petals lit up by the sun. I felt with her the same as the boy, and can only describe it as pure joy. The girl's mother was standing close by her and it was she who opened the door...

"The girl took a deep breath (so did I) as she opened the door. When the boy and girl finally were face to face they didn't say one word, instead I felt everything they 'said'. I felt every emotion of both of them and went back in time again, this time with her so I could feel her emotions and watch through the window as he approached the garden. We both could barely contain our joy and ran down the stairs as he was about to knock. I watched them as they looked at each other with young smiles. Suddenly I was inside the boy, seeing her through his eyes and also looking at him through her eyes. I then saw both their reflections looking back at me. What I felt next was simultaneously going through both of them and feeling their love." [69]

I'm not clear if the scenario in Cristine's experience was of a mortal place that she, as a spirit, was able to visit,

69   Cristine H, https://www.nderf.org/Experiences/1cristine.h.sobe.html

or if it all took place in the spirit world. Either way, her ability to jump back and forward in time seems to be an ability that is common (or possibly universal) to spirits on the other side.

Age in the Spirit World

Another aspect of time that sometimes comes up is the question of the age of people on the other side. Near-death experiencers have a lot to say about this question.

Carol Vengroff was 12-years old when she froze to death, but in her near-death experience, she felt older, wiser, and more mature.

"Though I was 12 when I died, you aren't any particular age when you pass. I don't know how it works —my 12-year old mind was able to absorb all this information." [70]

With only a few exceptions, experiencers I've studied say that everyone they met in the spirit world (with the exception of children) were in their prime. [71]

Robert, who met his grandparents in the spirit world, said,

"My Grandparents were there and Grandma Lucia had that same smile of love and harmony that she always

70   Carol Vengroff, IANDS NDE Radio Podcast, https://www.youtube.com/watch?time.continue=145&v=dI.C5GtJ9j8E

71   Tracy M, https://www.nderf.org/Experiences/1tracy_m_nde.html

had. Grandpa Pete was younger and more resilient. They all were younger than my memories held. They all appeared to be in their late 20's or 30's." [72]

Jeff spoke of his experience,

"So much love. Pure divine love around everything everywhere. I was totally engulfed in it. I saw things I can't even begin to describe. The awe factor was way off the charts.

"I saw a handsome young man who later was identified as my grandfather. I was shown a beautiful city that glowed a golden like aura. I felt like I was truly home again. This was very familiar to me." [73]

Nancy says,

"People should not be afraid of dying —you won't be alone, you have loved ones there waiting to guide you. And they are just like us, body and all, but in their prime and healthy." [74]

When Bob met his relatives, all of them were young and vibrant.

"The light was strong and somewhat unearthly at the end of a long tunnel. The light was as much love as anything in that it was pervasive.

"My relatives (all deceased) were there, all at their prime in life. They were dressed (I would say 1940's style

72   Robert N. https://www.nderf.org/Experiences/1robert_n_ndes.html

73   Jeff S, https://www.nderf.org/Experiences/1jeff_s_nde.html

74   Nancy P., https://www.nderf.org/Experiences/1nancy_p_nde.html

which would have been prime years for most). Relatives I knew of, such as my grandfathers, but never knew in life were there as well as uncles and aunts who passed before I knew them.

"The unconditional love was overwhelming and permeated all of us genuinely and richly." [75]

Not only are spirits young and vibrant, but in the spirit world, they don't show the physical limitations they had in the flesh. One woman who died from complications of childbirth saw her father in the spirit world. She says,

"Off to my left was my Father. I was overjoyed to see him as he had died when I was only twenty years old, and I'd missed him with all my heart.

"*Daddy*, I thought. All thoughts were telepathic. That had been a natural way of communication between my Father and I when he was alive. My father had severe Multiple Sclerosis and was quadriplegic my entire life. As with many people, when something is lost physically, something else is gained. He had a brilliant mind and I grew up talking to him without speaking. I never knew how unusual our method of communicating was until he was gone and unfortunately it became an ability of mine that had to be squelched. I found that people do not like their minds read. It is said that all humans have the ability to communicate telepathically, and I believe they do... The only thing that impedes telepathy is secrets, lies, and

---

withholds. These things shut us down.

"My father was also standing. I had never in my life seen him stand or walk. He looked vibrant and in the prime of his life and I was ecstatic. He was healed and we exchanged a flood of love from heart to heart." [76]

Space Travel and Touring the Universe

Many who have near-death experiences spend time exploring the universe, from a point hovering high above the earth to out among the stars, to other planets, to other galaxies, and so on, to the furthest points in space.

"It was as if I were in an invisible plane hovering over the San Fernando Valley and seeing the beauty of it all. At the same time, I was also looking down on earth from space and seeing how awesome earth looked from space. I went through the universe, understanding within me that this was a place I knew...

"Suddenly I was on a real, living firmament. A living place of pure love. The waters were living waters, the grass was living, the trees were living, and the animals were living, more alive than earth is."[77]

Carl G. Jung, a well known psychiatrist, died of a heart attack and had a near-death experience that altered his whole way of thinking about psychology. As part of his

---

76   *IT IS HERE IN OUR BODIES THAT THE LESSONS OF LOVE ARE MADE MANIFEST, 17 February 2017*, International Association for Near-Death Studies, https://iands.org/research/nde-research/nde-archives31/newest-accounts/1198-it-is-here-in-our-bodies-that-the-lessons-of-love-are-made-manifest.html

77   Diane, https://www.nderf.org/Experiences/1diane_c_nde.html

experience, Carl says,

"It seemed to me that I was high up in space. Far below
I saw the globe of the Earth, bathed in a gloriously blue
light. I saw the deep blue sea and the continents. Far
below my feet lay Ceylon, and in the distance ahead of me
the subcontinent of India. My field of vision did not
include the whole Earth, but its global shape was plainly
distinguishable and its outlines shone with a silvery
gleam through that wonderful blue light. In many places
the globe seemed colored, or spotted dark green like
oxidized silver. Far away to the left lay a broad expanse—
the reddish-yellow desert of Arabia; it was as though the
silver of the Earth had there assumed a reddish-gold hue.
Then came the Red Sea, and far, far back—as if in the
upper left of a map—I could just make out a bit of the
Mediterranean. My gaze was directed chiefly toward that.
Everything else appeared indistinct. I could also see the
snow-covered Himalayas, but in that direction it was
foggy or cloudy. I did not look to the right at all. I knew
that I was on the point of departing from the Earth.

"Later I discovered how high in space one would have
to be to have so extensive a view—approximately a
thousand miles! The sight of the Earth from this height
was the most glorious thing I had ever seen."[78]

During Joann's near-death experience, she describes
being given a tour of the universe:

"I was comfortably wafting along a black tunnel, no

---

[78]   Carl G. Jung, https://carljungdepthpsychologysite.blog/2018/02/03/carl-jungs-near-death-experience/
        #.WS3.qRNKgWS

specific direction since I had no body to gauge and noticed it was a blackness like I had never seen. It was full of love and joy and peace and just nurtured me along. Waves just came over me and gently guided me along. I was overcome by the love that surrounded me and that I could return the feeling.

"At some point, a being came along and took me on a tour of the universe. I had instilled in me, creation and how the galaxies were created. I got to visit places that were advanced beyond comprehension, and yet see places that are just starting out! I was met with such love and compassion that I [couldn't care less] what was going on to my human transporter. While the paramedics continued to work on me and get me ready for transport, I was too busy playing on a star and meeting my Maker! It never concerned me there were no bodies, and fear was not in my vocabulary. Things were assimilated instantly and within that instant, knowledge was completely consumed. These beings were not male or female. Since there is no way to measure time, I have no idea how long this went on. I was shown and told things unimaginable.

"Each time the beings were through with me, I would be back in the tunnel, floating along, only to be met by other beings. At some point I noticed a shining pinpoint of light. I floated towards it."[79]

During Roger's near-death experience, he was given the opportunity to not only visit another planet with people of great intelligence, but also to communicate with

---

79   Joann M., http://www.nderf.org/Experiences/rjoann.m.

them.

"In an instant, I was there on another planet! I was able to see my body there (I can't see my body in the light). *I'm in the presence of people, and am able to talk to them! How great*, I thought.

"They were amazed to see me in front of them. I was in some sort of city with flat ground; there were buildings with no windows nor doors, just like big boxes. They had a special way to enter them but it wasn't very important for me to know it. We weren't communicating with voice, but through the minds (telepathic), I was able to understand each word (in French, to me) and while I was talking, I know I was using another language with them. This was all done automatically.

"They where asking me where I come from? They wanted to see in my mind the stars I could see from my planet. The result was good.

"They where also asking me where on earth I was born, what was the area I liked to see and what I liked to do on earth? I told them I was born in a village called Caplan, and that I like scuba diving in Port Daniel and New Port, Quebec. They wanted to see in my mind what it looks like and a map of those areas. They asked me to show them—if I wanted to. The result, again, was good as I was capable of mentally showing them the map.

"They asked me where I was taking the energy to survive; I knew right away that they were talking about food in a strange way. I told them about the plants that we eat on earth and then they said, 'Are you also eating what used to be alive?'

"I said, 'Yes.'

"They told me, 'We knew there were primitive civilizations but not as bad as that!'

"They were really surprised that someone coming from such a primitive world could meet them on their own planet!" [80]

---

80   Roger, https://www.nderf.org/Experiences/troger_c_nde.html

Communication

From multitudes of accounts, it appears that communication between spirits takes place effortlessly, without misunderstanding. In fact, it appears that it tends to happen thought to thought—telepathically, and those thoughts flow freely, without conscious effort:

> "I remember that all of our thoughts flowed into and out of each other simultaneously. Despite this, I could still process my own thoughts. I knew that the lady near me was in her 30s, that she had died in a car accident leaving behind children but she was at peace with the fact that her husband would care for them."[81]

Franziska met her deceased brother during her near-death experience. Of the incident, she said,

> "I especially liked the way I could communicate with Andreas. I just needed to think a thought and immediately he knew exactly what I meant. He

---

81   http://www.nderf.org/NDERF/NDE Experiences/joschua.b.nde.htm

understood every facet of this thought, even including my corresponding feelings. The answer came back in each case without delay. To lie or hide a thought would have been impossible. Then we were sitting face to face in the grass and started to tell each other things or to discuss things.

"I can remember that in order to obtain an answer for a question, I just had to ask the question. After that I just had to follow the thread; I had access to all answers. I remember darkly a difficult mathematical task. I not only could get the answer, but I also understood very well and how everything was connected and was calculated. This amazed me. On the other side, there were no simple answers about what was/or should happen in the world. These issues we could discuss. I remember how we discussed certain structures of power in the Middle East. After some time, he stood up and told me that it was time to go back."[82]

The consistency of near-death experiencers describing communication is telling, as there are very few experiences that don't speak of it. Some even try to give more detail.

"She had communicated it with lightning speed, faster than computers can talk. It was instant and total knowing. I found that Grandmother and I could think on several levels at once and communicate them all simultaneously. You can't know something without knowing everything around it, what causes it, what

---

82   Franziska R. http://www.nderf.org/Experiences/1franziska_r_adc.html

sustains it. Knowledge dovetails in the spirit world, each piece fitting with other pieces. Every fact connected to it is seen instantly, in totality. We have nothing like it on Earth. We can't even approach it. Our knowledge and ability to communicate is like a child's who hasn't yet learned a language. We struggle to communicate, but we don't possess the tools. We're like little children." [83]

Lisa shares the following from her experience:

"The beings communicated with me, and one another in some kind of telepathic way. We spoke without words, directly, from mind to mind, or from spirit to spirit. None of us had any bodies. We were all made of some unknown substance, like a concentration of pure light, we were like dots of light in the light everywhere around us. Everybody knew what everybody else 'had in mind' instantly.

"There was no possibility, or need to hide anything from anybody. This kind of communication made misunderstandings impossible, and made us close in a way almost impossible to describe. We were all individuals, but at the same time we were all one, united by indestructible bonds of love forever, and also united with the light in the world of light around us, being part of it, and part of each others light." [84]

---

83   Wallace, Ranelle, *The Burning Within*, (Carson City, NV: Gold Leaf Press, 1994), pg. 99

84   Lisa, http://www.nderf.org/Experiences/1lisa_m_nde.html

Oneness and Unity

One thing that comes up again and again in near-death experiences is the mention of an incredible oneness and unity with God, other beings, and the universe as a whole. This unity appears to be so encompassing that many struggle to find words that even make sense to those of us who haven't had such an experience. Gratefully, many still make the effort. I think it's safe to say that while we can't comprehend the depths of unity available in the afterlife, we can recognize that there is incredible oneness available in the spirit world. Jennifer says,

"Yet another time, I was aware of being combined with all the other thoughts or shapeless and infinite souls of every person or creature who has ever lived or died, or been, or is, those waiting to be born and those who have already lived and died. I was aware of suddenly having infinite knowledge. I knew all languages, *all* languages at once, and all religious thought, all everything. I was one with the Creator and with Creation itself. I was the Creator. We all were; those who haven't come back still are. It's impossible to describe.

"I was aware that my earthly body, my container or vessel of my soul had been shed, and I was so much more. I knew all things. I was God along with everyone else, and yet God was still there in superior existence, too: A universal power that was gentle and kind, humble and pure. God lives in me; the soul of God was breathed into my dead body when I chose to live. I had individual thought awareness of one being, yet was one of the whole, without definition or separation away from each other. We were in, through, and with each other. It was incredible, humbling, beautiful beyond beauty, and powerful in the most gentle and kind of ways. It was loving and peaceful in a way that transcends all understanding."[85]

Josiane Antonette had a near-death experience, and experienced a profound oneness with everything.

"I feel such a wonderful release! I'm free! I can't resist this new and wonderful tide of energy sweeping my body upward. Now I'm on the hospital room ceiling gazing down! Everything appears so small: I see my bed; my body looks small and colorless; the people around the bed are tiny. Overwhelming grief and sorrow fill the room, and yet I feel completely disconnected from the scene below

---

85   Jennifer J. http://www.nderf.org/Experiences/1jennifer_j_ndes.html

me. I hover nearer and look at the strange form lying on the bed. I feel compassion beyond words. I understand everything, but I have no feeling of attachment to anyone. I look at each person standing at the bedside and feel tremendous love.

"I want to say to them, 'I'm all right. You don't have to worry. I'm all right. Look at me! I'm fine!'

"I am love; I am understanding; I am compassion!

"My presence fills the room. And now I feel my presence in every room in the hospital. Even the tiniest space in the hospital is filled with this presence that is me. I sense myself beyond the hospital, above the city, even encompassing Earth. I am melting into the universe. I am everywhere at once. I see pulsing light everywhere. Such a loving presence envelops me!

"I hear a voice say, 'Life is a precious gift: to love, to care, to share.'"[86]

In the spirit world, it appears that love pervades *everything*. It's as if love itself is a force of nature. Nancy Rynes explains from her near-death experience,

"The Beauty I saw and felt in those first moments really does deserve a capital B. It wasn't just pleasing to the eye, there was something deeper to it, more harmonious, more blessed, and more powerful. Everything felt tied together by an enormous amount of love and peace. Somehow I knew that the beauty of the landscape around me was the product of unconditional

---

86   Josiane Antonette, https://www.near-death.com/experiences/notable/josiane-antonette.html

love on a cosmic scale.

"While this beauty took my breath away, the sense of overwhelming peace and love completely ensnared me and made me want to stay here forever. I continued to feel a deep sense of unconditional love flow through all things around me: the air, the ground below my feet, the trees, the clouds, and me. I didn't know how it was possible to feel love as if it were a physical presence, but I did. My being vibrated with love to its core. Every molecule of me seemed bathed in love. I couldn't block it out, nor would I have wanted to. I continued to feel the energy of love flow around me like a gentle current, washing through me, and eventually capturing me by the heart. I felt supported by some kind of loving presence so powerful, yet so gentle, that I cried again. I had never experienced such unconditional love and acceptance in all of my years on this Earth.

"It felt as though this place were built from love on a very grand, cosmic scale."[87]

Mary Deioma explains from her experience:

"In that moment, a beam of pure white came out of the sky and came down and touched me on my shoulder. I was so filled with love—it's impossible to describe how much love there was in that moment. All the love of the world. It filled my whole, entire body—every cell of my body was completely infused with this love. It was the love of a parent for their precious child. And in the same moment, I recognized that I always knew that this truth

---

87   Rynes, Nancy, *Awakenings from the Light*, 2015, Solace Press, Denver: Colorado, pg. 23-24

was always there for me, and I was remembering (and not just learning something new—I was remembering): *I am part of this love. I am God, and God is me!* It doesn't really convey the truth to say the words. It doesn't come close.

"Anyway, as this beam touched me, suddenly I was viewing this scene of the road I was driving down from three different places. I was seeing it from my body, and I was seeing it from the passengers seat—and from the passengers seat, I could see it with my intellect. I was observing clearly the edges of the beam...

"And then my soul went out of my heart. My soul went up the beam, and as it went up the beam, I felt so connected to all souls! As I reached the top of the beam, I rippled out in concentric circles and I became one with every soul on the planet.

"And then my focus shifted, and I became one with all the trees on the planet. And specifically, I could feel that I was in a tree, and I was looking at another tree in the forest (which was me looking back at me!). It was so incredible! And then I was *all* the grass and I was looking at a blade of grass next to me, and it was a blade of grass looking back at me. It was amazing!

"My focus shifted, and I was a rock on a mountain. I was the earth, and that really surprised me, because I just never in my life imagined that inanimate objects were filled with God consciousness.

"And then my focus shifted again, and I was *all of the entire universe!* The complete, entire universe. So humungous!

"At the same time, I don't know how, but I could see the smallest, tiniest particle of what the universe is made out of. It was this massive, uniform field of particles, and at the tiniest level, the tiniest particle—smaller than anything that I know we could record, it was pure white —and this was a sort of radiant light. And this particle was pure energy, but more than that, this particle that *everything* in the entire universe is made out of is love! Like, a tangible love that is the stuff of God..."

"It was awesome! And I went beyond the universe into this pure consciousness... It's not anything you could describe (which is so frustrating), because I *so* want to let you know what it's like. It is pure potential—pure consciousness prior to actualization. It doesn't *look like* anything. It's outside of time and space. It isn't close to anything you can describe in the physical universe. But it was *so* amazing. So full of love. *So* incredible!" [88]

Landscapes and Cities

Among the most common elements of near-death experiences is entering a landscape of some sort. These landscapes vary about as much as they do on earth, but almost always seem to be somehow turbo-charged with love, life, and incredible detail.

Nancy shares,

"While my time on the Other Side (aka, 'Heaven') was brief in human terms, when I was there it felt as if weeks or months were passing. I observed an amazing amount in at most, a couple of human hours. The first wonderful thing that I experienced was the beauty of Heaven, both visually and in a feeling-sense. When I was there, a landscape of gently rolling hills surrounded me. Flower-filled grassy meadows spread out on the hills around me. There were huge, deciduous trees in full leaf. The trees

were larger and grander than any here on Earth and
surrounded the meadows. There was the barest sense of a
light mist, as if it were a humid summer morning clung to
the tops of the trees. The sky shown a very light blue,
similar to what you might see at the ocean's shore, with
wispy clouds and a very bright but somewhat diffuse
golden light.   That was the visual. But there is more to
Heaven than what we can see with our eyes. Below the
surface visuals was a well of feeling fueled by love, peace,
and an abiding Presence that I will call Spirit or God.

"Through the landscape around me I sensed a
profound feeling of peace, brightness, goodness, and love.
The Beauty I felt really does deserve a capital B. It wasn't
just pleasing to the eye, there was something deeper to it,
more harmonious, more blessed, and more powerful.
Everything felt tied together by love and peace, and the
beauty of the scenes around me were the product of this
unconditional love.   While the beauty of Heaven took
my breath away, the sense love completely ensnared me
and made me want to stay there forever. I felt a deep sense
of that love flowing through all things around me: the air,
the ground below my feet, the trees, the clouds, and me. I
felt the love flowing around me, flowing through me, and
eventually capturing me by the heart. I felt supported by a
loving Presence so powerful, yet so gentle, that I cried
again. I had never experienced such unconditional love
and acceptance in all of my years on the planet. It felt as
though this place were built from love and peace on a
very grand, cosmic scale.

"What I realized and was later told by my Guide was

that love formed the structure or underpinnings of Heaven. Each soul might see the 'landscape' differently, but all sensed and 'saw' the love that formed the basis for everything in the same way. That love and peace seemed to shimmer as glimmers of light beneath the surface, winking in and out of visual sight. It had colors and sparkle and texture. It seemed to take the form of what I saw, like trees, a meadow, etc., but at the same time it was also separate from the forms themselves."[89]

Tommy Lee Thomason shares:

"When I exited the other end of the tunnel, I was standing in a grassy field that had low gently rolling hills. There were a few large oak trees and flowering bushes. I realized I was standing on a narrow sandy path and started walking along it. I didn't know where I was going but felt compelled to follow it. It felt like I was home and had lived there for a very long time.

"The path lead over a slow rolling hill and when I got to the top, I could see the path lead to a small white bridge that crossed a small creek in the valley. I wish I could describe the vividness of the colors of the grass, flowers, sky, even the clarity of the water in the creek. It was like crystal. This is why I don't tell very many people. They can't comprehend and I can't explain.

"I followed the path toward the bridge. It was a wooden arch bridge about ten feet long and four or five feet wide. It had a wooden handrail on each side. As I got

---

to about fifty feet from the bridge, I noticed a figure dressed in brilliant white walking on the path on the other side of the bridge coming toward me. Just as I got to the end of the bridge, the figure was about ten feet from the other end of the bridge and he stopped and looked up at me. It was my grandfather who had died in 1966. I felt such warmth and peace and I never wanted to leave and started to go to him because I was so happy to see him again." [90]

Sharon describes,

"I felt at ease as they led me from the clouds to a beautiful garden that was to the left of a huge, glorious city.

"As I looked around, I noticed that the colors were so bright and vibrant, and the air was sweet and clear. I could hear birds singing. I heard water running, like there was a stream nearby. There were trees and flowers, and the grass was cool and soft on my feet. I felt a soft, silken breeze touch my skin. As I stood in this breathtaking place, I felt a huge presence all around me just pouring love out onto me. I felt such joy and all I could do was stand there in awe at the beauty and the love that was all around me...

"As I stood there in the garden, I noticed once again, how beautiful and brilliant the colors of the flowers, the trees and the grass were. The reds were redder, the pinks more pink, and yellows more yellow. The colors were so much more vibrant than any colors I had ever seen. The

90   Tommy Lee Thomason, https://www.nderf.org/Experiences/1tomy_t_nde.html

air was sweetly fragrant. It was so clean and clear. The grass felt cool to the touch, like on a beautiful spring day. There were birds singing in the trees, and I saw a stream where the water glistened like diamonds in the sun as it flowed over the rocks. I heard music, which was more beautiful than anything I had ever heard before. It was then that I noticed everything had its own pitch or sound. The trees had a sound, the leaves on the trees had their own sound, the grass had a sound, the rocks had their own sound, the water had yet another sound, and so on; and, when you take all of those individual sounds and put them all together, it sounded like the most magnificent symphony and choir ever created, and what's even more amazing, was, everything and everyone in Heaven was singing praises to God.

"It just poured out of every leaf, rock, blade of grass, and every bird. It was the most beautiful sound I have ever heard. I can still hear it, even now, after all these years. It is like a song in the wind. Every now and then, I still hear the Heavenly music, as the breeze blows through the leaves on the trees. It carries me back there and I feel that deep, all encompassing love again. It heals my soul and my spirit soars. There is no time in Heaven, so I have no idea how long it took for each different step of this journey...

"Then I moved to the edge of the garden to what looked like a wooded glen. I could see golden sunbeams pouring through the branches of the tall oak and pine trees. I noticed a log lying next to a stream with little flowers dotting around it here and there. There were pine needles and a few pine cones scattered about. I went over to the log and sat down listening to the water as it danced across the rocks. When I looked up, I saw a man sitting on the other end of the log next to me. The air was cool and comfortable and I could hear the birds singing their sweet songs.[91]

During his near-death experience, Scott was guided around the spirit world by his grandmother. Impressed by the incredible landscape, Scott asked,

"'What is this place Grandma?'

"She said, 'Son, this is where we all go when we die.'

"I looked around. I was so at peace. I could hear music. I could see the mountains in the background, the sky was a series of washed Alizarin crimson then faded to Prussian blues and then a beautiful darkness. Other than the Warm Golden light, the sky was the most beautiful 'sunset' I've ever seen. Behind me was darkness. It was night time and like space darkness. The ironic thing was that I felt like I was part of all of it and it was connected to me. I felt no fear. This was Heaven. I knew I had worked hard on changing my life. Years before, I had found faith in a power greater than me. I felt this feeling; I can only call love that knows no boundary of time, space or consciousness. It covers everything that has been, is and will be. I've read it, I've heard it, I have intellectualized it and believed. But never have I felt it in my soul, until then. Not because we can bribe love, by our acts or control it with penance or faith. It's just because we ARE

91   Sharon M. http://www.nderf.org/NDERF/NDE Experiences/sharon_m_nde.htm

and It loves us all no matter what." [92]

Among the fascinating details given about the details of heaven, many describe the colors as being more vivid than those on earth:

> "The next thing I saw was a meadow in the mountains with indescribable beauty. The sky was the bluest blue; the grass was the greenest green. All colors here are extremely pale compared to there. I saw my grandmother, running with children, towards me. She took me by the hand and we were at the beginning of a bridge over a small creek. We talked for what seemed like hours about my life since she had died." [93]

Howard Storm described the colors he saw in this way:

> "I'm an artist. There are three primary, three secondary, and six tertiary colors in the visible light spectrum. Here, I was seeing a visible light spectrum with at least 80 new primary colors. I was also seeing this brilliance. It's disappointing for me to try and describe, because I can't—I was seeing colors that I had never seen before. What these beings were showing me was their glory."[94]

Types of Landscapes

I haven't yet found a limitation on the types of

92   Scott W. http://www.nderf.org/Experiences/1scott_w_nde.html

93   Wendy G. http://www.nderf.org/Experiences/1wendy_g_nde.html

94   Howard Storm, https://www.near-death.com/experiences/notable/howard-storm.html

landscapes people encounter on the other side. It appears that if we have it here, they probably have something similar there. But here are a few examples:

Jungle:

> "I heard the nurse say 'no blood pressure.' I went unconscious. Suddenly I found myself in a boat, floating down a river in a jungle. In the background I could hear the most magnificent music I had ever heard. It was a jungle drum beat of incredible dimensions. I became very elated with its incessant melodic sounding rhythm. There were two paddlers steering the canoe and eight passengers. I was brimming over with delight. There was no feeling of pain or movement through the water. Then I came upon the distant shore. I was alone now. I do not remember stepping onto the shore. A radiant being in long white robes was there to greet me. I could not discern the sex of the being, or the face of the being. However the most incredible feeling of love surrounded me. It emanated from the being. We were communicating through mental telepathy. I have never experienced such joy. All of a sudden I was back in bed with incredible pain." [95]

Desert:

> "I remember seeing the bright light in the background and the foreground like a desert with tumble weeds. The light got brighter, closer, and wider as a form of a person was coming towards me (but kinda like looking at an

---

95   https://iands.org/research/nde-research/nde-archives31/newest-accounts.html?start=380

overexposed picture where you can make out forms but not details)." [96]

Mountain cave:

"I was looking down on myself again. There is a chunk of time I don't recall. During that time I was taken from the emergency room to ICU. During that time I had my Experience.

"I remember seeing these sparkles like jewels before my eyes. I remember trying to focus on the sparkles and as I did, this wall came into focus. The wall was alive with blues, purples, reds and oranges sparkling on it. I became aware of this golden sandy floor. My perception was of seeing from a height taller than my physical being. So in some part of my thought I knew I was floating. I looked around at the place I was and saw that I was in what appeared to be a huge cave or cavern. To my left and slightly behind me was this field of golden, sandy, boulders and beyond the boulders was this cliff wall that went so far up that the top was lost in the gloom above." [97]

Grassy Field:

"There was this grassy field... And as I went into that grassy field, I noticed off to my right that there was kind of river that went through. There was an embankment that went down. It was beautiful!

"There was music like nothing I can describe here on

96   https://iands.org/research/nde-research/nde-archives31/newest-accounts/1127-the-fall-from-mr-m-s-racehorse.html

97   https://iands.org/research/nde-research/nde-archives31/newest-accounts.html?
      task=blogcategory&start=375

this earth, that kind of wafted through everything: through the grasses, through the millions of little tiny white flowers that lay through the grasses, through the bushes, through the trees—it's almost as if everything that existed carried a sound. And all of that sound kind of wafted together, and it blended together. And it was a par of me. It was through me, it was out of me—it was the most peaceful thing that you can imagine.

"Along the water's edge there were probably somewhere about five to seven people, and I knew that they were there waiting for me. Someone looked up and noticed that I was coming. I was dressed in something that was long, and white, and flowing. I was moving across the ground rather rapidly. My hair was shoulder length. (My hair has never been longer than what it is right now my entire life, but it was long. And I felt such a peace, I felt such a fulness, such a completeness as I moved along heading toward this group of people that I knew were going to take me across that water if I decided to go with them. And I knew if I did go with them, I would never come back."[98]

Forest:

"I remember flying over a beautiful landscape. I saw a bright green forest, which seemed endless. I felt totally weightless and I had a strong feeling of invulnerability. I could see everything around me without having to turn my head. I could look behind me, straight ahead, and up above myself. Then I saw a bright light, like the sun

---

98   Elaine Durham, IANDS Utah meeting, 3 March 2004, https://iandsutah.files.wordpress.com/2013/02/iands-04-03-mar-2004-elaine-durham.mp3

except that it did not dazzle me. The light was everywhere! Suddenly I had the sensation of falling deeper and deeper. I landed on a stone floor and the impact stopped my fall, but it did not hurt.

"First I just closed my eyes, but after a while, I heard a voice calling, 'What are you doing down there? Get up!'

"I opened my eyes and saw someone who reached out his hand to help me up. When I was on my feet, I noticed that I did not have one scratch. I was OK. And I also noticed that there were other beings wearing long robes. These beings said to me, 'It is wonderful that you are here!' but I couldn't see their faces. Further away, I could see the forest from where I had come. I asked myself, *what is behind that forest?*

"The being who had helped me onto my feet responded that behind the forest is a wonderful little village. The being didn't speak; it was like telepathy. When I was near that being, I had a feeling of security and happiness, simply indescribably good. Suddenly, all the beings started moving in the direction of the forest. But the being that was helping me paused and asked, 'Are you coming with us?'

"I responded, 'Not yet.'

"I knew that, if I went with that group, I wouldn't be able to come back." [99]

Rural Countryside:

---

99   http://www.nderf.org/Experiences/1julia_b_probable_nde.html

"I was then aware of traveling through a dark tunnel. I found myself on a road winding down to a beautiful rural place, which contained a large rustic house set in a valley with a forest behind it. There was a sparkling river and the meadows in front of it were golden and peaceful. There may have been a mill wheel at the far side of the house, through which a stream flowed. The forest behind, looked safe and inviting and I was curious to see it and remain there. At some point, I found myself turned around on the road facing up towards where the tunnel had ended." [100]

Lakeside:

"I was instantly standing by this gorgeous lake. And the feeling I had was I wanted to fall into it, it was so beautiful! It looked like a combination of liquid silver and crushed diamond. And I knew if I went down into it that I could breathe under there…

"So many things caught my eye, I just wanted to see everything. I didn't have one care about the fact that I had departed earth, that I had left three children behind, family, friends, antiques—whatever! …this was such a fantastic place.

"As I turned my head away from the lake (the lake was to the right of me, I was standing to the left), it had these flowers, and they went all along the side of the lake that curved where I couldn't see past that because there were hills. And I was so curious about everything. I noticed there were just fields and fields of the most beautiful

---

100   https://www.nderf.org/Experiences/raustin_c_probable_nde.html

flowers, and their colors that we don't have in this world. I can still see them [today, in my memory] but I don't have names for them and I can't describe them. It's kind of like being blind from birth and trying to tell somebody what red is. I can't tell you. But they are so beautiful—colors that we don't have here. There were fields and fields of this plush, very brilliant grass. And the sky wasn't blue, it looked like swirling clouds of light. It was so incredibly beautiful! I can't imagine a place on earth that could look like this place.

"I saw a hill in the distance, and I thought, 'I want to go up on top of that hill.'

"And I had no sooner said that, I was up on top of that hill."[101]

I think it's fair to assume that if there is a desirable landscape that we like here, there is some form of it (probably a grander form of it) there.

Cities

Aside from natural landscapes, beautiful towns and cities are described by many experiencers.

During her near-death experience, Sharon Milliman had the opportunity to walk around with angelic guides, and after encountering some beautiful landscapes, she is shown a city. According her description:

101   Sarah Menet, Iands Utah Meeting, September 2017,
      https://iandsutah.files.wordpress.com/2013/02/iands-11-09-sept-2011-sara-menet.mp3

"I saw a beautiful, magnificent city, and there was a golden wall around the city. As I walked through the garden I saw a lot of the buildings that were on the outskirts of this glorious city. Some of the buildings seemed to be made out of a really beautiful marble. The one in the middle had a golden dome on it.

"I saw healing buildings with pools of water—and those were for soul healing, like for someone who had a traumatic death, or a sudden death and didn't know what was going on. And it seemed like each building had angels, and other people who were specifically trying to help the healing. They were trained for that.

"Then there was buildings for little children–babies. I saw the babies, and there were specific angels that were trained to take care of them as they grow—and they will grow.

"I saw schools. But these weren't schools like schools of science. This was like spiritual growth.

"I saw a library that had *tons* of books—I mean thousands and thousands of books on every subject you could possibly want. They were all in this beautiful building."[102]

During Kim Rives' near-death experience, she also came to a beautiful city:

"Up in the distance straight ahead, I saw this beautiful city that was shimmering with so much light that it was

---

102   Sharon Milliman, from a podcast interview, https://neardeathexperiencepodcast.org/sharon-millimans-near-death-experiences

just as brilliant as the sun, and rays that were coming off of it. And I said, 'Oh, I want to go there!'

"And when I said I wanted to go there, we were *in* the city, on the street. And it was kind of interesting, because if you know this—I landed in this direction, and I saw that the streets were paved in gold. Then I looked up and there was a beautiful building that looked like a temple, only much more magnificent. And even the temple was so beautiful, and there was a building on the side, and it had mortars in diamond—big mortars. And there were angels on the grassy areas on both sides, and they were talking, and they were conversing with one another.

"I wondered why they weren't coming and chipping the gold off the streets and putting it into a bucket, because I wanted to. But I guess they didn't need to!

"But what I enjoyed about watching the angels was they were so happy—contentment and peace. I didn't feel any strife or inner feelings of hardship. They just seemed like they were at rest, and happy to be with one another."[103]

Diane experienced cities and buildings during her near-death experience:

"After that we went about several cities, and I saw one quaint, another of like green glass, and then another like so many of our own great palaces or majestic buildings. The streets were indeed of gold, and this awesome

---

103   Kim Rives, from a Utah IANDS conference audio recording, 6 June 2010,
         https://iandsutah.files.wordpress.com/2013/02/iands-10-06-jun-2010-kim-rives.mp3

fountain was in front of one massive building, that just sparkled blue-green light giving love from it. It is something you never forget.

"He took me into this very massive structure, richer and more beautiful than anything we could ever create on earth. I realized that all paintings, all woven rugs, tapestries, carvings; all we create on earth that is beautiful has its seed from Heaven. We saw all this before we came to earth. We try to recapture some of Heaven while on earth. We deeply desire Heaven on earth. We miss Heaven deep in our souls...

"This palace the angel took me to, was spectacular and very, very high. I'd say the hallways were approximately three stories or more high. Very ornate and beautiful, marble hallways with exquisite paintings and these columns that were of gold and detailed with absolutely beautiful adornments on them. There was some form of writings on the doors, which were fully twenty-five feet or more high and automatic as well. The writings were more like ancient symbols but very familiar to me. I seemed to understand them. And suddenly we came to these two very magnificent doors which automatically opened and this awesome presence filled the marble floored throne room. It was definitely the throne room and I was acutely aware that I was only being permitted to view the reflection of God's Light. Not the full force of His Awesome wonder."[104]

Sylib, while being guided through the spirit world

---

104   Diane, https://www.nderf.org/Experiences/1diane_c_nde.html

with Jesus Christ as her guide, said,

> "I felt sad because I wanted to stay there with Him. I
> don't know if it was heaven or not, I just know I was the
> happiest person in the world. He showed me briefly a city
> with lots of people. Green grass grew and children were
> running, laughing and playing. Older men in white robes
> were teaching young children as if in a school. Women
> were very busy getting ready for what looked like a great
> event. They were all dressed in white as well. Flowers
> bloomed and green trees with lots of fruit stood along a
> river of running water, like a rippling stream but larger.
> Its water was clear as glass. Such a site I saw. Everyone
> was busy. Even the air smelled sweet like a rose. I was
> then send back to Earth." [105]

Roy Mills describes memories from before coming to
earth, as he experienced with a spirit guide.

> "Very early in my pre-birth training, before I had
> looked into the life books, or even chosen my life
> experiences, or met some of my future family and friends,
> I was taken to an extremely large auditorium—larger than
> a grand stadium. My guide led me across the most
> exquisite floor I have ever seen. The floor didn't glow, as
> some of the others I'd seen, but it reflected the room's
> bright light, and in it, I could see my own reflection.

> "My guide had not told me why I was being brought to
> this place, but she had seemed very excited. There were
> many other angels inside, bustling about, preparing the
> auditorium, and they seemed to share an excitement.

---

[105] Sylib, https://www.nderf.org/Experiences/1sybil_s_nde.html

And I saw in this section of the auditorium faced a large, elevated platform. A very large, pure white chair sat in the center of the raised floor. The chair was simple in design. It glowed with a powerful white light. I was in the throne room area where the audience of souls was to stand before the Spirit Father. I was going to *see the Father!*" [106]

Ricky Randolph describes from his near-death experience:

"Faster, and faster the speed was increasing. I saw other star systems and galaxies as I raced onward. I entered what seemed to be a hole of some sort. It was long and dark. However around me I saw streaks of light made up of every color in the spectrum. I saw a faint light growing brighter and brighter in the distance up ahead. As I entered the light I felt it all through my being. I was not afraid anymore.

"Then all of a sudden I was standing before a massive set of steps. They led up to what seemed to be a bridge or walk of some kind. In the distance I saw a sight so magnificent and astounding—a city made up of what seemed to be glass or crystal!

"The lights were of many colors that radiated from it. Never have I ever seen such a sight. I began walking toward the city in a daze of unbelief.

"So many questions raced through my mind. I had to know where I was. What was happening to me?

106   Roy Mills, *The Soul's Remembrance*, (Onjinjinkta Publishing, October 25, 1999)

"I reached the front of the city and saw a double door that looked to be about thirty feet or so in height and width. It shined as if it was polished. As I stood there wondering, the doors began to open. I took a step back and looked inside.

"I could see what appeared to be people walking about on the inside, much like they do in a mall here on Earth. These people though were dressed very different. For one thing, they all seemed to be dressed in some sort of robes with hoods.

"I entered through the doors in amazement at what I was seeing. The inside was massive. It seemed to be square in shape, with a balcony all around that led down to different levels. I walked up and looked downward over the balcony. It seemed to go on forever! [107]

Cecil L. Hamilton talks about several cities he saw in his near-death experience:

"A long way off there was a pinprick of light. I moved toward it, slowly at first, then faster and faster as if I were on top of a train accelerating. Then I stopped and stepped fully into the light. I noticed everything—sky, buildings, glass—emitted its own light and everything was much more colorful than what we see here. A river meandered around. On the other side was a city, and a road running through it to another city, and another city and another and another.

"Right in front of me but across the river were three

---

men. They projected themselves to me. They didn't walk
or fly; they projected over. I didn't recognize them, yet I
knew one was Lynn Bibb. (I was named after him. He
died a matter of weeks before I was born.) I knew these
three men were looking out for me, like a welcoming
committee to escort me over the river to the first city. I
had the feeling that if I went with them, there would be
no coming back, so I hesitated.

"The first city was like first grade. People stayed there
until they were ready to go to the next city—your eternal
progression, from city to city."[108]

Discussing her experience in the spirit world, Linda
Allen describes:

"It had golden colors and there was what looked like a
big explosion coming up from the city. There were colors
that we do not have on earth. These colors were so
brilliant and intense that they would hurt our eyes if we
looked at them on earth. But not there. It was a glorious
glowing city of buildings and streets. The streets had
bricks. They were like golden bricks. The buildings (and I
know that this sounds really strange) were smart. They
were intelligent. They were buildings of knowledge."[109]

That gives an interesting view of what may be meant
by the streets of heaven being paved with gold. But from
Larry Tooley's experience, we find that the gold is not just

---

108   Harold A. Widdison, Trailing Clouds of Glory, (Cedar Fort, Inc., Springville, Utah) December 6,
        2011, 22

109   *Harold A. Widdison,* Trailing Clouds of Glory, (Cedar Fort, Inc., Springville, Utah) December 6, 2011,
        22

in the streets:

> "As we approached the light I was told, 'We can go no farther. Just ahead lies the bounds of our travel.'

> "The hillside ahead continued its ascent, ending at the base of a mountain. Cliffs rose steeply, disappearing into a hazy mist. Very high mountains protruded through the mist as fleecy clouds slowly drifted across their craggy peaks. Regal splendor crowned this celestial scene.

> "At the base of the mountains lay a glorious city. Tall spires and pinnacles rose in exalted splendor, challenging the clouds above for dominance.

> "Light radiated, undulating from the pearlized buildings. A thousand different shades of color filled the spectrum. I struggled to comprehend the sheer immensity of the city that lay below me. At first I failed to see the delicate details of the domed spires until I studied the scene in more detail.

> "Each spire's dome was capped in pure gold. Pinnacles the color of platinum rose among the spires.

> "My emotions overcame me as I sank to my knees in the tall grass at my feet. Through each arched doorway and window shimmered a faint blue light."[110]

Many experiencers see a great wall around a beautiful city:

> "Next thing I remember was going through this dark

---

110   *Harold A. Widdison*, Trailing Clouds of Glory, (Cedar Fort, Inc., Springville, Utah) December 6, 2011, 25-26

passage. I didn't touch any of the walls. I emerged out into an open field and was walking toward a big white wall, which was very long. It had three steps leading up to a doorway in the wall. On a landing above the stairs sat a man clothed in a robe that was dazzling white and glowing. His face had a glowing radiance also. He was looking down into a big book, studying.

"As I approached him I felt a great reverence and I asked him, 'Are you Jesus?'

"He said, 'No, you will find Jesus and your loved ones beyond that door.' After he looked in his book he said, 'You may go through.'

"And then I walked through the door, and saw on the other side this beautiful, brilliantly lit city, reflecting what seemed to be the sun's rays. It was all made of gold or some shiny metal with domes and steeples in beautiful array, and the streets were shining, not quite like marble but made of something I have never seen before. There were many people all dressed in glowing white robes with radiant faces. They looked beautiful. The air smelled so fresh. I have never smelled anything like it. There was a background of music that was beautiful, heavenly music and I saw two figures walking towards me and I immediately recognized them. They were my mother and father, both had died years ago. My mother was an amputee and yet that leg was now restored! She was walking on two legs.

"I said to my mother, 'You and father are beautiful.'

"And they said to me, 'You have the same radiance and you are also beautiful.'

"As we walked along together to find Jesus, I noticed there was one building larger than all the others. It looked like a football stadium with an open end to the building where a blinding light radiated from it. I tried to look up at the light but I couldn't. It was too brilliant. Many people seemed to be bowed in front of this building in adoration and prayer.

"I said to my parents, 'What is that?'

"They said, 'In there is God.'

"I will never forget it. I have never seen anything like it. We walked on as they were taking me to see Jesus and we passed many people. All of them were happy. I have never felt such a sense of well being." [111]

Sara Menet said:

"Far, far off in the distance I could see a beautiful, beautiful city. It could have been a hundred miles away, but I could see it very well.

"I looked about, and I saw this beautiful little cottage, far to the distance and to the left. And it kind of looked like a Hansel and Gretel cottage. It had this little, stone walkway, and a stream that ran by it that had that silvery, crystal water. And I thought, *That's the kind of house I want to live in. I don't want one of those big mansions that I could see...* I thought this cottage was so beautiful...

---

111   https://www.near-death.com/archives/ndes/an-accountant.html

"The little voice in my mind said, 'You can have that. You can have any kind of house you want—if you've earned it…"

"I looked down into this beautiful city. My eyes could focus like a telephoto lens, and I could see it like I was standing close to it, and yet I knew I was quite a distance. The buildings are very shimmery, very brilliant. To me they look like this light, pink hue of alabaster marble, but so thin I could see through the building. (Or maybe it's just because your spiritual eyes can see through buildings.)

"And I could see all kinds of activities. I could hear music playing in the building. I saw this beautiful library with these *huge*, gorgeous books. I don't know what they were bound with, but I noticed there were no chairs there. There were tables, and rows and rows and rows of these beautiful books. And I understood when you cross to the other side—I was only there for seven minutes, but I learned more there than I could learn here in a lifetime, just in a few minutes. I learned how pyramids were built. I saw other things which I never have shared, and probably won't…

"I learned incredible things. So I knew there was learning, and you learn more rapidly over there. Because I started asking questions about what was going on there, the city, and the people and everything. And I noticed as I asked questions, I could ask more than one question at a time. And I could get several answers at the same time, and assimilate everything perfectly..."[112]

During Nancy Rynes' near-death experience, she visited a beautiful landscape, and felt energy coming from each element of the landscape.

"I abruptly found myself standing in a spectacular landscape unlike any I'd ever experienced. Warm breezes drifted across my skin. Beautiful vistas of meadows and distant mountains surrounded me. And a pervasive, loving presence overwhelmed me in its intensity.

"Surrounding me was a landscape of gently rolling hills, flower-filled grassy meadows, towering deciduous trees in full leaf, trees taller and more grand than any here on Earth, and a sense of a light mist floating through as if it were a humid summer morning. The sky gleamed a very light, pearly blue, similar to what you might see at the ocean's shore, with wispy clouds and a very bright but somewhat diffuse light...

"Below the surface forms and colors of everything in the landscape, I somehow also or sensed vibrating energy. I'm not sure how to describe it. It seemed I could see the surface of a leaf, for example, yet also see below it to an energy, a vibration of love or compassion or kindness that made the leaf take on a subsurface radiance. Everything had this radiance: trees, grass, sky, flowers, and clouds. Colors seemed intensified by this radiance. The feeling of love flowed through everything and heightened this

---

112   Sarah Menet, Iands Utah Meeting, September 2017,
       https://iandsutah.files.wordpress.com/2013/02/iands-11-09-sept-2011-sara-menet.mp3

radiance."[113]

So what can we conclude about what kinds of landscapes they have in the spirit world? It appears from hundreds of near-death experiences that if we have it here, it's likely there, too—and more. From deserts to jungles to cities to countryside, it's all there.

I'm therefore left to wonder if people designed cities in the spirit world after leaving this earth, or if (and I consider this FAR more likely) that cities on earth were inspired by the cities that already existed in the spirit world. After all, if we lived for eons in a beautiful landscape with massive cities, wouldn't we be likely to attempt to recreate that here? Whether people caught glimpses of such structures and brought their visions here, or whether spirits from the other side just inspired designers on earth to create them to be like those in the spirit world is unclear. Maybe some of both.

Obviously as far as natural landscapes go, nature on earth must have been designed by God to look like and emulate nature in the spirit world.

The thing that astounds me the most about all of this is how everything seems to contain life: from the obvious, such as people, animals, and plants, to the less obvious, such as water, rocks, and even buildings. What is that kind of life, and does it have some sort of intelligence?

---

113   Rynes, Nancy, *Awakenings from the Light*, 2015, Solace Press, Denver: Colorado, pg. 23-24

Obviously we can only assume from these experiences that they do indeed have some sort of life, intelligence, and consciousness, though we're obviously not equipped to measure it here in the mortal world.

And if inanimate objects (such as buildings and water) have some form of life, might we conclude that *everything* in existence has some form of life?

It's something to think about, to be sure.

Bodies, Food, etc

From near-death experiences, we learn that there are different forms the spirit body can take, but that the most comfortable form tends to be that of adult prime. But our spirit bodies are not made of mortal physical matter. It appears that the most consistent explanation is that those bodies are somehow made of light.

Diane, while traveling with a loving, angelic guide, was given answers to questions she had about her spirit body. She explains:

"I was so filled with love and wanting to hug Him with joy. And His voice came within my mind and He commanded me to stretch forth my hands and arms to see that I was made of solid light. And I did so. And then He infused within my mind the knowledge that we all are of solid light, male and female, each with our own identity and purpose. Each created before entry to earth and each was male or female prior to that entry. He contains both sides, and this is the truth of it. For it is not the sexual side but the strong and the gentle of each side of Him that determined who we'd be created as. A balance of His being."[114]

This question of the structural makeup of a spirit body is an interesting one. There are those who's spirit body seems about the same as their physical body (minus the injuries, of course).

Don died at age 12, and says,

"I died and left my body. While floating above my body, I looked at my hands and they were there. I had a body. I could hear the men in the room saying 'He sure is young to have to die.'

"I tried to tell them I'm not dead. But they could not hear me. Out of the corner of my eye, I saw a small light coming at me or I was going to it." [115]

I've heard of near-death experiences where everything on the other side felt so "physical" that they seemed even more physical than they did in mortality— more tactile, providing more sensation than the person had ever felt on earth.

Jeff Olsen was in a terrible car accident that killed his wife and son, and he survived (but had part of his leg amputated), but had a few near-death experiences following the accident. In one experience, he saw his baby son who had died.

---

114   Diane, https://www.nderf.org/Experiences/1diane_c_nde.html
115   Don, https://www.nderf.org/Experiences/1don_nde.html

"As I walked, on two healthy strong legs, I entered into a long hallway. It was a lovely corridor that seemed to stretch forward almost into eternity, yet I moved down it rapidly and with ease. I saw where it came to a stop, and at the end of the hallway was a baby crib. I rushed to the crib, and peeking in, saw something beyond joyful.

"There lying in the crib was my son. It was little Griffin! He was alive and well. He slept peacefully. I looked at him and took in every detail. How his chubby little hands lay so peacefully beside his perfect face. How his mouth drew breath, raising his small back up and down. How is hair lay gently across the tops of his ears. I reached into the crib and swept him up into my arms. I could feel the warmth from his little body. I could feel his breath on my neck and the smell of his delicate hair. He was so familiar and so alive! I held him close and cried tears of joy as I laid my cheek against his soft little head as we had always done. I felt him breathing as he snuggled into me. His ribs rising and falling with each inhale and exhale. Not only did I feel him physically, but I also felt him spiritually. Every cell of his perfect little body was full of light and life. I felt the energy of his soul and how connected we were. I was his dad. I had taken part in creating him. He was perfect.

"It was Griffin! He was alive, and I was with him, holding him in this wonderful place. It was real, even super real. I had never felt anything so intense. We were tangible. I could feel his body solidly against mine. I felt the life in each of my own cells as they melted together with his in a love exceeding our earthly bond.

"I sobbed with joy, holding my little son. I closed my tear-filled eyes and breathed in how he smelled and how he felt and how everything seemed to disappear except us." [116]

Others see their body as looking just like their physical body, but transparent or made of light. Jeff describes,

"We stopped so I could listen to how the universe sounded as it expanded. Like a deep hum all around me. Everything was so alive all around me and I felt I was part of everything and everything was a part of me. We were one. I now understood how we were all connected to each other. All this knowledge was opening up in me. So beautiful. So endless. Sounds I have never heard before. Colors so intense and new, unlike anything I have ever seen.

"I remember seeing myself as this transparent being of pure light. And when we communicated our whole being would flash different colors depending on our response. I realized then there was nothing I could hide from anyone.

"So much love. Pure divine love around everything everywhere. I was totally engulfed in it. I saw things I can't even begin to describe. The awe factor was way off the charts." [117]

I've also heard of others who looked down at themselves and saw no body at all. They might be in the

---

116   Jeff Olsen, http://kennethcope.com/we-saw-him-part-18/

117   Jeff S, https://www.nderf.org/Experiences/1jeff_s_nde.html

midst of light or hovering over a landscape, but can see no body of their own.

As Casey explains from her experience:

"I was floating down a long white corridor like a tunnel. I was moving towards the most beautiful white light that I had ever seen. It was so beautiful that our words cannot describe it. I was experiencing complete peace and tranquility with no fear or worry. Then I realized I had no body. In fact, my consciousness was floating slowly towards the beautiful light and I was ready to go." [118]

Still others have described being a ball of light, or simply some kind of orb, floating about without any real body or extremities of any kind.

Daphne explains:

"I saw the white tunnel and went through it very quickly. I exited into white light and saw a variety of Beings off to the left-hand side. I told them I was not going to stop, that I was going further on. I turned to my right and found myself in utter blackness. I was very calm and remarked to myself, 'I guess I am dead.'

"I thought that I should tell someone that I was dead and headed to the nurses station to ask them to look in room 16. I saw everyone who was on duty and told them. Then I realized that that was silly because I wasn't in a body. I was a light orb.

---

118   Casey W. https://www.nderf.org/Experiences/1casey_w_possible_nde.html

"Upon realizing this, I returned to the Void. I then thought about who I should tell and I thought of my Mother who was wintering in Harlingen, Texas. As soon as I thought this, I saw a window appear before me with a man and woman sleeping on a bed. I entered the window and stared down at them. There was no emotion and I didn't feel any attachment to them. I said to the woman, 'Well, I just thought that I should tell you that I have died and I will be going on.' Then I went back through the window into the Void." [119]

Debra died during surgery, and says,

"I was not in my body as they rolled me into surgery. I actually stood next to the surgeon and the emergency room doctor as they spoke. I stood next to the surgeon as he performed the surgery. The next thing I knew, I found myself in a waiting room. It was not gray, white or blue, but a mixture of those colors. I knew I wasn't alone, but I felt rather than saw anyone. I felt the words, *go back*.

"I said 'No' because I finally felt like I was out of my hell on earth.

"Then I felt a shove. Irritated, I found myself at the ceiling of the intensive care unit room (ICU) I was in. I was looking down on my body, fully aware that I was an orb. I saw myself in the bed with monitors, tubes, and a nurse working over me. That's when I felt an overwhelming feeling of curiosity. The next thing I knew, I felt a whoosh and found myself gliding under the bed

---

119   Daphne B, https://www.nderf.org/Experiences/1daphne.b.nde.html

coming up through my chest while gasping for air." [120]

Then others see their body as transparent, or described as woven light or simply being made of light.

Robert saw himself similar to this. He says,

"I was going to enter this light. It was now what might be like standing before a sun, except it was of a pure white light. As I was about to enter it two large swirling energy forms with human like shape emerged from it. They asked me (in my mind) 'What are you doing here?'

"I said 'I'm going into the light'.

"They said 'It is not your time'.

"I tried to assure them I was going into the light but they denied my passage. They were adamant it was not my time.

"I then noticed I was a ball of light. I no longer had the shape of a human being. My consciousness was spherical in all directions at once, and I had a God-like knowing. All at once I saw my entire life pass before me in minute detail." [121]

These various types of spirit bodies have led me to a hypothesis about the structure of our bodies on the other side.

It appears that there are at least two basic forms that we may take on in the spirit world—that of a basic

---

120   Debra P. https://www.nderf.org/Experiences/1debra_p_probable_nde.html
121   Robert C, https://www.nderf.org/Experiences/1robert_c_nde_4239.html

intelligent consciousness, and that of a body in the likeness of the mortal, physical body. And while a person may alternate between various aspects of these two forms, it seems that even outside of our physical body, we can generally be reduced to two basic forms—the intelligent consciousness and the spirit body. I emphasize that I came up with this idea of quantifying the spirit form in these two ways. I haven't heard anyone who's been to the other side confirm or deny this idea. I may be totally wrong. Take this with a grain of salt, but this is the idea.

Intelligent Consciousness

The intelligent consciousness seems to be the most essential part of our nature—the part that can be independent of the physical body AND independent of the spirit body. It is the part of a person that is the deepest individual identity of any being. It is eternal and has always existed. As far as I can tell, this part of a person has no distinctive form. It may look like nothing, or it may look like a beam of light, an orb, or some kind of mist or cloud.

In many near-death experiences, people speak of "merging into the light" and describe stepping out of their own 'ego' and becoming fully and entirely one with God, the universe, or the light. They describe it as if they are no longer an individual, no longer separate from anything. They describe having no body, no face, no hands—just existing as a consciousness that merges into the infinite light of God. I suspect when this level of merging is taking place, it is because they are in the intelligent consciousness form.

Others describe drifting over landscapes without any form of body—being completely invisible. They are still themselves, still thinking, feeling, and being, but they are in a form that can shrink into the smallest parts of quarks and atoms, or it can expand to the size of the entire universe. Again, there is a oneness with everything, but there is still the individual within that oneness. Again, I would suggest that this form is the intelligent consciousness form.

Sometimes the senses of sight, sound, smell, etc, can be a little blurred in this form. Perception is every bit as keen in this form, but not via the same sensing organs. In some near-death experiences, people will describe not 'seeing' or 'hearing' anything at all—that no senses were used, yet they might still be in a wide open landscape with people, forests, or buildings. They "sense" everything perfectly without seeing, hearing, feeling, tasting or touching anything. I would suggest that this form is the intelligent consciousness form.

Yet others describe incredible sensations of hearing, seeing, and smelling in this form. Cristine, during her experience, seems to have experienced both the spirit body form and the intelligent consciousness form. And if

I'm understanding her words correctly, it appears that her intelligent conscious form (her actual conscious self) is able to separate and see her spirit body for a time. When her spirit first leaves her body, she seems to be in the spirit body, but then her spirit body goes to sleep, and her intelligent consciousness emerges. She says:

"I began falling through a blackness that quickly turned into super fast moving streaks of brilliant, colored light. The 'ride' was smooth despite the speed that I was falling at. I felt invigorated and was without fear. To me it was an adventure and I looked forward to what would happen next.

"What happened next is a little hard to describe. I was through the tunnel and suddenly landed and watching the creation and birth of everything (earth to plants and animals) one, right after the other. It was shown in such an extreme fast forward that my eyes became 'fast' so that I could view it all. I remember a seed then suddenly had roots which spread furiously fast through the soil and then it's life force pushed through and the petals unfolded to became the most beautiful red rose—I noticed the color was more vibrant as if it had life as well. The flower seemed to grow from seed to complete flower in less than a second. It was like seeing everything being born from conception to birth in the blink of an eye. I can not say in words what it truly all was like. The colors I was seeing had evolved from dark hues of blacks, grays and browns to blues, greens and then reds and yellows. Next I found myself in a room. The room was filled with sumptuous pillows where I sat down and was treated to a show. I can only describe it as being inside a gigantic kaleidoscope, where the colorful images were changing designs rapidly...all breathtaking. Afterwards feeling very drowsy, I quickly fell asleep on the soft pillows.

"In the next moment I was waking up in a placid blackness in space. There were tiny pinholes of starlight giving the impression of floating in outer space. I felt well rested and very calm after what seemed like a long sleep. I looked over to see myself in the distance. I watched myself wake up. I (the self I watched) was curled up in a fatal position. When I became aware that I could move about freely, I 'opened up' and gently floated downward through the night above a new place while I waited for the sun to rise. I am now in a flower garden, a large and very crowded mass of colors in full bloom. The flowers were very tall and looked beautifully old world. This garden was the perfect greeting to the house it belonged to. It was a happy garden, it was alive with a child like excitement.

"Here, my physical body was now completely gone. I was light and getting smaller but becoming much more than before. I could fly all about the garden, my vision was extraordinary and I could zoom in on the tiniest details. I felt very natural here and the garden's joy made me feel like I belonged. There was always the me with the body (although not seen) watching the other me (a small, ball of light) while experiencing everything the other did. I took notice of the flowers, of how they were alive and they were immersed in a love that was pure. To this day I can cry thinking of it. The garden's colors were also alive with hues that made every other colors at 'home' dull." [122]

If my understanding of this is correct, this intelligent consciousness is as much a part of our spirit body as our spirit body is part of our physical body in mortal life.

The Spirit Body

In the spirit body, a person looks like themselves. They have hands, face, feet, clothing, and individual features that generally match well their physical, mortal body in the prime of it's life.

Bonni Burrows speaks of interacting with a spirit on the other side:

"I'm greeting him, and he's greeting me, and we're hugging. And we had substance. That substance was different than this substance, but it *was* substance. We could hug, and we could enjoy each other. We could communicate and we could love each other." [123]

The spirit body is can be experienced by the senses of others (seen, heard, smelled, etc), and it experiences all of the major senses of the physical body plus many more. It is refined and distinct. Vision through the spirit eyes is keener and more sensuous even than the physical eyes. So

---

122   Cristine H, https://www.nderf.org/Experiences/1cristine_h_sobe.html

123   Bonni Burrows, IANDS Utah meeting audio recording, April 2013, https://iandsutah.org/archive-2013/

with the spirit ears, nose, etc. Senses are distinct and precise. The senses of the intelligent consciousness are still present, but are added upon by the spirit body.

When people describe near-death experiences where they are seeing family, embracing people, eating, smelling flowers, or any other sense-based experience, I believe they are in the spirit body form. They are still an intelligent consciousness, but that intelligent consciousness is clothed in a spirit body.

My understanding is that this spirit body was formed, created, or birthed by God. And this spirit body is necessary to house a physical, mortal body. It very likely influences the features that win out in the genetic lottery of our conception and birth. And while there may be many glitches and mistakes made in the formation of the physical body, the spirit body housing it is both perfect and flawless.

While I can't prove this theory (that there are two forms we might take on in the spirit world), it does account for many of the seeming contradictions in near-death experience explanations, and actually opens the door to better understanding the most basic nature of our existence. It provides a possible explanation of how we might have been created and yet always existed. It explains how we can be both one with everything and yet uniquely individual.

The Spiritual Illusion of Form

There is one more aspect to the appearance of the spirit
body that I should mention. There seems to be something
of an ability that many have to see other people in a variety
of forms: that is to say, a man may initially see his
grandmother in the form he last knew her—old and gray,
but later sees her vibrant in her prime, and still later sees
her as merely a light or orb. That itself is interesting
enough, but some even seem to be able to see people in
other imagined forms. For example, the man may choose
to see his grandmother in a funny, even monstrous form, if
he chooses. It's as if the perception of the viewer has an
influence on how people and places look. But even in such
cases (such as when a person makes everyone around him
look like little monsters), it appears that the easiest, most
relaxed way to see people is in their bright, prime adult
form. Anything else takes a level of concentration—which
suggests to me that seeing things or people in any other
way than their true form is probably just an illusion.

Let me give you an example of what I'm talking
about. Natalie Sudman was in a vehicle that ran over a
land mine, which exploded, and she found herself
instantly on the other side, in a grand stadium, sharing
information with white-robed people in the stadium. At
the same time (perhaps because there is no perception of

time on the other side), she seemed also to be in another setting where she was just at rest, which she calls the 'rest environment.'

The insights she has about the spirit form here are interesting. She says,

"I was surrounded by a whole stadium full of other beings, or people... I was 'downloading' information to them, and they were absorbing that information, and they were sending me gratitude. Then I communicated that I wasn't going to go back into my body, and they communicated to me that they would really like me to return... and I said, 'Sure, I'll do it!'

In describing what she looked like there in that setting, she says,

"...I wasn't really physical. I just had that shape [human shape], while being energy. In the *rest environment* I didn't have any form. I didn't have any form at all. I was just awareness, or just consciousness. And it doesn't mean that I was totally dissipated. I was still *a something*, but I wasn't a form.

"...It's like you could take on any form you wanted to there. It was a little farther from the physical world, and so you could take on form if you wanted to, but you didn't have to have a form."

Then describing the reasons that the people in the stadium looked like white-robed figures, she says,

"It was just a very comfortable way for me to perceive them. I talk about playing around with turning them into little monsters and stuff. I could do that. I mean, I could see them that way. And I think that just seeing them as humans in white robes was just a very comfortable way that wouldn't sort of distract my human mind...

"It could be really distracting to be looking at bugs or something, instead of looking at people in white robes."

Then describing the human mortal form we have while living a mortal life, she says,

"It takes so much focus to be in this and stay in this physical awareness and in this physical body..." [124]

Likewise, it appears that spirits have the ability to take on different forms—such as the man's grandma looking like her older self, even though she's now in her prime. Perhaps she chooses to appear to him that way so he'll recognize her. In such cases, it again seems to be that taking on any form besides your natural, prime self, takes a level of concentration.

This may explain some of the strange forms that lower level spirits seem to sometimes take on—such as a demonic form, or a monster, in order to scare people. This is probably not their real form, but rather an illusion in order to frighten or bother people. Likely it takes concentration for them to maintain that frightening

---

124   Natalie Sudman, *What Near-Death Experience Teaches Us About Suffering, Souls, and Spiritual Guidance,* from an interview with Bob Olson in his program, *Afterlife TV.* https://www.youtube.com/watch?time_continue=1&v=PCyQi-7jx4A

image.

When it comes down to it, I'm not exactly sure what to make of all of that, except to say that it seems our imaginations have a much more potent and direct influence on our experiences in the spirit world than they do here.

Sleep

This mention of Cristine's experience (above) also brings up something I've only come across a couple times in my near-death research—the idea of sleep in the spirit world. One thing seems fairly clear; sleep is apparently not *necessary* there like it is here. In fact, upon asking many near-death experiencers if they new of sleep in the spirit world, most insisted that they never saw anything like sleep, because you don't need it there.

But from a few experiences that I've found, it does appear that sleep is possible in the spirit world. Cristine's experience (from the last section) is the most potent spirit-world sleep experience I've heard of, but Jeff, another experiencer, also mentions it in his account. After being buried alive in a workplace accident, Randy entered a realm of light. Says he:

"So much love. Pure divine love around everything everywhere. I was totally engulfed in it. I saw things I can't even begin to describe. The awe factor was way off the charts.

"I saw a handsome young man who later was identified as my grandfather. I was shown a beautiful city that glowed a golden like aura. I felt like I was truly home again. This was very familiar to me.

"Then I was taken even higher. In a flash, I was on a floor in a vast room. There were these vast steps in front of me and my eyes slowly followed them up until I saw what was above me. I immediately hit the floor face down saying 'I am not worthy to be here. I should not be here' over and over again.

"I was before the Holy Trinity. I couldn't look at it. It was so blindingly bright. In a flash, the Christ told me to stand up and I did. He then pulled me into himself and I was gone.

"When I came to, I was being cradled in this huge energy like ball that felt endless and was truly feminine in nature. Like the best-est mom in all the universe. I knew that it was the Holy Spirit. The female aspect of the G-D. The Mother of the Universe. She assured me and rocked me to sleep.

"I was then placed back into my body. When I opened my eyes, I saw and felt the sunshine on me. I was still in that wonderful connection. The sky was an intense blue and the clouds so white and beautiful." [125]

Whether Jeff's sleep was a genuine unconsciousness in the spirit world, or whether this was just a way to "ease"

---

125   Jeff S, https://www.nderf.org/Experiences/1jeff_s_nde.html

him back into his body is unclear. But it does appear that sleep is at least possible in some form in the spirit world, albeit not a necessary regular recharge as it is here.

Food

While it appears that eating is not necessary for the spirit body, it's still both possible and common. Sara Menet found herself in a beautiful place during her near-death experience, and shares:

"Then I saw into a room which struck me a little unusual. There were a lot of ladies, and it looked like they were preparing fruit on these big, beautiful trays (I think it was fruit). One of them looked like a hard-boiled egg, only it had little craters in it. And the one lady (they're all so happy and having so much fun) would cut off slices of this thing, and every once in a while she'd take a bite of it, and you could tell it was just like, 'Oh, that's so good!'

"And so, as I was standing on the hill, I said, 'I wonder what that tastes like. I wish I could taste that.'

"And just out of nowhere I could taste it in my mouth. It's incredible! The only thing I can kind of equate it to is maybe baklava—that kind of melts in your mouth—only it's so much better than that! So I understood that they eat there. They eat for pleasure, not for sustenance. They do not eat meat (there'll be no killing of animals or anything like that in the world to come). But they do eat for pleasure, and there's no waste.

"Everyone that I saw in the city—*ever person*, they were

beautiful. Everybody. The men, the women. It's like seeing Angelina Jolie everywhere, it was so beautiful. Which gave me an understanding that regardless of what shape or size our bodies are or were here, that we are beautiful spiritual beings. And we will be that again when we leave this mortal tabernacle. Everyone is beautiful. No person should ever think, 'I'm not as pretty as this person.' You're *all* absolutely divine—just beautiful. Everyone was happy." [126]

Sharon Milliman describes a similar setting that she saw during her near-death experience:

"I saw this one (building)—it was like a banquet hall, and there people inside having a party—or what seemed like a party. The women were wearing beautiful gowns and jewels, and the men were in tuxes or suits. It was so lavish! There was a chandelier and there was this beautiful, plush, pink carpet on the floor. There were tables with linens, and flowers the colors of the women's dresses, and the tables were just laden with fruits and vegetables, cheeses, meats and breads. Everything you could think of was on these tables! There was a man walking around like a butler, and he was carrying a silver tray, passing out champaign glasses.

"And there was a gentleman over in the corner, and he was playing this gorgeous piano. There was a candelabra on this piano, and this vase of roses just spilling out all over the place...

---

126   Sarah Menet, Iands Utah Meeting, September 2017,
      https://iandsutah.files.wordpress.com/2013/02/iands-11-09-sept-2011-sara-menet.mp3

"You can eat in Heaven, but you don't have to. It's not to sustain life, it's only because you enjoy it." [127]

I have heard some suggest that we're all vegetarians in heaven. I don't know if that's true, since some people have clearly seen meat served there. Some have even eaten it there. Where the meat came from is the bigger question —obviously nothing spiritual would have had to be killed to get the meat, since death of that sort is not even possible in the spirit world. But if you're going to ask that question, you should also ask it about plants. After all, doesn't eating a leaf "kill" the plant?

Clearly there is much still to learn on this subject, but it's fair to assume that first, nothing dies in the spirit world, and second, that the foods we loved here will be available there.

My suspicion is that there is more to spiritual composition that a kinetic construction of parts. Perhaps thought itself (which clearly has more direct influence there anyway) can create the ingredients or even the final product that makes food. Or perhaps eating in the spirit world is the perfect illusion—that what you see, smell, touch, taste, and finally swallow is no more than a "trick," but which still provides everything that makes the actual experience of eating.

I don't know. No idea, but again, something

---

127   Sharon Milliman, from a podcast interview, https://neardeathexperiencepodcast.org/sharon-millimans-near-death-experiences

interesting to think about.

The point is, is there food in heaven? Yes. Do we *need* it for survival? Apparently not. Can we eat food if we want to in the spirit world? All the evidence I can find says, absolutely.

Homes

Are there houses in the spirit world? Yes. In fact, it appears that the houses in the spirit world are quite nice. A woman named Rebecca described in her near-death experience:

"As we walked my eyes drank in the splendor of my environment. The houses, as we approached and passed them, seemed wondrously beautiful to me. They were built of the finest marble, encircled by broad verandas, the roofs or domes supported by massive or delicate pillars or columns; and winding steps led down to pearl and golden walks. The style of the architecture was unlike anything I had ever seen, and the flowers and vines that grew luxuriantly everywhere surpassed in beauty even those of my brightest dreams.

"Turning to the left, my escort led me through the beautiful marble columns that everywhere seemed substituted for doorways into a large oblong room. The entire walls and floor of the room were still of that exquisite light gray marble, polished to the greatest luster; and over walls and floors were strewn exquisite long-stemmed roses of every variety and color from the deepest crimson to the most delicate shades of pink and yellow."[128]

Spencer had a remarkably detailed near-death experience in which he saw the spiritual home he grew up in:

"Instantly we were in another place. I recognized it immediately. It was my home, where I had spent all of my spiritual childhood.

"The building before me was made of a stone-like material, white in color, but more like pearl, with gold and silver streaks that seemed to be moving slowly around larger emerald veins, as if they had occurred in natural stone. Each block of stone was about as tall as a man.

"A long-ago memory arose in my mind of watching Father create it. It had come to its present form over a long period of time—though time was just the limited way my mind understood it. It was just a continuation of the eternal now in my memory. The building had taken shape with purpose. God wanted a room to teach me in, so the building had obeyed His desire. He loved columns, and representations of the beauty of His earthly creations near the tops of the columns along the ceiling and over the doors, and it had all obeyed. I realized that some

128   Harold A. Widdison, *Trailing Clouds of Glory*, (Cedar Fort, Inc., Springville, Utah) December 6, 2011, 26-27

rooms had been "created" to teach me my first lessons of things I would encounter on earth. Others had been shaped to allow me to see and touch objects to teach me, such as books, art, tools, and many other things needed to prepare me for earth life.

"It was less of a building than a divine place that had assumed the shape of an earthly building for my education. I could take any shape God conceived. It did not require work, workmanship, tools, or trades to change it. It simply flowed, in joyful obedience, into any shape He wished.

"My guide opened a large door that was made from a single piece of wood. There were no joints or seams, as if God had asked a single tree to assume the shape of this elaborate door. The wood was unpainted and beautifully carved with natural wonders from earth—flowers, animals, children, men, and women in loving moments.

"The room beyond was a familiar entryway. The whole of what I saw radiated a sense of vibrant excitement that I was ack. The walls and columns were of the same divine stone as outside. The ceiling was vaulted, resting upon four fluted columns with light radiating from everything. The floor was darker, more like the natural marble of a dark emerald green. There was a close door to my right, a wide hallway directly before me, and another closed door to my left.

"My guide led me to the corridor before us. It was about twenty feet long and ended in an arched window that looked like pearl. It appeared to be fluid, with smoky white colors shifting in it. As we approached it, it turned clear so that I could see through it. The large room beyond was again familiar to me.

"He looked at me and asked, 'Do you know this place?'

"I said with tears of joy streaming down my face, 'I'm back home!' In my mind I thought, *this is where I used to live before I was born.* I knew I was back in the spirit world, where I grew up as a spirit child. Many sacred memories and scenes flowed through my mind of my spiritual childhood, which I choose not to relate here. I stood there for a long while, never entering but watching and remembering my past."[129]

What can we conclude about homes in the spirit world? That we have them! And they are custom built to our needs, wants, and education.

---

129   Pontius, John M, *Visions of Glory*, (Cedar Fort, Inc., Springville, UT, 2012), pp. 94-95

Work and Technology

It appears that work continues in the spirit world. Though clearly a much more refined and more meaningful version of such, spirits still have occupations.

These may be as simple as blessing lives, as Waylan experienced during a near-death experience:

"Instantly, I was in the presence of God and I was hearing that I was not to fear as I was all right, instantly all fear was gone and I knew that I was all right. I do remember many other people being there, some I recognized and some not although I was aware that I knew them all. It is impossible to explain the love God has for us. No one would ever voluntarily leave God. I ache to return.

"Then a female preacher, whom I had met once about

a year before, stepped forward and our task was to pray with and for specific people in different areas of Baylor Hospital in Dallas where I was located. We went to these people through space, walls and closed doors. I could not tell that I was out of my body. Everything looked and felt normal."[130]

Or, they may involve some sort of manual labor. Betty J. Eadie, during her near-death experience, was given a tour of the spirit world, and while in a beautiful city, Betty was shown some of the work some spirits were doing:

"Everybody was happy. Although there was a vast difference in the light and power between these women and Christ, their love was unconditional. They loved me with all of their hearts.

"The memory of that tour has been partially taken from me. I remember being taken into a large room where people were working, but I don't remember how we got there or what the building looked like from the outside. The room was beautiful. Its walls were made of some kind of substance, perhaps like a very thin marble, that let light come in, and in places I could see through it to the outside. The effect was very interesting and beautiful

"As we approached the people, I saw that they were weaving on large, ancient-looking looms. My first impression was, *how archaic to have manual looms in the spirit world*. Standing by the looms were many spiritual

130   Waylan, https://www.nderf.org/Experiences/rwaylan_nde.html

beings, male and female, and they greeted me with smiles. They were delighted to see me and moved back from one of the looms to let me have a better look. They were anxious for me to see the workmanship of their hands. I went closer and picked up a piece of the cloth that they were weaving. Its appearance was like a mixture of spun glass and spun sugar. As I moved the cloth back and forth, it shimmered and sparkled, almost as though it were alive. The effect was startling. The material was opaque on one side, but when I turned it over I was able to see through it. Being transparent from one side and opaque on the other—similar to a two-way mirror— obviously had a purpose, but I wasn't told what the purpose was. The workers explained that the material would be made into clothing for those coming into the spirit world from earth. The workers were understandably pleased with their work and with my gratitude for being permitted to see it.

"We moved from the looms, my two companions and I, and went through many other rooms where I saw amazing things and wonderful people, but I have not been allowed to recall many of these details. I remember the feeling of traveling for days or weeks and never tiring. I was surprised at how much people like to work with their hands there—those who want to. They enjoy creating devices that are helpful to others—both here and there. I saw a large machine, similar to a computer, but much more elaborate and powerful. The people working on this too were pleased to show me their work. Again, I understood that all things of importance are created spiritually first and physically second. I had no idea of this before." [131]

After traveling through a tunnel with a guide at her side, Diane Goble burst into the light, which brought her to a beautiful landscape.

"Suddenly, we burst into the light and a whole new reality was revealed to me, similar to the physical world, but, in this higher vibration, more colorful, more beautiful, more amazing. I saw plants, trees, mountains, lakes, animals, and shimmering crystal-like buildings, some very large and ornate. I saw beings moving about, light beings, going about their daily lives. They don't have physical bodies, but they are distinct fields of energy. They don't walk, they float. They have lives much like ours, but without the struggles and sorrows. They are artists, musicians, dancers, singers, inventors, builders, healers, creators of magical things... things they will manifest in their next lifetime in the physical universe." [132]

It also appears that some carry on with pre-mortal work after they return—as if they got "time off" for their mortal experience. Anna shares the following in the midst of her near-death experience:

"My aunt, father-in-law, and grandmothers were all there. Yet, the remaining ones weren't relatives I'd known from earth. They were light beings I've known before being born into the Earth. They guided me to a 'library.' I

131   Eadie, *Embraced by the Light*, (Gold Leaf Press: Carson City, Nevada, 1992), 74-76

132   Diane Goble, http://www.nderf.org/Experiences/1diane.g.nde.html

place this word inside quotation marks because it was a multidimensional composition: I cannot even call it a structure. Apparently, I had a 'job' up there and had left it 'briefly' when coming to Earth because I'd needed to experience certain things and learn certain things in order to be able to continue my work. There were stair-like features, which we could move by the will of our minds.

"By the way, everything I'd learned: languages, subjects, nature observations, while being on Earth, were absolutely useful up there.

"I had then floated onto my unfinished manuscript that looked like some form of tablet except it would only appear by my mind's command. It had data from way before, but since I already knew it, I didn't even look back. I simply stared at it. Out of where my forehead is placed now that I'm human again, appeared these strange characters/letters, round and perfect, a language I'd known seemingly eternally. By sheer thinking of these thoughts, these characters stamped themselves onto the manuscript. I cannot call these characters 'language' as we know it. One doesn't need to speak it or write it. It's simply a thought process. However, these thoughts I'd inserted into the manuscript had and served a great purpose, which as a Light Being I knew.

"However, back in my human body, I don't have a clue, as if there was a veil administered upon my return.

"There were many other light beings conducting similar work, and yet I knew that not every soul or light being is given such a task. Ours was a team destined to do this. Others were destined for other 'work'.[133]

While it may be tempting to assume that technology such as computers and machines are unique to this life, there does seem to be evidence of such devices on the other side. Whether our technology was inspired by those on the other side, or whether they are brought about for some other purpose is unclear. One thing appears certain: the technology in the spirit world is far more advanced than what we have here. Diane shares this from her near-death experience:

> "This angel took me to a place like a coastal community, where I flew above it without wings or plane and it was colorful, alive and so beautiful. And then he (I was aware this angel was male) took me to a place where there was a computer.
>
> "Now you can image how difficult in 1958 it was to describe after I came back what I now have words to describe. So, I will give you both what I saw and then how I tried to explain what I saw. He showed me God's computer! You got that! Heaven has a computer we will never catch up with on earth. And the angel and I were discussing my choice to enter earth in 1936 versus the other choice, I'd debated, or that of the Civil War period. So, he went over to a wall area (this room was white and very clean and orderly) and took a tiny case, which I now know is what we call a jewel case for CDs. At the time, I

---

did not know how to describe this tiny case, but clearly, it was the Civil War era. And he took from the case this less than half dollar sized CD (which I described as a metallic record without a hole in the middle) and he slipped it into the table top (it wasn't a desk at all).

"Suddenly, the entire wall in front of me, I'd say that it must have been a good fifty feet or better, just opened up and it was like looking down on earth during the civil war. And I was in it as a human being, female, and all this killing was going on. And I said in my mind, 'Oh, I can't stand killing at all. This is why I didn't want to go to earth then.' And as quickly as I thought this, I was back by the angel and out of it, the wall closed and the metallic disk popped out which he replaced in the case and put back on the shelf."[134]

Though not using the term *computer*, Christian Andreason described something that somewhat matches the description:

"When I arrived in Heaven (in my experience) I found myself in a huge room where the walls and ceilings were made of pure crystal and they had Light coming from the inside of them. The effect was amazing. Then as I looked up, I saw four translucent screens appear (and form a kind of gigantic box around me). It was through this method that I was shown my life review... Without ever having to turn my head, I saw my past, my present, my future and there was even a screen that displayed a tremendous

---

amount of scientific data, numbers and universal codes."
135

Spencer, during his near-death experience, was privileged to see the home that his premortal spirit grew up in. While visiting his room, he reminisced on lessons he learned that included some spiritual technology unknown on the mortal earth. After spending some time standing before his pre-mortal home, Spencer finally went inside.

"When I was satisfied and again ready to move on, my guide took me back to the entry and to the first door I had seen. The door opened for me as I approached. I recognized it as "my room," almost like a bedroom for a mortal child, but there was no bed here. The room was about twenty square feet, with a high, flat ceiling. The walls and floor were of the same material as the foyer, but with slightly different colors, lending more toward blue and mauve. I loved this room, and I felt as if it was all "mine."

"The only furniture in the room was a large rounded-top chest sitting in the middle of the floor. It was about three feet by four feet, with an arched lid and rounded corners. The top was a beautiful red with highlights of burnt orange. It was made of the same material as the rest of the home, but it was thinner and brightly colored. The sides of the chest were a vivid canary yellow. I knew that I had picked these colors and changed them often to suit my childhood whims. The lid could be opened, but there

135   Christian Andreason, https://www.near-death.com/experiences/notable/christian-andreason.html

were no visible hinges.

"I stepped to it, and after walking around it, I glanced at my guide questioningly. He smiled, and I slowly raised the lid. The substance gave my mortal memory the message that it was heavy, but it felt feather-light as I opened it. Within were strange objects I had never seen in mortality. There were utensils of strange shapes and different sizes, white clothing, and tools that I had used. I knew exactly what each tool and object was for as I stood there in the Spirit, but since returning to mortality, that information has not remained with me.

"I realized that I 'owned' them, but also that such things were common to our premortal experiences. Still, their connection to me had been a part of my early experiences. I picked up each one, looked at it, and remembered what it was for. Every object in the chest was an achievement of mine. Each object represented an accomplishment, like a trophy of sorts, of a lesson learned, ordinations I had received, stages of development that I had achieved. These objects signified my worthiness and preparation to participate in the object of the lesson—not just in this world but in the mortal world as well. These things were like certificates, authorizing me to actually do those things. Each ability and authority was gained by a long process of qualifying for and earning that authority.

"I had received these objects as tokens of lessons I had learned, and qualifications I had achieved. Some of the objects were actual tools to assist me in that act. To my memory of these things, they seemed to me to be divine technology, objects endowed with power by God to allow and assist me in doing some necessary service or act, like the Liahona that assisted Lehi's family or the Urim and Thummim that enabled seers to see the future. The white clothing was carefully folded and was sacred and ceremonial in nature. It was all part of my matriculation to spiritual maturity.

"As I picked them up, the lesson learned, the process of learning, and the joy I felt in the achievement returned to me. I treasure each object with all my heart and pondered on them and then placed them carefully back in the chest. Nothing in the chest was a toy or whimsical object. Everything had deep, eternal meaning to me. Each object recognized me and was happy to see and interact with me...

"I realized that I had possessed the ability to change the room into anything I needed. If I desired to read a book that belonged to mortality, like scripture or a scroll written by a mortal prophet, I simply desired it, and the room would change to provide that thing to me. It came in the setting it had been used, in a palace, a cave, or on a desk; this is how it appeared to me. I could touch it, pick it up, and read it. I could feel and even smell it. It was not the actual object summoned from some eternal storage vault but a flawless spiritual re-creation or representation of it. Each object was perfectly like the original, including all of the memories and history a spiritual individual could experience from the object.

"If I wanted to see something large, such as the birth of Christ or the creation of the earth, that event would surround me. I could watch it and learn from it, interact with it, see the angels and divine beings who had enacted the original events. I could move arount it and see it from every angle with perfect clarity and experience everything and everyone involved in the initial event. In short, it was magnificent, and it was the most perfect classroom in eternity—and all who desired it had one just like mine."[136]

Like the discussion on cities, we are left to wonder if technology in the spirit world is an extension of the development of technology from mortal earth or if earth's technology is inspired by technology on the other side. My gut is that technology has always been far more advanced there than it is here.

That isn't to say it's not at least partly a two-way street. As silly as it may sound, consider the emoji, for example. Not a complex technology, of course. A simple, silly, yet effective way of communicating simple emotions. But were there emojis in the spirit world before they were here? No idea. Are there emojis there now? Well, it's hard to imagine that text-happy teens dying today wouldn't carry the tradition into spirit world if it's not already there.

What about art pieces? Dance moves? Songs?

While many musical compositions were probably inspired by music from the other side, there is also

---

136   Pontius, John M, *Visions of Glory*, (Cedar Fort, Inc., Springville, UT, 2012), pp. 96-97

doubtless beautiful music here that wasn't previously in the spirit world.

Of course, when I consider the whole "time doesn't exist" thing, I'm left to rethink this "chicken and the egg" question. We'll obviously never understand it all here, but I'm confident our knowledge will continue to expand with each person that returns from death with new insights about the spirit world.

House of Learning

Though people in the spirit world seem to have a great ability to learn with very little effort, it appears that there are places designated as places of learning, where even more knowledge and wisdom are available. Their descriptions make me think of a sort of library, and they are often described as a "house of learning," "Hall of Records," "Temple of knowledge," or similar names.

During his near-death experience, after his life review, Ned Nougherty described such a place:

"As the movie-like scenes of my future life ended, I found myself in a building, which became known to me as the Hall of Records. I was sitting on a marble bench and waiting. From there I could look outdoors through a large opening at the side of the room. I could see columns of large pillars supporting an archway of the building in which I sat. In front of the columns, there was a long stairway leading to a large open courtyard." [137]

Edgar Cayce had a near-death experience, and of the moment rushing through a tunnel, said,

"As I pass on, there is more light and movement in what appear to be normal cities and towns. With the growth of movement I become conscious of sounds, at first indistinct rumblings, then music, laughter, and singing of birds. There is more and more light, the colors become very beautiful, and there is the sound of wonderful music. The houses are left behind; ahead there is only a blending of sound and color. Quite suddenly I come upon a Hall of Records. It is a hall without walls, without ceiling, but I am conscious of seeing an old man who hands me a large book (which he calls the *Book of Life*), a record of the individual for whom I seek information." [138]

Dr. George Richie also describes such a place of learning:

"I began to perceive a whole new realm! Enormous buildings stood in a beautiful sunny park that reminded me somewhat of a well-planned university. As we entered one of the buildings and doorways, the air was so hushed that I was actually startled to see people in the passageway. I could not tell if they were men or women, old or young, for all were covered from head to foot in

137   https://www.near-death.com/experiences/notable/ned-dougherty.html
138   https://www.near-death.com/science/research/temple-of-knowledge.html

loose-flowing hooded cloaks which made me think vaguely of monks.

"But the atmosphere of the place was not at all as I imagined a monastery. It was more like some tremendous study center, humming with the excitement of great discovery. Everyone we passed in the wide halls and on the curving staircases seemed caught up in some all-engrossing activity; not many words were exchanged among them. And yet I sensed no unfriendliness between these beings, rather an aloofness of total concentration. Whatever else these people might be, they appeared utterly and supremely self-forgetful—absorbed in some vast purpose beyond themselves. Through open doors I glimpsed at enormous rooms filled with complex equipment. In several of the rooms hooded figures bent over intricate charts and diagrams, or sat at the controls of elaborate consoles flickering with lights. Somehow I felt that some vast experiment was being pursued, perhaps dozens and dozens of such experiments. And something more... In spite of his obvious delight in the beings around us, I sensed that even this was not the ultimate, that he had far greater things to show me if only I could see.

"And so I followed him into other buildings of this domain of thought. We entered a studio where music of a complexity I couldn't begin to follow was being composed and performed. There were complicated rhythms, tones not on a scale I knew. 'Why,' I found myself thinking. 'Bach is only the beginning!'

"Next we walked through a library the size of the whole University of Richmond. I gazed into rooms lined floor to ceiling with documents on parchment, clay, leather, metal, paper. 'Here,' the thought occurred to me, 'are assembled the important books of the universe.' Immediately I knew this was impossible. How could books be written somewhere beyond the Earth! But the thought persisted, although my mind rejected it. 'The key works of the universe,' the phrase kept recurring as we roamed the domed reading rooms crowded with silent scholars. Then abruptly, at the door to one of the smaller rooms, almost an annex: 'Here is the central thought of this Earth.'

"'Is this heaven, Lord Jesus?' I ventured. The calm, the brightness, they were surely heaven-like! So was the absence of self, of clamoring ego. 'When these people were on Earth did they grow beyond selfish desires?'

"'They grew, and they have kept on growing.'"[139]

Jan Price also experienced music in the Temple of Knowledge:

"Quickly we approached a structure of supernal beauty. It was vast, of the purest white, and somewhat Grecian in architecture. Paths led into the structure from all directions, and I observed many people coming and going. Over the archway through which we entered the structure, I saw the words TEMPLE OF KNOWLEDGE and felt a gentle power drawing me into itself. There were pillars of varying heights, becoming higher and higher

---

139   https://www.near-death.com/science/research/temple-of-knowledge.html

toward the center. Turning back to the interior of the
temple, I saw that creative activities were taking place in
different areas. There were a number of individuals
sitting at easels painting, and I saw one man playing a
flute-like instrument that emitted the sweetest of sounds.
Farther on, dancers moved with ethereal grace,
performing with a lightness impossible to the physical
human form. As I watched in utter delight, I became
aware that the musical background for this visual feast
came from what I would call a celestial choir—an
orchestra of voices creating heavenly music for the dance.
This Music of the Spheres was indeed singing the praises
of the Creator. A little tug from Maggi reminded me that
there was more here in the temple to investigate. Moving
in toward the center, it was quieter, and the gentle power
that I had felt earlier was stronger. Here were individuals,
wise ones, it seems, stationed at intervals and waiting to
assist those who chose to approach them."

This theme of music regarding the place of learning
seems to recur, with many people hearing music or seeing
the learning, playing, and performing of music. Dr. Allen
Kellehear described a choir in the hall of learning in these
words:

"This time we were audience to a choir of angels
singing. Angels were totally outside my reality at the
time, yet somehow I knew these beautiful beings to be
angelic. They sang the most lovely and extraordinary
music I had ever heard. They were identical, each equally
beautiful. When their song was over, one of their number

came forward to greet me. She was exquisite and I was
mightily attracted, but I then realized my admiration
could only be expressed in a wholly nonphysical manner,
as to a little child. I was embarrassed by my error, but it
did not matter. All was forgiven in this wonderful place.
Instantly we arrived in an art gallery. It contained the
work of the great masters of all time and all places. The
display was both classical and modern. Some of the great
works seemed familiar. Others were unlike anything I had
ever seen, indescribable. The beauty and form of the
sculpture and paintings on display were beyond words. A
lifetime could be spent in this place, but to see everything
I needed to see during this visit, we must move on.

"Next we materialized in a computer room. It was a
place of great activity, yet peace prevailed. None of the
stress of business was present, but prodigious work was
accomplished. The people seemed familiar to me, like old
friends. This was confusing, because I knew there to be
present those who lived on Earth still, and those who had
passed on. Some of them I knew by name, others by
reputation; and all had time for me, to teach me if ever I
need help understanding.

"One of them was Albert Einstein, whom I had always
admired greatly but distantly, and this great man took
time away from his duties to encourage me. He asked me
if I would care to operate the computer, which was very
complex and beautiful and designed to guide the path of
destinies. I was flattered, but felt incompetent and unsure
of myself in the presence of such greatness. I told him I
would like to try, but I was afraid of making a mistake. He

laughed greatly, and reassured me, saying that error was not possible in this place. Encouraged, I seemed instinctively to know how to operate this unusual machine, and waved my hand in a pattern over the large keyboard, rather like playing a piano without touching the keys. I knew instantly the task had been performed perfectly, and it had somehow been of great benefit to someone. I was suffused with the joy of a job well done. I would gladly spend eternity here at this rewarding work if only for the tremendous feeling of well-being I had experienced as a result.

"We continued our tour and arrived at a library. It was a vast old traditional building, containing all of the wisdom of the ages, everything ever said or written. Room upon room, shelf upon shelf of books stretched away as far as the eye could see. By that time I had growing doubt I was destined to stay in this mysterious yet familiar place, even though I knew in my heart it was home. I had the uncomfortable feeling I must return soon to resume my life. My guide, for by now I thought of him as such, told me I must study and learn from the infinite array of wisdom before us. I was dismayed, and said there was no way I was capable of such a task. I was told to simply make a beginning, to do the best I could, and that would always be good enough. There was plenty of time."[140]

Whether there is only one temple of knowledge or many is unclear. But many who see this building describe

---

140   https://www.near-death.com/science/research/temple-of-knowledge.html

it differently, suggesting that either they are seeing it from different angles, it looks different to each individual, or (and more likely, I suspect) there are many such buildings. Diane Goble, who died in a rafting accident, describes:

"Again, the Being of Light told me it was my choice to stay or go, but that there was more for me to do in that life and it wasn't quite time for me to leave. Still hesitating, I was told that if I chose to go back, I would be given certain knowledge to take back with me to share with others. After much discussion, I agreed to go back and suddenly found myself in front of a tall cone-shaped building; so tall, it seemed to go on forever. I was told this was the Hall of Knowledge. I entered the building and flew, spiraling upwards, through what appeared to be shelves of books, like in a library, many millions of books, and I flew through them all. When I reached the top, I burst through it into a kaleidoscope of colors and, at the same time, my head popped out of the water. I was down river about ten yards from the raft."[141]

Karen Brannon describes,

"I was in a library in an ethereal temple or atrium, similar to ancient Greek or Roman villas. Everything was airy and light. I had the impression that there were other souls studying in the next room. I gathered all this information instantaneous. While I was getting the information of the library and school at the temple, I was aware of a very tall Master or Spiritual Guide with long

---

141   Diane Goble, http://www.nderf.org/Experiences/1diane.g.nde.html

white robe, and long white hair and beard." [142]

Though I haven't discovered the purpose for the robe-like clothing worn by many of the administrators of these buildings, one man attempts to learn the reasons for it, but fails to get a full answer:

> "I was snapped back to the task at hand—the life review. It was judgment to be sure, but more like fact-finding than fault-finding. The only condemnation was me regretting some of my mistakes. Then the movie stopped abruptly. The end of my life had been reached. The Being of Light was surprised and I felt it. There was something missing...
>
> "With no movement at all, we were now at a large library. The one who had been doing my life review was no longer a ball of light but now a hooded and robed figure. And still inscrutable. 'Look what I found out there,' it said to the library staff. One of the clerks went to large bead rack, much like an abacus, and began calculating. One clerk wore a short robe with a classic Greek pattern decorating the lower edge. His robe had a hood, as did the robes of all the others. I concluded that his hood was not for warmth and asked my guide. The guide confirmed my observation, the hoods were not for warmth. When I pushed to know the purpose of the hoods I was informed that I would know when it was time to have that information. I sensed that my guide disapproved of the non-traditional attire, but had no cause to criticize as the work done by that individual was

---

142   https://www.near-death.com/science/research/temple-of-knowledge.html

always excellent.

"Another clerk observed the placement of the beads on the top row and thought, 'Oh, no! The Old section.'

"That was clay tablets to be moved and sorted through. A moment later, two of the beads in the top row were moved again. It would be in the section written on hides stretched over wooden frames. Much easier to sort through. When the calculation finished, we set off through the stacks counting rows as we went. I observed stacked sheets of papyrus, then scrolls. Then came rows with stacked wooden frames. We passed these quickly and came to a row with hides stretched over sticks.

"A clerk was now counting bays, then shelves, then hides. One hide was selected and pulled from the stack. Another clerk carefully counted the entries until he found the right one. The writing was like none I'd seen before. It reminded me a bit of Hebrew and runic writing. I couldn't read it. But I could read the mind of my guide! Hah! Blocked. I tried to read it through one of the clerks. Frustrated again. I tried to memorize the shapes of the letters but was frustrated there as well. My guide informed me that I wasn't supposed to know what the entry said. I asked what was I allowed to know? I was informed that the entry described my life. It was hardly larger than a business card." [143]

This doesn't seem to imply that answers in general aren't available to those in the house of learning.

Generally, most answers *are* given.

"I navigated around for a second or two at the speed of thought and realized in the distance there was an open library. A library in the sky without walls... In a blink of an eye, I was within the confines of this learning area and I came to the understanding that this area contained all of the answers of the universe. I was so elated! I opened myself to the knowledge gate and answers began to play through my mind like the pictures in the movie The Lawnmower Man. I saw pictures and diagrams of our entire universe being created and all the fabrics within it. I began to see wisdom and knowledge of man and spirit. I even saw Einstein's Theory of Relativity and understood holes in the theory because true spirituality had the real answers (They were big). I began to truly understand everything and it was bliss. I wanted to take all of the knowledge I could back with me, but I knew that this knowledge was knowledge of the spirit and could not be taken back into my little material brain."[144]

Damien Spaulding recorded this experience:

"I navigated around for a second or two at the speed of thought and realized in the distance there was an open library. A library in the sky without walls... In a blink of an eye, I was within the confines of this learning area and I came to the understanding that this area contained all of the answers of the universe. I was so elated!

"I opened myself to the knowledge gate and answers began to play through my mind like the pictures in the

---

144   https://www.near-death.com/science/research/temple-of-knowledge.html

movie *The Lawnmower Man*. I saw pictures and diagrams
of our entire universe being created and all the fabrics
within it. I began to see wisdom and knowledge of man
and spirit. I even saw Einstein's Theory of Relativity and
understood holes in the theory because true spirituality
had the real answers (They were big). I began to truly
understand everything and it was bliss. I wanted to take
all of the knowledge I could back with me, but I knew
that this knowledge was knowledge of the spirit and
could not be taken back into my little material brain. I
would have to stay dead and be with God in order to keep
it forever and I wanted that. I was enjoying myself so
greatly. I wanted to stay for a long time." [145]

In Bettie Eadie's experience, she describes a similar
library:

"I was taken to another large room similar to a library.
As I looked around it seemed to be a repository of
knowledge, but I couldn't see any books. Then I noticed
ideas coming into my mind, knowledge filling me on
subjects that I had not thought about for some time — or
in some cases not at all. Then I realized that this was a
library of the mind. By simply reflecting on a topic, as I
had earlier in Christ's presence, all knowledge on that
topic came to me. I could learn about anybody in history
– or even in the spirit world—in full detail.

"No knowledge was kept from me, and it was
impossible not to understand correctly every thought,
every statement, every particle of knowledge. There was

145   https://www.near-death.com/archives/stress/damien-spaulding.html

absolutely no misunderstanding here. History was pure. Understanding was complete. I understood not only what people did but why they did it and how it affected other people's perceptions of reality. I understood reality pertaining to that subject from every angle, from every possible perception; and all of this brought a wholeness to an event or person or principle that was not possible to comprehend on earth.

"But this was more than a mental process. I was able to feel what the people felt when they performed these actions. I understood their pains or joys or excitement because I was able to live them. Some of this knowledge was taken from me, but not all. I cherish the knowledge granted me of certain events and people in our history which were important for me to understand.

"I wanted still more experiences in this wonderful, incredible world, and my escorts were delighted to continue helping me. It was their greatest joy to give me joy..." [146]

Considering the knowledge that many gain while standing in the light, or in the presence of God, it's unclear the reason for the library of learning (or temple of knowledge), except that perhaps in the library, knowledge may be obtained on demand, whereas God's personal presence might not be. And perhaps there are nuances of knowledge, or details about history (or any other subject) that are uniquely found in the library.

---

146   Betty J. Eadie, *Embraced by the Light*, (Gold Leaf Press: Carson City, Nevada, 1992), 76-77

Regardless, it becomes quickly apparent that knowledge is readily available on the other side, and that some sort of writing, record-keeping, and book work continue to take place. And from the experiences discussing the placing of words into books, it appears that the recording and writing process is not as clunky and laborious as it is on earth. As a writer, I would very much appreciate this change!

Abilities and Knowledge

While it becomes clear from near-death experiences that you will still be you after you die, that doesn't mean you'll have all the same capacities. And while some abilities are taken away (consider the ability to experience physical pain and suffering), others are greatly expanded.

We've mentioned the ability to hear thoughts, feelings, intents, etc, as well as the ability to go from one place to another without effort. But there are many other senses and abilities that come with being in the spirit form.

Many who have near-death experiences speak of walking through walls or windows without even feeling them. Others describe passing through physical objects in such a way as to suggest that the objects simply vaporize before them, and then reappear after passing through. But this begs the question of whether spirits likewise walk through each other.

Another capacity that is enhanced is the comprehension of things. Russell Ricks said:

> "When I would focus on a particular object, such as a flower, I would comprehend and experience everything about it—from how it was created and by what power it was made to everything and everyone who had smelt, touched, or appreciated its beauty. I could feel the joy that flower had in the measure of its creation when it pleased all those who appreciated its beauty...
>
> "While in this dimension, my own perception of things seemed heightened far beyond my eight-year-old understanding. It was as if pure intelligence continuously flowed into my mind, and I comprehended many things in an instant. Whatever I focused on, I could learn and experience everything about it." [147]

There is an incredible sense of freedom that many feel when they enter the spirit world. They are able to do so many things they couldn't do in the mortal body that it's almost overwhelming. Lisa says,

> "I felt as though I was finally being my true self. There were no limits or limitations whatsoever. I could go wherever I wanted, know whatever I wished, do anything. The sense of freedom was inexplicable. I was also

---

147   Russell Ricks, Remember: *A Little Boy's Near-Death Experience*,

strangely aware that the thing we ordinarily call *time* now was suspended, and no longer existed." [148]

Flying is one of the most common abilities mentioned in near-death experiences. James was dying in a hospital when he saw his grandmother (who had long-since died) with others around him. He explains,

"I was also aware that there was some sort of barrier between my grandmother and me. I do not know whether it was a river, rift, or what, but I knew I could not get over there. I also became aware of a beautiful city behind them all somewhat in the middle distance. I am not certain, but there may have been hills behind the city. The city was golden, either from its own internal light or from a golden light at sunset. There were beautiful trees and flowers and lovely smells. The city awakened in me a desperate yearning to go there, though I don't exactly know why. I could somehow see that there were busy people in the houses, which had windows and flat roofs.

"Suddenly I could cross the divide! I felt simply wonderful, with no pain, and I was full of powerful feelings of peacefulness. I flew right over [my grandma's] head and the heads of the other people with no apology. I could fly and I seemed to have no mass. (I did not look at my body or any part of it, so I don't know what I looked like or even whether I was in my body.) I wanted to get to the city with great intensity. The landscape rushed toward me and grew ever more beautiful as I approached.

148   Lisa, http://www.ndert.org/Experiences/rlisa_m_nde.html

I could hear the most beautiful music I had ever heard." [149]

Another person, shortly after the moment of death, says,

"Then I was flying... I could see where everyone was positioned on the ground. I was flying about 14 feet off the ground. I flew to the front of the house where I could see my mother chatting to my aunt out the front of the house by the car. I could see her leaning on the car door while it was open.

"I then travelled to the back of the house where I was being revived by my cousin. I could see him performing CPR on me and I could see where everyone was positioned around me. Then I came back." [150]

Another ability that seems to be common in spirit form is the capacity to see in all directions at the same time.

Michel says,

"I suddenly found myself floating upwards from the bed, towards the ceiling of my hospital room where I remained, lightly floating and weightless. I could see all around me without turning my head: 360 degrees of panoramic vision." [151]

Henry Likewise explained:

149   James S. https://www.nderf.org/Experiences/1james_s_nde_5011.html

150   IANDS, *Drowned at Three*, https://iands.org/research/nde-research/nde-archives31/newest-accounts/1109-drowned-at-3.html

151   Michel, https://www.nderf.org/Experiences/1michel_l_nde.html

"I was amazed at the sharpness of the room around me and the vividness of the colors. I could perceive an energy surrounding everything. The books, desk, furniture of the room all seemed to have a slight glow that radiated from them. No sooner had I noticed this than I realized I could see 360 degrees around me. I didn't need to turn my head I just looked and I saw." [152]

Similarly, many speak of being able to hear and comprehend many things at the same time. Amy describes:

"I remember being in a vanilla, pink-colored, and misty tunnel. I could hear the prayers of people. Some of the people I knew, like my youngest son. Many people I didn't know. But these prayers I could hear them individually and as a whole at the same time. They were also displayed like a silver audio play-button on a sound file as I passed through this tunnel. I could reach out and touch these files and hear them. It was an overwhelming feeling of love and caring." [153]

Another person describes sounds as being somehow magnified:

"There was a glow from the east horizon that leads me to believe dawn was breaking, but what I remember most is the feelings. I was me, but I wasn't. I was not afraid, and normally, I was terrified of the dark, and was not at all concerned about being outside our kitchen window. I remember I light glow from the window, probably our night light, and I had no interest in going back inside. I

152   Henry W, https://www.nderf.org/Experiences/1henry_w_probable_nde.html
153   Amy C. https://www.nderf.org/Experiences/1amy_c_nde_8259.html

could hear everything, the sound of crickets I remember, and other sounds, as if they were magnified. I could look around me, and I did a slow peripheral once around, although I do not remember how." [154]

Understanding Minute and Complex Details

It appears that as a spirit, our senses are not only amplified, but we actually have many more senses than we have in the body. We can comprehend minute details beyond what we see or hear with our natural senses alone. While drowning in the ocean and drifting in and out of his body, one experiencer had the following experience:

"Soon, I simply could no longer keep my head above water. Then I found I was not swimming any more. I was looking down at myself from above! At first, I did not even recognize that it was me. There I was unmoving and floating in the water. I saw my wristwatch on my arm, reflecting the sun. However, even though I thought I was far above the watch, I also seemed to be looking at it from no more than three inches away. I could see the tiny details of numbers and letters on the dial and even the smallest details of the works inside it. I mean, that I really was inside the wristwatch and observing the cogwheels of the watch machinery moving. I understood each movement while observing the battery feeding the mechanisms with energy to the cogwheels. The

---

154   IANDS Archives, September 2003, https://iands.org/ndes/nde-stories/640-archive-through-
       september-28-2003.html

molecules of the moving cogwheels had like an infrared color, and the pieces that were not moving had like an ultraviolet color. I believe the difference in color was between Kinetic and Potential energy. It was so weird and wonderful. Then I found myself back in the water and inside my body floating somewhat below the surface."

It also appears that in the spirit form, our perception, or ability to perceive, can even extend beyond time. Celso continues,

"When I began to see under the water, towards the seashore I saw a small sunken wooden boat that resembling a buccaneer ship. The ship was probably a fake sunken ship for tourists. Then I looked to the floor of the ocean. First, it was totally black, not a blackness as like lack of light but as a blackness full of life. At that instant, the notion of time and space vanished. I have seen in front of my eyes a macabre parade of natives, pirates, sailors, women, children, drowning (yes, drowning in present tense) in this very place during centuries. Their fear is the dreadful darkness that makes us afraid.

"During the parade, I was about 10 feet under the water. I saw them one by one. For example, I heard a person splashing on the surface and beginning to drown. The person was taking in water, gasping, and struggling to go up. I do not know if they fell down from a boat, committed suicide, or was killed, or running away from a battle or a hurricane. I do not know that. I saw them passing in front of and near me, going down to the

bottom of the sea. Only after reaching the bottom of the
sea, then begins the drowning of another person. Maybe
in another time, maybe centuries after the last one I saw.
It is so difficult to understand how the vector of time
works in this reality. They were not translucent as ghosts.
They were normal human beings.

"I knew they were natives, sailors, or pirates. I knew
not only by their clothing, but somehow, we were
connected to each other by our thoughts. I felt each one
of them as a part of me. I observed their facial expressions
however, I was paying more attention to their feelings,
their suffering, and their fear of death. The knowledge
was more emotional than visual. I saw about 40 humans
drowning.

"One person impressed and amazed me most of all.
She was a pregnant woman, perhaps European and in a
long white elegant skirt. She had long brown hair. Her
dress resembles the style from the 1900's. She was not
struggling for her life as the others before and after her. I
could understand her thoughts. She was deeply
concerned about her baby and not about her life."[155]

After stepping out of his body and realizing that he
had an expanded ability to know people's feelings and
thoughts, Spencer decided to walk around the hospital
where his medical procedure was taking place.

"I had already experienced walking through walls and
was curious to experience that again. I felt comfortable

doing this because I continued to be completely aware of what my body was experiencing no matter where I was in the hospital.

"I turned away and walked to the nearest wall, paused a moment, and then stepped through into the next room. I found myself in a doctor's office, having walked through a wooden desk, a wooden chair, and a leather couch.

"I paused for a moment to let the flood of information settle into my mind. As I had passed through the desk, I realized that it had been made from three different trees. I saw each tree. I knew them from the moment their seed germinated until they were harvested, milled, and crafted into this desk. There was a living component in the wood. It was intelligent but had little will. It was content to be wood, and it was pleased that someone had chosen it to be shaped into this desk. It was a rolltop desk and quite beautiful. I knew that the desk understood the love the craftsman had put into his work on the desk. The desk also felt pure and worthy because it had never been used in anything that offended God.

"I want to say much more about this phenomenon, of understanding physical things, but words fail me. I understood the emotion and motive of the man who cut it down and knew his name and all about his life too, as I did everyone who every touched or used the desk. I understood everything about the cotton stuffing in the seat and the leather from the sofa. All of it welcomed me and was pleased to communicate to me its life and how it had come to be that couch. I understood the several cattle whose hides covered the couch and their lives and their sacrifice. They had left all that information with their hides but the spirit of the cow was elsewhere, not in the leather, but still pleased and content with the benefits to mankind that its life and sacrifice had rendered. It was pleased that it was of benefit to the children of Adam...

"I was quite interested in rocks and natural stonework, whose voice was ancient, predating the formation of the earth. It remembered its creation and luxuriated and rejoiced in being beautiful and useful to man. I found that I liked rocks. They all magnified Christ. I liked their company and sense of timeless patience and eternal worship of Christ..."

"I found a few items in the hospital that were saddened by how they had been used by their owners. A few things had been used in crimes or for violent or immoral purposes, and their voice included a cry for redemption and justice. It was not a shrill or piercing or unpleasant sound—but it was unending, and carried the vivid details of the injustice. I knew that the object itself was not diminished or condemned, but it waited with patient expectation for the day of redemption.

"I walked through a wall and into a nice office. It was more nicely furnished than the others, with beautiful pictures on the walls and ornate wooden furniture. I considered going out the door to see whose office this was, but as I walked through a desk I was stunned by what I felt. It was longing for redemption. I realized that recently a series of love letters had been written at this desk promoting an affair that ultimately would injure many people. I knew the content of every letter and the true emotion and manipulation of the writer as well as the reaction of the reader. I moved away, not wanting to remain in that stream of torrid details. I went through the couch, and it likewise testified of the same affair and unrighteous events that had occurred here, some recently. I could not find any place in that beautiful office that was not saddened or offended or crying for redemption."[156]

It appears that the level of a person's abilities on the other side can correlate with the present level of their spirit. Amy Call says:

"We were traveling upward, I suppose. My own vibration was changing. There was a big change in frequency. Like I was tuning into a different radio station on a grand scale. I was out in the Universe, and I was being given a kind of show. Like having an astronomy teacher speak on the beauty of the Universe while laying under the stars at night. But I was out there amidst them. And this part seems to have been made foggy for me since my return, but I remember vaguely that during this scene, I saw something like holographic words and numbers move in front of me past the stars... and it felt like I was being downloaded with information. I felt at that time that I understood *everything*. That I felt the full truth of Laws and Order in the Universe.

---

156   John Pontius, Visions of Glory: One Man's Astonishing Account of the Last Days, Utah, Cedar Fort, Inc. (November 13, 2012), chapter 1

"One thing that I held onto was the beautiful *math* of the Universe. I remember coming to understand that there was a supreme and perfect kind of *math* that was in and of *all* things that existed. I remember being told something about Einstein! I was so excited. It was such a pleasant experience. I was also shown how there is a kind of clock-work in the sky. How the stars themselves actually hold a sort of map or mathematical Key to everything that is! 'You are written in the stars,' I was told! *Everything* is! I recall how *thrilling* this part of my NDE was for me.

"I want to add that in my life, I have always had a mental block when it came to math. Even the simplest math ideas, starting from the time I was only six years old were difficult for me to approach. I would shut down when anything with numbers was presented to me. So, in my NDE, while being shown such an enormous array of gorgeous mathematical equations and facts... and visual numerical splendor, I was overjoyed at my own ability to thoroughly comprehend all of it. Unfortunately, at my return, I was discouraged to find that I could not relay or bring with me the expansive amount of math understanding and knowledge I'd been so anxious to share with others. I was and still am, in love with numbers. That was a big leap forward!"[157]

Sharon similarly had knowledge poured into her:

"On one hand, it seemed like everything happened so fast, and, on the other hand, it seemed that time stood

---

still. I began feeling as if I was attached to a giant IV
bottle of knowledge. I was being fed all this knowledge,
and I didn't even have the words to ask the proper
questions. I felt such joy and elation; it was one 'Aha'
moment after another. And, it all seemed so simple and
so logical. I remember at one point saying with a huge
smile on my face 'Wow, is that all there is to it? That is so
cool.' God, you are so awesome! We are the ones who
make everything so complicated. I saw angels, and they
spoke to me showing me a lake and, in the lake, they
showed me future events that would take place on earth;
which have, in fact, taken place."[158]

Jean learned in her experience that this access to all
knowledge isn't exclusive to just a few.

"I knew that what I had found was the sum total of all
'knowing' or wisdom of all people for all time—past,
present and future. All wisdom comes from this pool of
collective knowing and all we learn goes into the pool for
the use of everyone." [159]

Like many mentioned previously, Deborah got
something of a tour of the universe prior to receiving
incredible waves of knowledge:

"Then in the blink of an eye, I wasn't in the 'room'
with my brother anymore. I was suspended in the cosmos
amidst a vast and beautiful field of stars. It was absolutely
breathtaking. I could see the planets glowing and
orbiting silently and I was suddenly struck by the

---

158   Sharon M. http://www.nderf.org/NDERF/NDE Experiences/sharon m.nde.htm
159   Jean , http://www.nderf.org/Experiences/1jean_nde.html

knowledge that the universe wasn't chaotic at all, in fact it was a highly synchronous realm that had been painstakingly created by a loving and intelligent creator. That realization touched me to the core of my soul.

"Suddenly, I began getting hit with a vast amount of knowledge. It was coming at me very rapidly and my mind began absorbing everything that there was to know about science, music, art history, physics and math. It was a huge burst of knowledge and I understood everything despite the rapid speed at which it was flowing. I was never very good at math, especially throughout grade school, but I found that I was able to comprehend some very complex mathematical calculations in this other realm. I knew that those calculations had some kind of universal significance. I remember thinking that everything about life and the universe made complete sense and that I finally had the answers to everything that I ever wondered about. It was an amazing feeling of infinite knowledge and it was wondrous and breathtaking beyond description."[160]

During her near-death experience, Carol Vengroff was guided by many wise and powerful beings to a place where she was taught and shown many things. Of the experience, she shares:

"...as a human being, we're incapable of even digesting or understanding even the most minute parts of what they had taught me—what they told me, and what they had shared with me. And I actually started laughing. I

---

160   http://www.nderf.org/NDERF/NDE_Experiences/deborah_l_ndelike.htm

did! Because I thought, 'This is amazing! No wonder why humans can't talk about this place and can't talk about this experience...'

"And I got the answers to every question imaginable. And I knew I could never take all of them back in the human form because we just don't have the vocabulary, the words, or the experiences for what is going on.

"I did register, and I was able to make a mental note: *anything is possible.* So I know that for a fact, because I got to experience that on the other side."[161]

But even with all this access to knowledge, Howard Storm learned that much of the knowledge we receive comes a little at a time based on our readiness to receive it. While walking with a friend, whom he believed to be Jesus Christ, Howard asked about this.

"I asked my friend, and his friends, about death— what happens when we die?

"They said that when a loving person dies, angels come down to meet him, and they take him up— gradually, at first, because it would be unbearable for that person to be instantly exposed to God.

"Knowing what's inside of every person, the angels don't have to prove anything by showing off. They know what each of us needs, so they provide that. In some cases it may be a heavenly meadow, and in another, something else. If a person needs to see a relative, the angels will

161   Carol Vengroff, IANDS NDE Radio Podcast, https://www.youtube.com/watch?
time_continue=145&v=dLC5GtJ9j8E

bring that relative. If the person really likes jewels, they will show the person jewels. We see what is necessary for our introduction into the spirit world, and those things are real, in the heavenly, the divine sense.

"They gradually educate us as spirit beings, and bring us into heaven. We grow and increase, and grow and increase, and shed the concerns, desires, and base animal stuff that we have been fighting much of our life. Earthly appetites melt away. It is no longer a struggle to fight them. We become who we truly are, which is part of the divine.

"This happens to loving people, people who are good and love God. They made it clear to me that we don't have any knowledge or right to judge anybody else—in terms of that person's heart relationship to God. Only God knows what's in a person's heart. Someone whom we think is despicable, God might know as a wonderful person. Similarly, someone we think is good, God may see as a hypocrite, with a black heart. Only God knows the truth about every individual.

"God will ultimately judge every individual. And God will allow people to be dragged into darkness with like-minded creatures. I have told you, from my personal experience, what goes on in there. I don't know from what I saw anymore than that, but it's my suspicion that I only saw the tip of the iceberg.

"I deserved to be where I was—I was in the right place at the right time. That was the place for me, and the people I was around were perfect company for me. God allowed me to experience that, and then removed me, because he saw something redeeming in putting me through the experience. It was a way to purge me. People who are not allowed to be pulled into darkness, because of their loving nature, are attracted upwards, toward the light.

"I never saw God, and I was not in heaven. It was way out in the suburbs, and these are the things that they showed me. We talked for a long time, about many things, and then I looked at myself. When I saw me, I was glowing, I was radiant. I was becoming beautiful not nearly as beautiful as them but I had a certain sparkle that I never had before." [162]

Bonni Burrows, speaking of how easy it was to gain knowledge in the spirit world, said,

"I asked questions. They were questions that I don't even understand how to ask here. No matter what it was that I wanted to know, it was just like moving my consciousness to that thought, and the answer in the totality we can't even understand [here] came to me. So there was this being able to tune in to the universe and know everything.

"One analogy; it's kind of like if you were asking about that bottle of water there, you wouldn't only just know about that bottle of water, you'd know every molecule in it. You'd know where it had been when it was evaporated and how it came down and where it came from and all of the processes —every person that ever

162   Howard Storm, https://www.near-death.com/experiences/notable/howard-storm.html

touched it—everything that ever happened to it—if it had been part of a rainbow—and then that's just the *water* in the bottle. We aren't talking about the label and the plastic.

"In *total fulness*, every answer was there of everything. And I could just keep going on and on with all of that."[163]

Mathematical Understanding

Interestingly, one of the things that seems to come both easily and comfortably to a person in spirit form is mathematics—everything from formulas, geometry, and calculous to Einstein's theory of relativity. While the discovery of this understanding may be different for different people, the depth of mathematical understanding gained in the spirit world is expansive.

That knowledge seems to point in experiencers toward a sort of wholeness—a grand plan or mission that everything points toward. Jean shares,

"I saw that life on this planet was not random, there is a giant plan. The plan, however, is on a scale that is incompressible to us. Our minds are too finite to grasp it. I was shown a ball that was convoluted and contained all surfaces. For years after my experience, I looked for someone who could explain this to me. I would take a strip of paper and twist and attach the two ends together. 'What is this?' I'd ask.

163   Bonni Burrows, IANDS Utah meeting audio recording, April 2013, https://iandsutah.org/archive-2013/

"Finally, years later, I met a physicist who told me it was a Mobius strip. I told him I had seen a solid round ball that was like this Mobius strip. The physicist said that would be a Mobius solid. 'Pure mathematics has proven a Mobius solid can exist,' he said, 'but our three-dimensional minds could not envision one.'

"I told him I had seen one.

"He just shook his head.

"During my experience, I was told that all time is *now* and all space is *here*. I believe there was more to this middle part of my experience that will be revealed to me when the time is right." [164]

The Basic Senses

Some people describe the experience as ultra-visual, while others describe it as not being a mere visual experience. I am led to suspect that the senses that excel in the spirit form are so potent as to drown out much of the visual experience. Think of it this way: consider of the last time you went to a theme park. What did it smell like? Certainly it had a smell, probably many smells, several rather strong, but the senses that were being most heavily stimulated (sight, and possibly hearing) were so strong that you may not have paid much attention to the smell. If then, in the spirit form, there are senses and emotions that are more potent and overbearing than sight and hearing,

---

164   Jean, http://www.nderf.org/Experiences/1jean_nde.html

then that would explain why people struggle to describe aspects of the experience using the senses, even though sight and hearing are still more potent there than here.

Reading Thoughts, Feelings, and Intentions

Many experiencers record having had the ability to hear peoples thoughts, feelings, history, and intensions. Immediately following her death, Diana records this incident:

"I lost consciousness at some point. That is when I experienced being outside of my body and was watching how frantically they were working to get me to breathe on my own.

"My next realization was that I was no longer frightened about not being able to breathe on my own. I was at peace and very aware of the steps the doctors and nurses were taking to save my life. I understood all the terms they were using and could comprehend that I was not alive as far as they were concerned. I became aware of is the state of each person's relationship with others in the room. There were suddenly no secrets and yet, there was no judgment on my part, but rather an unconditional love. I felt very much loved at this time and I wanted to extend that to the others in the room. But they could not hear me. I could hear and see everything! It made me think of the scripture that says, we 'will fully know as we are fully known.' Oddly, this ability continues today in terms of knowing the truth about people's relationships with others."[165]

Spencer had a similar experience just following the moment of his death, where he stood next to his body and began to somehow just *know* things.

"The nurse tried to find a pulse and couldn't. She swore and shouted back at the control room, 'I'm losing him! I'm losing him!'

"A male technician rushed into the room.

"Immediately people assembled to try to revive me. A doctor I had not seen before ran into the room, and for some reason, I immediately knew that he was having an affair with the nurse who started the IV. It came as a complete surprise to me that I knew this. I found my mind full of new information that was coming at me more from my heart than from my usual senses. I also knew that this nurse was recently divorced. I knew how much she valued and also feared this relationship with the doctor who was now working beside her to save me. I knew how hard she struggled to be good at her profession and still be a good mom to her two sons at home. I knew she had terrible financial problems. I knew everything about her, actually every detail of her life, and every decision, fear, hope, and action that had created her life. I could hear her mind screaming in fear. She was praying for help, trying to take control of her fear and remember her training. She desperately did not want me to die.

---

165   Diana H, Near Death Experience, http://www.nderf.org/NDERF/NDE Experiences/diana.h.nde.htm

"I looked at the other people in the room and was astonished that I could hear their thoughts and know the details about their lives just as vividly as the nurse.

"There is a heightened spiritual sensitivity that comes from being dead that I had never anticipated or heard of before. I knew what everyone was thinking. Actually, it was greater than just knowing what they were thinking. I also knew every detail of their lives. I knew if they were good people or bad, if they were honest or corrupt, and I knew every act that had brought them to that state. It wasn't something I felt or could see, it was just knowledge that was in me.

"What was even more interesting to me was that I felt no judgment of them. I simply knew these things. It was like knowing a rose is red; it isn't something to judge, it is just the way that flower is.

"What I did feel, which was totally new to me, was a rich compassion for them and their circumstances. Since I knew so much about them, I also knew their pains and their motivation for everything they had done that had taken them to this moment in time. I also felt their fear of losing me." [166]

Knowing Everything

While it's hard to imagine an ordinary person gaining access to *all* knowledge, this seems to often happen during people's brief visits to the spirit world. Steven says,

---

[166]   John Pontius, *Visions of Glory: One Man's Astonishing Account of the Last Days*, Utah, Cedar Fort, Inc. (November 13, 2012), chapter 1

"Then came a feeling like I was in utopia with complete knowledge of everything. If I began to ask a question, I had the answer before I finished the thought. It was during this time when I wanted to know Jesus/God better and get as close as I could to him. The thought was, 'If you listen to Thomas, seek out Thomas...'

"When I woke from my coma, I told the nurse that if she wanted to know the answer to anything, to ask now because the knowledge was fading fast. It was like a dream when you first wake you remember every detail and then it fades and you only remember the basics of the experience. But that thought, 'search out Thomas (the book)' was vivid. At the time, I knew that he was one of the 12 disciples, but his importance or that there was a book of Thomas, was not known to me at the time." [167]

Expanded Attention Capacity

Not only does expanded knowledge and increased capacity to comprehend multiple things increase in the spirit form, but so does the person's ability to focus on multiple things at once.

Spencer, while standing over his body as the medical staff worked on him, had the experience of expanded attention capacity.

"The next awareness I had was that I was able to comprehend many things simultaneously. I didn't need to focus on any one thing, because they were all clear to my

---

[167]   Steven D, http://www.nderf.org/NDERF/NDE.Experiences/steven.d.nde.htm

understanding. I felt like I could understand limitless amounts of knowledge and focus upon an infinite number of matters, giving each my absolute attention. This was amazing to me and so different from my experience as a struggling graduate student, trying to memorize volumes of information."[168]

Bonni Burrows also learned that in the spirit form, she had expanded attention capacity.

"My dad is still with me at that point. He's still there, and there are all of these other people that I know belong to me. They're relatives, people who have passed on, people I've never seen, but I know that they're are part of me. They're connected to me.

"And there's something that happens on the other side... [Here on earth] if you're in a crowd, and there are a lot of things going on—or even if you're in a quiet crowd, you can be distracted. It's more difficult, maybe, to focus. But on the other side, it was like having all those people made me *more* able to focus, to understand. They weren't a distraction, despite the fact that there was so much that was new."[169]

Learning Without the Body

While some lessons, such as those listed above, are easy to learn in the spirit form, others are much more difficult without a body. You might call this one of the limitations

---

168   Pontius, John M, Visions of Glory, Springville, UT, Cedar Fort, Inc., 2012, pp. 6-7
169   Bonni Burrows, IANDS Utah meeting audio recording, April 2013, https://iandsutah.org/archive-2013/

of the spirit form. Amy Call had a near-death experience, and found herself in a room or place with many people who seemed rather caught up in their own problems or self-importance. As she approached the group's guide, or teacher, who was there to help them overcome their self-centered mindsets, she conversed with him on the subject.

"He looked at me and I realized he was a kind of teacher or Guide for this group. He explained that he had died in a truck accident. He had been a truck driver by profession. He was a Latino man. He told me that he was not a perfect man, but that he had Mastered Humility. I know that sounds ironic, but when I was with him, I could feel truly, that he hadn't a shred of self-regard or as we'd say, *pride*, about him. He explained, that he had come to help teach them importance of humility to this group of people, because they had been so self-absorbed in their lives, they hadn't been able to learn vital lessons and had aborted their own lives. He seemed to be telling me that in one way or another, these people had 'Committed Suicide.'

"This made me wonder, as I hadn't noticed anyone in the room who had hung themselves, intentionally overdosed on drugs, shot themselves, or things like that. I was a bit confused by how the term, 'Suicide' could come to me with these people. But I came to understand that the casual disregard for life, and the flagrant and selfish risks that one might take, whether involved in drug use, drunk driving, or any kind of action that could essentially lead to one's own demise is what is considered, 'Suicide,' at least where I was. When a human takes their own life in desperation, due to emotional or mental imbalances, or physical agony, or depression so severe, this is very similar to when a very old person gets so tired of "hanging on" that they *will* themselves to go... simply stop eating and breathing, etc... This is not punished, so to speak, on the Other Side. It is different. It is just the human, willing themselves out of this life cycle.

"The teacher continued to offer more information. He explained how in aborting their own lives, these people would have a rest period, but that learning what they needed to learn would be difficult. I came to understand that as much as they were taught and infused with good and helpful information there, and even if they agreed 'wholeheartedly' with what was being taught, or what they needed to learn, that learning without a body is like learning to get over an addiction to drugs with no opportunity to do the drugs! Or like learning to love one's own enemy without having enemies to deal with. He explained how he needed to teach this group of people how vital it is to let go of themselves. How to lose their obsession with themselves. How they will be stagnant in all progress if they cannot unchain themselves from their own self-obsessions. He had to teach them the importance of humility. And yet, he shook his head, smiling slightly, and he implied that there was still very little he could help them with, without their bodies. His hope was to instill more of a passion for what he had to teach, strong enough that it would leave a seed of Light that might stay with them through their sojourns." [170]

---

170 Amy Call, http://ndestories.org/amy-call/

Clothing

What do people wear in the spirit world? We've briefly mentioned the wearing of white, or robes of white or brown. But are these the only things people wear in the the spirit world. When Sharon died, she found herself in the very clothes she'd died in.

> "I also remember, I looked down the front of my body. I could see that I still had a body and it looked the same as it always had. I had on the same clothes as before and I noticed my long blond hair falling down below my shoulders. I could see my jean shorts and my feet. But I also noticed that my body felt much lighter, it felt kind of 'floaty'. It was not heavy, like it is here on earth. On earth, we are weighted down with gravity. Everything seems very heavy, but there it was a light body. And I also noticed that I was no longer concerned about my body, how it looked, or if I fit in or not." [171]

---

171   Sharon, http://www.nderf.org/NDERF/NDE_Experiences/sharon_m_nde.htm

Sometimes people wear clothes that have personal meaning to them. Deborah shares:

"I don't remember the exact date of my experience, but it was several weeks after my brother passed away. The experience happened shortly before what would have been my brother's 45th birthday. I know that it was a Saturday night and I went to bed like any other night. I began dreaming. All of a sudden, the dream began to fade and something began nudging me to turn. Everything began to feel very different from a dream.

"I turned halfway around and saw my brother standing before me. He looked wonderful; he had a glow about him and his face was very relaxed, calm and peaceful. He was perfectly healthy and he was wearing an outfit that he had worn only once about a year or so before he died. It was a black turtleneck shirt, white jeans and black and white sneakers. His hair was short and he had a nicely-trimmed goatee. What amazed me is that I had liked his outfit the day that he wore it and I thought that he looked very handsome; but I never said anything to him. Of course, I never thought about that outfit again. It really struck me that he was standing before me wearing it.

"My brother began speaking to me, but it was telepathic. He was speaking directly to my mind. It struck me as a much more efficient way to communicate and it seemed very natural." [172]

---

172   Deborah L. http://www.nderf.org/NDERF/NDE_Experiences/deborah_l_ndelike.htm

Ranelle Wallace, during her near-death experience, noticed the clothing on the people she saw, and observed,

> "My feet and hands were perfect and whole. They radiated this glistening, beaming light, and I looked at my grandmother and saw that her light was brighter than mine. Every part of her was more brilliant. Even her dress was glowing white. And I recognized the dress. It was the dress that she had been buried in. My mother had bought it for her funeral. I thought about what Jim had been wearing, and I understood that people there wear what they want to wear. They wear what they're comfortable in, and I knew that my grandmother must have loved this dress my mother bought for her. Although she had never worn it in life, Grandma was wearing it now, and she was radiant."[173]

That experience seems to sum it up. From everything I read, it appears that people wear what they want in the spirit world.

Which, of course, brings up the question of why so many wear white. I've read many experiences where the people on the other side of the veil are wearing colors other than white, but white does seem to be the most common clothing color. Which is interesting, since it's not the most commonly worn color here (and not *just* because it shows dirt more than other colors).

One possible reason for this has to do with our

---

173   Wallace, Ranelle, *The Burning Within*, (Carson City, NV: Gold Leaf Press, 1994), pg. 99-100

attitudes and feelings about one another there. Here, there tends to be an intense level of competition and comparison in how we present ourselves. But that doesn't seem to be the case there.

When all thoughts and feelings are open to the viewing of all (which they often are in the spirit world), perhaps outward expressions of self become less important. And if beauty is measured in love, kindness, and glory, then perhaps people tend to wear colors that best reflect the bright light emanating from their true being. White probably does that well.

Those are just speculations, but if we tend to wear what we want in the spirit world, and we tend to *want* to love, serve, and bless one another, then outside of genuine preference, we probably wear what best reflects our truest selves.

Music

Many who have near-death experiences report hearing music on the other side. Many such instances we've already shared. Their descriptions vary, and from what I can guess, there is probably as much (or more) variety of music there as there is here. So let's discuss some of the more interesting aspects and details about people's experience of music in the spirit realm.

Some hear music being sung in praise of God, or singing to the light at the end of the tunnel. Nan says,

"As we got very close to the light I saw tens of thousands of beings dressed in white gowns all facing the Light and singing a music I had never heard the likes of before. They were in the service of The Light and apparently, 'singing' praises to The Light. The Light was filled with the most extraordinary, overwhelming and indescribable feeling of LOVE. Then I came directly in front of The Light and The Light spoke in a man's voice, firm and direct, saying only, 'Go Back!'" [174]

Carol Vengroff describes the music she heard in this way,

"It is sound, absolutely, but not like we know it. It *is* like we know it, and then it's, much more. And the sounds, the notes, take on lives of their own. And each note has meanings, and oh, it just goes on and on!"[175]

Some people, during the early parts of their experience, speak of a tone, chime, or voice that seems to extend forever, or continue without ceasing. Pam Reynold's, a singer/songwriter, describes this "note."

"The next thing I recall was the sound: It was a Natural 'D.' As I listened to the sound, I felt it was pulling me out of the top of my head. The further out of my body I got, the more clear the tone became. I had the impression it was like a road, a frequency that you go on... I remember seeing several things in the operating room when I was looking down. It was the most aware that I think that I have ever been in my entire life" [176]

During a near-death experience, Sylib also experienced heavenly music:

"I could feel my spirit come out of my body and I saw my body lying there as if asleep. I was carried as if my angels, though I did not see them, far up into the heavens

174   Nan A, https://www.nderf.org/Experiences/1nan_a_nde.html

175   Carol Vengroff, IANDS NDE Radio Podcast, https://www.youtube.com/watch?
      time.continue=145&v=df_C5GtJgj8E

176   Pam Reynolds, https://www.near-death.com/science/evidence/people-have-ndes-while-brain-
      dead.html

and at a great speed. I was taken to a place surrounded by
music. It was like no music I have ever heard. More
beautiful than all the best music my ears have heard and
it came from everywhere." [177]

Bonni Burrows described the music this way:

"The music was incredible! Like nothing I had ever
heard. It's like that's what hearing was created for. It's not
like I'm just hearing it with my ears—it's like I'm hearing
it with my ears and my very being." [178]

A man named David describes heavenly music this
way:

"The sounds of the Angels' singing was so beautiful,
and thunderous and Glorious above me, I felt as if their
sound vibrations were filled with wisdom, (so
sophisticated) that these sound vibrations were actually
creating life and myriad possibilities in the universe: that
Angelic sounds were not just singing for the fun of it
alone, but were creating with sounds." [179]

Sharon Milliman:

"Oh, the music! When I was in the garden, I could
hear the music, and it was like each blade of grass has a
sound. The leaves on the trees have a sound. The birds
have a sound. The water has a sound. The rocks have a
different sound. And when when you put all these
individual sounds together, you have the most

---

177   Sylib, https://www.nderf.org/Experiences/1sybil_s_nde.html
178   Bonni Burrows, IANDS Utah meeting audio recording, April 2013, https://iandsutah.org/archive-2013/
179   David, http://www.nderf.org/Experiences/1david_nde.html

magnificent orchestra you have ever heard in your life! The choir—everything was singing praises to God. It was so magnificent! And I could hear the piano notes, and I could hear the string instruments. But it was a vibrational sound that was coming off each individual leaf, or blade of grass, or rock, or whatever.

"I noticed that each color had a vibrational sound, like a rainbow—each color had a different sound.

"The music in Heaven is magnificent!"[180]

I hope in further research to find more details about the music people hear. Do they hear string instruments? Trumpets? Pianos? Flutes? We learn from previous chapters that there are individual instruments. Sharon Milliman saw a man playing the piano, and was impressed by the beauty of the sound.

My suspicion is that if we have an instrument here, there's a version of it there, and it probably sounds even more full and beautiful than it's earthly counterpart.

From many experiences, we also learn that there is music learning—such as classes, choirs, music theory, etc. That suggests to me that this life isn't our only chance to learn to sing or play an instrument. But one thing is for sure, if we learn it here, we may find ways of creating heavenly music to leave on the earth for other mortals to enjoy!

---

180   Sharon Milliman, from a podcast interview, https://neardeathexperiencepodcast.org/sharon-millimans-near-death-experiences

Relationships

Of the few things we can take with us into the next life, relationships are one of the most important. Not only because they continue into the next life, but also because love is known there to be the most important and vital attribute. Relationships are the result of the love we carry. Gratefully, those relationships are fully in tact on the other side—even when the time spent together on this side was so short.

This is especially true with family relationships. It appears that family relationships are so essential that even family members you don't recognize have an important relationship with you. Sharon says,

"Then, two men appeared and stood one on either side of me. They were young men, maybe in their 20's or early 30's. They had blond hair and blue eyes. They wore what looked like cream-colored linen clothing. There was a brilliant glow around them; they seemed to be illuminated, and their joy seemed to pour from every cell in their bodies. I noticed the linen clothes they wore were very detailed. It was a very tightly woven cloth and very soft to the touch. I could see the tiny weave pattern of the linen. Why that seemed important, I do not know, but it stood out very clearly.

"At first, I thought these men were angels, but, then, I realized who they were. These two men were my younger brothers who had died as babies. I was only age 1 when my first brother died shortly after birth and I was age 2 when my mother lost the other one due to a miscarriage although she was far enough along to know she was having a boy. I knew of these men but was too young to have remembered anything about them. My parents never spoke of them.

"We were so happy to see each other; it was like a family reunion. They had beautiful smiles and they both looked so much like my dad. I knew he would be so proud of them both." [181]

Many who have near-death experiences have expressed a deep connection with ancestors and family history. Whether those things mattered to the individual before, after the experience they have a deep love and appreciation for their families going back many generations. Leonard K. says,

"After the introductions and all settled down I spent some time chatting with grandma and grandpa, my living

181   Sharon M. http://www.nderf.org/NDERF/NDE_Experiences/sharon_m_nde.htm

grandmother's parents. They both said that someone very special was coming to greet me. I don't remember if they mentioned who it was. A very pleasant woman dressed in a tunic that resembled a loose weave type of sack material soon joined us. Her gray hair looked chopped and very uneven. Up until this woman joined us all of my other relatives looked like they wore clothing from the time period they lived in. This special woman explained that she would take me to a place where she could show me something very important.

"From this point forward I think it would be best if I call her Mother, because that is exactly how she felt to me. It was as if she knew more about me than I did. I had no problem going with Mother when she asked if I was ready. She possessed a concentration of love in her that I was immediately attracted to. My relatives had the same love, but Mother was stronger. As we moved together she started to glow, and soon we came to a place where Mother explained that I belonged to a family that went back multiple generations. Mother simply waved her arm, and a round, grayish tunnel opened before us. It went very deep, and it went straight back as if we could walk into it if we wished. She pointed out that I could see many generations of my family going back through this opening. I could see people, most of them couples. They went back into the tunnel in steps that represented each generation that had lived before me.

"The first person that stood out was a woman sweeping the entrance to her home. I somehow knew that she never married. Some of the previous generations

were aware that we could see them, and they appeared to
know who we were. I remember one particular couple
sitting in some chairs, and the woman smiled as she
waved from the distance. It was obvious that she was
pleased to see us. I'm not certain, but I think the people in
the chairs were my great-great-grandparents from
Denmark. I was viewing a heavenly history of my family.
It did go back a very long distance like Mother had
explained.

"Then Mother pointed to the very center of the
tunnel, and she explained there was a powerful light at
the far end. Suddenly the light was before us. Mother had
me stand alone while the light penetrated every part of
me. I felt complete and taken apart at the same time. The
best simple explanation I can give for how it felt would be
like standing in front of a powerful fan while soaking wet.
An incredible warm, penetrating wind entered me like
life itself. I glowed with the light now, and I was
extremely happy. I was in the form of a toddler, Mother
and I were laughing together as she held me.[182]

Christy speaks of encountering her stillborn child:
"...the doctors put me out with anesthesia to do an
emergency hysterectomy. I remember waking up in a
large field that was filled with grass and beautiful pink
flowers. The sky was so blue. There were mountains in
the background and a large forest on the other side of the
field. What I remember most is how warm I felt. It was a
very comfortable warmth like on a Spring or fall day
when the weather is perfect and the sun is shining; like

182   Leonard K. http://www.nderf.org/Experiences/1leonard_k_nde.html

that. Sitting next to me was a little girl. We talked for a long time. She was a daughter I lost to stillbirth several years ago. I knew that's who she was and I felt happy to see her and talk to her. She was about 7 or 8 years old which is how old she would be now if she had lived." [183]

Carol Vengroff encountered a grandfather who had died before she was born.

"And I got to a place where my grandfather was there, and he greeted me. He was sort of in a life form, but he was also the essence of my grandfather, and it was wonderful to be with him again. And as he was greeting me, we caught up on everything that had happened. And the ironic thing—the really bizarre thing is: he died before I was born, but yet I recognized him, and we had missed each other. And it was such a joyful reunion again!" [184]

There appears to be a special link and responsibility that we have for our ancestors, both in the next life and here on earth. One woman says,

"I noticed a line of lights behind [my father] winding away into the distance and I asked my father, 'Who are they?'

"He looked at me gently and said, 'These are your ancestors... They have come to greet you. Didn't you know that you were the living hope of your ancestors? What they couldn't accomplish during their lives, they

---

183   https://www.nderf.org/Experiences/1christy.h.nde.html
184   Carol Vengroff, from an interview on IANDS NDE Radio, https://www.youtube.com/watch?v=dLC5GtJ9j8E

counted on you to resolve. You got as far as you did because you were able to stand on their bones.'

"I could see my lineage stretched out in front of me and I was awed and humbled. I could never feel alone again." [185]

Romantic Relationships

Some people mention physical attraction (though the term may be something of a misnomer in this case) towards spirits they meet on the other side. Steve, who is married at the time of his near-death experience, says of his experience,

"I had a near-death experience at age 25, during a minor surgery. I awakened from the surgery, blinded by a river of white light. I thought it was an aftereffect of the general anesthesia. I thought it was odd that it pushed beyond my optic nerve and went through my entire body. I immediately rose to my feet, and looked at the nurse who had helped me up. She wasn't a nurse. She was clothed in light, extraordinarily beautiful, and loving. She was the most beautiful woman I had ever seen, and I almost cry when I think about it. I fell in love the instant I looked at her. I was in ecstasy. She wore a loose-fitting, white gown, and it gave off light of its own. Her light was golden and white. She was thin, blond, with shoulder-length hair. She was about 5'7", and fair but golden in her

185   *IT IS HERE IN OUR BODIES THAT THE LESSONS OF LOVE ARE MADE MANIFEST*, 17 *February 2017*, International Association for Near-Death Studies, https://iands.org/research/nde-research/nde-archives31/newest-accounts/1198-it-is-here-in-our-bodies-that-the-lessons-of-love-are-made-manifest.html

skin hues. She was definitely female, but radiated power and intelligence, as well as love and care. She was responsible and carried massive authority.

"I looked behind me, and saw my body still asleep in a post-operative rest area. She said not to worry, that I wasn't dead. My heart was still beating. I could see into it. She was concerned about my breathing because the anesthesia was too strong for my central nervous system. It was depressing my respiration. She was there to stabilize my respiration and watch over me.

"Not a word was spoken—all communication was by shared thoughts and feelings.

"She told me that my life was too important to take any chances on my survival, and that's why she was there. I had to be guarded. I was too important to risk.

"She led me off to the side, and I realized that we were looking through a wall at my sleeping body, from another room. After calming me, which didn't take long, she showed me some amazing views. There was a curtain of light around her, a veil of energy behind her. I wasn't allowed to pass through that veil. I was in a resting area between worlds. to our sides, there was a multi-colored halo of glittering lights in geometric shapes. They seemed electrically charged, moving, and shimmering, like a ragged border between her world and mine. Through a fog-like mist, we peered into the physical world.

"I felt wonderful, and not too surprised—this was not the first time I had met someone like her. Her light was a signature that identified her, and I had seen that light before. To see her was to fall in love with her instantly. I never wanted to leave her. It may be that she felt the circumstances provided an unfair comparison with my wife. She showed me some details about my children, and revealed a view of another woman even more lovely and desirable—the wife I was married to. She then said it was time to return, that my breathing had stabilized, and that my nervous system was able to work on its own."[186]

A couple points I think worth making here: first, learn to control your thoughts while in the mortal body. That's not an easy thing to do, but controlling thoughts will be much easier to do there if you've mastered it here. Why would you want to learn to control your thoughts? Well, for one thing, if you get to the other side, and find yourself attracted to a spirit you don't immediately recognize, you'll want to be able to keep your thoughts clean and diverted from your attraction. Thoughts aren't secret there, so the person will immediately recognize your attraction to them. Which for some people may not sound like a big deal except for the fact of the second point...

Most of the time, when you die and encounter a spirit you don't immediately recognize, it is a family member, such as a grandparent, great-grandparent, or sometimes even an unborn or future child.

I only mention this to save you the potentially laughably embarrassing situation you may find yourself in

---

186   Steve, https://www.nderf.org/Experiences/1steve t possible nde.html

when you realize the spirit you've just unintentionally openly confessed romantic love for is your grandma, or (heaven forbid) your daughter. Talk about heavenly awkwardness—sheesh!

Another fun (though more innocent) example of this comes from Kim Rives, who, after a remarkably in-depth visit to the spirit world, returned to earth to get ready to return to her body, and visited her sister's home.

"I was then taken to the last place that I would be going to, and it was a totally different scene. My sister, she's three years older than me and was going to Utah State University to become a therapist, and when I landed here in this new scenario, I was sitting with my body half-way in the building dorm room, and half-way out. I remember looking at myself in this wall, and I thought, *this is interesting, I'm in a wall, and it doesn't even hurt. How do I get out of it?*

"And then I noticed that she was working on her computer—working on her thesis. So I'm sitting here, stretched out, and I see this beautiful angel, and I'm telling you, this guy was handsome! And I was single, so he was rather appealing. He had this reddish hair, he had on a white toga that was bare at the shoulder, and he had some sort of thing on his head—leafy thing, and I don't know what that meant.

"As I was looking, he was floating above the ground, and I thought, *you know, I wonder what kind of power it takes to float.* Well, then I got myself and I pulled myself through, and looked down and noticed that I was floating, too. It didn't take any power at all, you just do it. You just float.

"Well he looked at me, and I said [thought], 'You are cuuuute!'

"I did think that, I have to tell you, but once again I was embarrassed, because I realized then that he heard me. Well, he didn't say much about that. He just said to me, 'Kim, you need to get back in your body. Your mission is not yet complete.'" [187]

Apparently there is still romantic attraction on the other side.

Relationships with Premortal and Post-mortal Spirits

During her near-death experience, Bettie J. Eadie was privileged to see the spirits of those preparing to come to earth.

"I returned to the garden and met my earlier escorts again. I had seen people progressing in the worlds I had visited, working toward becoming more like our Father, and I was curious about our development on earth. How do we grow?

"My escorts were pleased with my question, and they took me to a place where many spirits prepared for life on

---

187   Kim Rives, Utah IANDS conference, 9 May 2009,
       https://iandsutah.files.wordpress.com/2013/02/iands-09-05-may-2009-kim-rives.mp3

earth. They were mature spirits—I saw no children spirits during my entire experience. I saw how desirous these spirits were of coming to earth. They looked upon life here as a school where they could learn many things and develop the attributes they lacked. I was told that we had all desired to come here, that we had actually chosen many of our weaknesses and difficult situations in our lives so that we could grow. I also understood that sometimes we were given weaknesses which would be for our good. The Lord also gives us gifts and talents according to his will. We should never compare our talents or weaknesses to another's. We each have what we need; we are unique. Equality of spiritual weaknesses or gifts is not important."[188]

Though they seem to live together in harmony, there does seem to be some difference between spirits that have lived a mortal life, and those who haven't yet.

Ranelle Wallace, upon meeting dear friends she'd known before he mortal life, describes:

"The younger spirits, the ones who hadn't been to earth, were then called away. They seemed younger only because they hadn't gained the experiences of earth life yet. We all looked the same age, somewhere in our twenties. After they were gone, the rest of us spoke on a higher level, sharing things we could not share with the others. Life on earth does something to us. It strips away a naivety, an innocence, and infuses our eternal selves with maturity and wisdom. With the other gone, we

---

188   Bettie Eadie, Embraced by the Light, (Gold Leaf Press: Carson City, Nevada, 1992),

could now bare all of our lessons and experiences from earth. We looked forward to the future in a way we hadn't before, knowing better what the whole plan entailed."[189]

---

189   Wallace, Ranelle, *The Burning Within*, (Carson City, NV: Gold Leaf Press, 1994), pg. 109

Goals, Dreams, and Ambitions

There seems to be a great deal of progression that takes place on the other side. One man named David, finding himself in the light, describes various levels of glory.

"In the light I heard the thunderous fluttering winds and the most beautiful sounds of angels voices singing louder than the thunderous winds. My body was becoming paralyzed with the power of the Light. The Love was overwhelming to me...

"When it swallowed me whole, an explosion of Ecstasy and Love started from my belly and expanded into the light itself. Soon, I became the Light and became Innocence, Love, Ecstasy, Peace, Power and Beauty and Wisdom of the Light. Like a mother carrying a child in her arms, the light carried me upwards and at tremendous speed. The Light itself spoke to me and I knew it was God, the Power that created the whole universe. The Light told me this first clear light heaven I was in (which was a million times brighter than any love I ever felt on earth), was filled with countless paradise planets. I looked down at my body and it was made of white light but still had a luminous human form.

"I spent some time there, but was taken higher, where the Joy and Glory of God was crushing me to the point that I could not bear the Ecstasy any longer, thus I exploded into a new light and Glory of Innocence, Love, Ecstasy, Peace, Power and Wisdom one million times brighter than the first Heaven was. My new body was brighter and clearer and could somehow withstand this exponential increase in Glory. I was told this Second Heaven was filled with countless paradise planets.

"In each ascending Heaven, the Glory of these qualities in the light, multiplied another million times. It is inconceivable how bright and beautiful life is in these heavens to any mind alone, separate from this light. I was taken to the point where the Ecstasy and Love were so overwhelming; I could barely stand the levels of cosmic energy and Ecstasy any longer.

"I exploded into a new light one million times brighter than the Second Heaven; thus the Third Heaven. Here, my body was still human but so much white light shining from it I could not believe my eyes. I could see for millions of miles with perfect clarity...

"I sped through this Third Heaven and was taken into

the fourth where the Glory of God was so bright. I felt any being here was beyond even inconceivable Glory. My body was so bright here that it had little remains of the human form. The Glory was so bright and filled with these qualities; I told God 'I can't take any more. You are far greater than I ever imagined God to be by inconceivable measure.'

"Whole Galaxies of energy could be created by this light.

"I asked God to not take me higher, but God did. At this point, because the Glory was so bright and beyond my abilities, this amazing quality, descending down from the even brighter light above me. I do not think there are any planets up here, but perhaps beings live inside of stars here. The Grace of God, the most beautiful and poetic quality of God came down like millions of leaves falling in harmony and stilled and purified the Ecstasy and Glory to the point that I could bear it. I could write a whole chapter on Grace and not do it justice.

"Then I was taken into the Fifth Heaven. My body was now like a giant sun. It had no human form any more. The Glory here was unspeakable. What goes on here is truly unbelievable for human beings.

"I stayed there for some time and was taken into the Sixth Heaven, which is a million times brighter than the Fifth. I will not speak about how bright God is here. The Angels were singing so loud that no human ears could hear this music of the universe. My body was an even brighter sun merged into the central light of God.

"I was then taken into the Seventh heaven, and what happens there is so far beyond my abilities, God brought me down. I only lasted ten seconds in the Seventh Heaven. Whole galaxies could be created with the light there with total ease. Any beings that can go there are millions of years more evolved than I am. To think that in each of these higher heavens the Light and Glory of Innocence, Love, Ecstasy, Peace, Power, Beauty, Grace and Wisdom multiplies a million times over the preceding heaven, makes it so difficult to pass through and live in."[190]

Carol Pope had a near-death experience. When asked later about future events, and the situation of spirits after this life, she said,

"What I saw is so exciting! As a matter of fact, if you guys had seen it, this whole room would be standing up ten times more excited than you are right now. Seriously! And you would get up in the morning, ready for your day ten times more excited than you've ever lived your life before, because of what's coming. It is SO great!

"Anybody who's out there in life, and they're really doing life, and playing in life, and their creating—just get ready, because it is SO GREAT! I didn't see the bad stuff...

"It was really interesting, because as I started to watch it, I was really stunned that Father was so wanting me to have like everything that a young egoic spirit would want. So, in other words, (I will just admit) I always wanted to

190   David, http://www.nderf.org/Experiences/1david.nde.html

be famous. I wanted to star on Broadway. I wanted to have all the money that I needed so that I could do charity, and tithing, and help people, and still have all the toys that I wanted to have. And when Father showed me that that was all coming, I'm like, 'What? You mean I'm not bad to want those things? You mean it's okay that I really truly down deep in my heart, I would love to have that stuff?

"And Father just laughed and laughed. He thought that was so funny. Like, He said that just like your mother and your father—and you're a mother, and you know how you love to dote over your kids and give them all the stuff. You know how we do that at Christmas (my goodness do we go overboard or what?)—it's because we *love* to give those things to our kids...

"That's how Father is with us. He's so okay with it! At least that's my experience."[191]

If I'm understanding this correctly, there are levels beyond levels beyond levels we work toward in attributes, learning, experiencing, adventuring, and expanding. So too are all things available to us in time. God wants us to have everything he has, just as a parent wants their child to obtain everything they have, and become everything they're capable of being. The biggest things that hold us back from obtaining it all are our own attitudes and choices—and, of course, our temporary mortality.

Beings, Animals, and Plants

It seems that our connection with animals, plants, and other life forms are much more meaningful on the other side of the veil.

Frances describes:

"There were so many flowers and trees. They were alive. The flowers were so bright; they had colors I had never seen before. The blue ones seemed to be polarized light. Yellows felt as if the sun was inside them. Their brightness was as intense as looking at the sun in this world, except that there, it didn't hurt my eyes. They were incredibly beautiful and they were made of light."

Sharon Milliman said:

"Our animals do go to Heaven. There are rolling plains, valleys and hills, and places for horses to run, cows to run, and dogs to run, and cat's to play, and whatever. Heaven is so huge! If you think earth is huge, multiply it by twenty billion, it's so big!"[192]

During her experience, Cristine found herself in a beautiful garden. As she describes,

"I took notice of the flowers, of how they were alive and they were immersed in a love that was pure. To this day I can cry thinking of it. The garden's colors were also alive with hues that made every other colors at 'home' dull.

"The flowers moved as if a gentle wind always was present. It was sunny but the sun never hurt my eyes. The temperature was perfect and I felt a sense of wellbeing as I never have. The sun lit up the petals and wings, making them transparent and I would fly in to enjoy the intricate designs (like I did inside the kaleidoscope). The garden was entertaining me and I felt not only love and joy there but also a sense of fun. My ears could make out each bird and insect but there was a particular sound—a buzzing, that was actually becoming obnoxious in it's impatience for my attention. I flew to it and was face to face with a big fat bumblebee. It went into a flower and then suddenly was blown out by a tremendous explosion of pollen. I could see each tiny grain floating in slow motion. The expression on the bumblebee's face was hilarious— like it had the best [sensation] ever—It looked me straight in the eyes, smiled and flew off as I laughed out loud. The

---

192   Sharon Milliman, from a podcast interview, https://neardeathexperiencepodcast.org/sharon-millimans-near-death-experiences

garden felt like the entire universe and everything it held I could see in a single dewdrop on a flower's petal. I thanked God for letting me come here." [193]

This fascination with the colors, textures, and energy of the plants and life-forms in the spirit world is incredibly common among near-death experiencers. Betty Eadie shares:

"When light strikes an object here, the light reflects off that object in a certain color. Thousands of shades are possible. Light in the spirit world doesn't necessarily reflect off anything. It comes from within and appears to be a living essence. A million, a billion colors are possible.

"The flowers, for example, are so vivid and luminescent with color that they don't seem to be solid. Because of each plant's intense aura of light, it is difficult to define where the plant's surface starts and stops. It is obvious that each part of the plant, each microscopic part, is made up of its own intelligence. This is the best word I can use to define it. Every minute part is filled with its own life and can be reorganized with other elements to create anything in existence. The same element that now resides in a flower may later be part of something else – and just as alive. It doesn't have a spirit as we do, but it has intelligence and organization and can react to the will of God and other universal laws. All of this is evident as you see creation there, and particularly evident in the flowers.

---

193   Cristine H, https://www.nderf.org/Experiences/1cristine_h_sobe.html

"A beautiful river ran through the garden not far from me, and I was immediately drawn to it. I saw that the river was fed by a large cascading waterfall of the purest water, and from there the river fed into a pond. The water dazzled with its clarity and life.

"Life. It was in the water too. Each drop from the waterfall had its own intelligence and purpose. A melody of majestic beauty carried from the waterfall and filled the garden, eventually merging with other melodies that I was now only faintly aware of. The music came from the water itself, from its intelligence, and each drop produced its own tone and melody which mingled and interacted with every other sound and strain around it. The water was praising God for its life and joy. The overall effect seemed beyond the ability of any symphony or composer here. In comparison, our best music here would sound like a child playing a tin drum. We simply don't have the capacity to comprehend the vastness and strength of the music there, let alone begin to create it. As I got closer to the water the thought came to me that these could possibly be the "living waters" mentioned in the scriptures, and I wanted to bathe in them.

"As I approached the water, I noticed a rose near me that seemed to stand out from the other flowers, and I stopped to examine it. Its beauty was breathtaking. Among all the flowers there, none captured me like this one. It was gently swaying to faint music, and singing praises to the Lord with sweet tones of its own. I realized that I could actually see it growing. As it developed before my eyes, my spirit was moved, and I wanted to experience its life, to step into it and feel its spirit. As this thought came to me, I seemed to be able to see down into it. It was as though my vision had become microscopic and allowed me to penetrate the rose's deepest parts. But it was much more than a visual experience. I felt the rose's presence around me, as if I were actually inside and part of the flower. I experienced it as if I were the flower. I felt the rose swaying to the music of all the other flowers, and I felt it creating its own music, a melody that perfectly harmonized with the thousands of other roses joining it. I understood that the music in my flower came from its individual parts, that its petals produced their own tones, and that each intelligence within that petal was adding to its perfect notes, each working harmoniously for the overall effect – which was joy. My joy was absolutely full again! I felt God in the plant, in me, his love pouring into us. We were all one!

"I will never forget the rose that I was. That one experience, just a glimmer of the grander joy that is available in the spirit world, in being one with everything else, was so great that I will cherish it forever." [194]

Ranelle Wallace speaks of an interaction with the flowers in a garden that she had during her near-death experience, with her grandmother at her side.

"A garden cannot exist on Earth like the one I saw. I had been in gardens in California that had taken my breath away, but they were stuck into insignificance by the scene before me now. Here was an endless vista of

---

194   Bettie Eadie, Embraced by the Light, (Gold Leaf Press: Carson City, Nevada, 1992), 79-81

grass rolling away into shining, radiant hills. We have never seen green in our world like the deep, shimmering green of the grass that grew there. Every blade was crisp, strong, and charged with light. Every blade was unique and perfect and seemed to welcome me into this miraculous place.

"And the whole garden was singing. The flowers, grass, trees, and other plants filled this place with glorious tones and rhythms and melodies; yet I didn't hear the music itself. I could feel it somehow on a level beyond my hearing. As my grandmother and I stopped a moment to marvel at the magnificent scene, I said to myself, 'Everything here seems to be singing,' which was woefully inadequate to describe what I felt. We simply don't have language that adequately communicates the beauty of that world.

"I noticed something unusual about the flowers near us. My grandmother waved her arm and, without speaking, commanded them to come to her. Although it was a command, the flowers took joy in obeying her. They floated through the air and came to a stop, suspended within the circle of her arms. The bouquet was alive. Each blossom was able to communicate, react, and actually enlighten others near it. 'Grandma,' I said, 'they have no stems.'

"'Why should they have stems?' she said. 'Flowers on Earth need stems to receive nourishment, to grow to their fullest potential. Everything God has made is spiritual and is designed to grow towards it own spiritual potential. A flower reaches its fullness in the blossom. Here everything exists in its fullest form. These flowers have no need of stems.'

"'But they just float.'

"'Should they fall? Everything here is perfect.' She took one of the flowers and handed it to me. 'Isn't that beautiful?' she said. The whole blossom was filled with various shades of light, and its beauty was incredible. Then the flower became part of me. Its soul merged with mine. It experienced everything I was doing, or had done before. It was acutely aware of me, and at the same time it changed me with its delicate spirit, with its own existence and life. It affected my feelings, my thoughts, my identity. It was me. I was it. The joy that came from this union was more pervasive and delicious and fulfilling than any I had known until that moment, and I wanted to cry. The scriptures say that one day all things shall be as one. That statement has great power for me now. My grandmother commanded the flowers to return, and they floated gently back to their places just above the ground. The one in my hands also returned, but its essence remained with me.

"'All this comes from God, and the power to sustain it comes from him. It is the power of his love. Just as the plant life on Earth needs soil, water, and light for nourishment, spiritual life needs love. All creation springs from God's love, and everything he creates has the capacity to love in turn. Light, truth, and life are all created in love and are sustained by love. God gives it love. We give it love. You give it love. And thus creation grows. And, RaNelle,' she said, 'I love you!'

"As she said the words, I felt her love charge into my
being, filling me with incredible warmth and joy. This
was life. This was true existence. There had been nothing
like it on Earth. I felt the plants loving me, the sky, the
fragrances, everything. And as I received my
grandmother's words and this love, I knew that now I
would be responsible to increase and heighten all love
around me, whatever my circumstances. She was teaching
me love, its definition, its extent and power, not just so I
could take pleasure in receiving it, but so I could express
it to others. I was being filled with love in order to
become a source of love."[195]

This idea of flowers not having stems may have been
unique to Ranelle's experience, since stems are sometimes
elsewhere mentioned regarding flowers in the spirit world
—or perhaps there are some flowers with stems and some
without. Regardless, seeing the flowers without stems
appears to have had the desired effect of teaching Ranelle
the perfection of the place.

It also appears that there may even be plants and
animals in the spirit world that are not found here on
mortal earth. Diane describes,

"I first came to an absolutely serene and beautiful
countryside. This is where I saw animals (including
unicorns) and they were so beautiful and contented, so
full of LOVE. The grass, trees, and flowers were all so

---

195   Wallace, Ranelle, *The Burning Within*, (Carson City, NV: Gold Leaf Press, 1994), pg. 101-104

exquisite that my mind said so and in return, a vibration of Love flowed back to me from them. The water was so spectacular that I expressed this in my mind and the waters were living and sparkled back to me with love.

"There was melody or music all around, not unexpectedly, and perhaps because I love music so much. And God has permitted me several times in this life to hear this awesome music, fully more melodic and more beautiful than anyone could write while here on earth. Just suddenly playing and filling my soul with joy.

"This angel took me to a place like a coastal community, where I flew above it without wings or plane and it was colorful, alive and so beautiful."[196]

Arelene describes:

"The grass was such a lovely shade of green and the stems of flowers grew up out of the grass. I did not recognize any of the flowers but they were exceptionally beautiful, colorful, and delicate. They were so beautiful that when I returned to earth I set out on a quest to learn as much about flowers as I could, and searched in every botany book I could find. But the flowers I saw were not of this world. Their petals are very sheer, but brilliant in their colors. They seem to have the loveliest parts of many different flowers I have seen on earth combined. There are no words to describe the beauty of the flowers I saw."[197]

---

196   Diane, https://www.nderf.org/Experiences/1diane.c.nde.html

197   Harold A. Widdison, Trailing Clouds of Glory, (Cedar Fort, Inc., Springville, Utah) December 6, 2011, 28

Sometimes when a person is next to their body (which is dead before them), they interact with their surroundings on a level not possible in the body. Such interactions can be potent and deeply meaningful. Jennifer shares this experience:

> "I had a tree outside my window in PCU, and I communicated with it the whole time I was in PCU. I knew it by name, for I had touched and been one with its soul during an NDE. I can still feel it along with the sister wind that caressed its leaves and branches. Seeing with the heart, through the heart, in and of the heart. Our hearts are where the soul originates, and all our sense and essence and flowing and being. A week later, on December 12, I was released from the hospital with a clear bill of health. It really was a miracle."[198]

In the Spirit world, it appears that communication with animals is also easy. One experiencer shares:

> "During the wait in the ER at some point I slipped away. It started with a darkened area (which was not a void) that was kind of a roadway with different colored streaks and sparks. I had the sensation like I was riding one of those airport level moving things. Then the next thing I knew I was in a kind of desert-like place and I could see a stream of people going toward a building. At that point I knew what had happened and went to the building. It kind of looked like a cross between an old 19th century church and a barn. There were people there (none of whom I knew) and some small animals. No one

---

198   Jennifer J. http://www.nderf.org/Experiences/1jennifer_j_ndes.html

would talk to me because they were occupied with whatever they were doing. I finally found a badger who would talk to me. I was there for a very long time but he told me that I would eventually go to where I needed to go." [199]

Another writes:

"During my surgery, I became aware of myself, walking in a grassy clearing that was surrounded by trees. At the time, I thought that I was seeing a light-grey sky in the distance. But now, I believe it was a dim light. As I continued looking at it, the light became a pure white. I wanted to go there, to where the white light was, and so I kept walking toward it. As I walked, I noticed how lush and green the grass and the forest were. I was at peace and I felt content.

"Then, I heard dogs barking and I could understand what they were saying! They were playing, and planning to go somewhere to continue their game. I turned a corner and there was the group of dogs! I became very joyful when I saw that two of my deceased dogs were part of the group! I called out the name of one of my dogs, wanting to hold and pet him. The other dogs took off, racing towards the light. My dog turned, looked right at me and barked. And again, I could understand him. In a very scolding tone he said, 'You're not supposed to be here!' He took off and joined the other dogs, and soon they were all engulfed by the light. I could see figures there, but I could not move.

---

199   https://iands.org/ndes/nde-stories/iands-nde-accounts/422-learning-with-being.html

"It was then that I woke up." [200]

Roy Mills shared,

"This exquisitely beautiful scene appeared to stretch before me forever. Everything had spirit about it. I could sense not only life in the grass and flowers, but they also radiated a knowing—a communication that conveyed love, peace, and joy all blended together. And the colors! Even the colors radiated life, knowledge, friendliness, and good will. They were beautiful beyond earth description —brilliant, yet at the same time soft, gentle, twinkling; luxurious pastels that seemed to send their beauty right into my soul." [201]

In her book, *A Greater Tomorrow: My Journey Beyond the Veil*, Julie Rowe tells her near-death experience, and describes walking with her guide, John, through a beautiful field.

"We came upon the most incredibly beautiful lake. It was crystal clear and of a silvery blue color that sparkled in the bright sunlight. We stood together on the shore, and John encouraged me to gaze into the water.

"In the lake I could see all manner of fish swimming around. There were varieties I have never before seen on this earth. There were varieties of every kind in several different sizes, shapes, and species. The lake was so clear but so so deep that it went beyond my vision and I could not see the bottom—as if it went on and on forever.

200   https://www.nderf.org/Experiences/tdon_possible_nde.html

201   Harold A. Widdison, Trailing Clouds of Glory, (Cedar Fort, Inc., Springville, Utah) December 6, 2011, 27

"The water was seemingly alive, and the fish and other organisms that lived in this lake were full of energy and intelligence. I felt as if they were communicating with me. I could sense that they too felt the love and peace that I felt.

"It quickly became apparent to me that every living thing, the grass, the flowers, the trees, the animals—all that I saw—were able to communicate with me and with each other telepathically. There was a feeling of true joy and completion emanating from the water and from the intelligences all around me. It was exquisite. It was made known to me that this was Living Water."[202]

We've already heard of many experiencers describing animals and plants as *alive*. As a gardener and hobby farmer, I can attest that both animals and plants here on earth are *alive*. But obviously experiencers are trying to express something beyond what is known or obvious in this life. And perhaps Bonny Burrows comes a little closer in her description of these things when she describes them as being *sentient*.

"The grass was sentient. The flowers were sentient. The water was sentient...

"The flowers were sentient. They were welcoming me. The streams were welcoming me. The rocks were welcoming me.

"The colors were incredible! And the colors were

---

202   Julie Rowe, *A Greater Tomorrow*, Spring Creek Book Company, Provo, Utah, 2014, pg. 11-12

sentient. It wasn't like having a red rose—it was like, there was a rose, and the color gave itself to the rose because the colors loved the rose so much that it gave itself to the rose. Multiply that by a billion with every flower and every blade of grass and everything that's there. It was just incredible! It's a constantly increasing feeling of love!"[203]

Anthony also described the sky, mountains, and ground as being alive:

"Everything in this other world was made of what I can only describe as liquid light. Everything was alive, the ground, the mountains even the sky. The voice was still with me and during this experience never left me. It told me that where I was the 'real' world and that I had a job to do whilst I was there." [204]

Sara Menet explains what she learned in her experience about animals:

"I learned a lot about animals. I learned that when you have stewardship over a pet in this life, that pet will be with you in the world to come. They will find you there. You don't have to be looking for your pets or your loved ones. There's like, what I call a spiritual radar where they know you're there, and they find you. And that was a great comfort to me because I'd had so many critters growing up: frogs and turtles and cats, and everything you could think of—even a baby duck. So I was happy to

---

203   Bonni Burrows, IANDS Utah meeting audio recording, April 2013, https://iandsutah.org/archive-2013/

204   Anthony N, https://www.nderf.org/Experiences/1anthony_n_nde.html

learn that." [205]

When Jacqueline died, she went into the light, and as she did, she met someone she hadn't seen in a long time:

> "Upon experiencing the tremendous light, which to our normal eyes would seem almost blinding, I first saw our dog, Mr. Miyagi, who had passed six months earlier. He had died of old age, but upon that meeting, he was like a lion, in his prime, and sitting in a meadow. He radiated love for me and for our time that had been spent together on this earth. We didn't communicate through words; it is just a knowing." [206]

Bryce Bond had a fatal allergic reaction to pine nuts, and after passing through a tunnel into a bright light, shares,

> "I hear a bark, and racing toward me is a dog I once had, a black poodle named Pepe. When I see him, I feel an emotional floodgate open. Tears fill my eyes. He jumps into my arms, licking my face. As I hold him, he is real, more real than I had ever experienced him. I can smell him, feel him, hear his breathing, and sense his great joy at being with me again.

> "I put my dog on the ground, and step forward to embrace my stepfather, when a very strong voice is heard in my consciousness. Not yet, it says. I scream out, Why? Then this inner voice says, What have you learned, and whom have you helped? I am dumb-founded. The voice

205   Sarah Menet, Iands Utah Meeting, September 2017, https://iandsutah.files.wordpress.com/2013/02/iands-11-09-sept-2011-sara-menet.mp3
206   Jacqueline HW, https://www.nderf.org/Experiences/1jacqueline_hw_nde.html

seems to be from without as well as within. Everything stops for a moment. I have to think of what was asked of me. I cannot answer what I have learned, but I can answer whom I have helped.

"I feel the presence of my dog around me as I ponder those two questions. Then I hear barking, and other dogs appear, dogs I once had. As I stand there for what seems to be an eternity. I want to embrace and be absorbed and merge. I want to stay. The sensation of not wanting to come back is overwhelming." [207]

Learning these things about both animals and plants in the spirit world, I am inclined to better reverence every type of life form around me here. Perhaps it doesn't suggest that we should be vegetarians (though I can't help see that as an honorable gesture of love), since the spirit of plants are also sentient and loving in their own sphere of life, but it does suggest that we may want to treat all living things with respect and dignity.

And just think how much richer life would be if we were to simply treat the world around us with greater love, respect, and dignity. Clearly, our pets will be with us in the spirit world, as will all the beautiful and wild creatures that surround us—along with many we don't have here.

We can argue to the ends of the world about whether mortal plants and animals have the same level of feelings and experience as we do, but when it comes to the

---

207   From Atwater, P. M. H. *Beyond the Light: What Isn't Being Said About Near Death Experience: from Visions of Heaven to Glimpses of Hell*, (Kill Devil Hills, NC: Transpersonal Publishing, 2009), pp. 13-14

spiritual side of any life form, clearly, there is more going on there than instincts and evolution.

Symbolism and Metaphor

There is a point worth making here regarding the kinds of things people see in near-death experiences, and that has to do with the use of symbolism and metaphor in the spirit world. While some experiencers see visions that are represented by something intended as a metaphor, others see actual events, people, and places intended to teach a lesson.

As an example of this, Erika Mckenzie, while in the presence of God, was told to put on a pair of glasses before her. She looked, and discovered a pair of glasses the size of a bus in front of her. Confused, and unsure how she was supposed to proceed, she managed to lift the glasses and put them to her face. The glasses resized as she drew them to her eyes. Once she was wearing them, she could see the events, memories, and prophesies around her from God's perspective.[208]

One is then left to ask from that, "Does God wear glasses?"

I think it's fair to say that He probably doesn't. What was given to Erica seems to have been a metaphor. Does that mean she didn't put on glasses? No. It means that the glasses she put on were there to teach her something. Would it be fair to suggest that the glasses weren't there before Erica needed the lesson? I don't know, but I'm not sure it matters. The lesson was taught *beautifully*.

Many, when they first leave this life, find themselves on a path, a bridge, a train-station, or some other landscape with a clear sense of travel or the crossing of a barrier. Does the metaphor of a path, for example, which is clearly there to lead the person into the afterlife, negate the possibility of the actual spiritual existence of that path, with all it's surrounding landscape? Does the fact of it being a metaphor mean it can't be also real?

I'm under the impression that in the spirit world, the actual "factual" existence of a thing, and the mere "symbolic" or "metaphorical" imagery of a thing, are not mutually exclusive things. Something can be both a metaphor, and a real thing. We're not foreign to that idea.

---

208   Erica Mckenzie, NDE Talk 2016, https://www.youtube.com/watch?v=K6udn-HTleM

A shepherd *really does* lead, guide, and protect their sheep. But so does God *really* lead, guide, and protect His children. Using sheep as a metaphor doesn't mean that the idea of sheep and a shepherd aren't real—that they are only symbols, lacking substance.

We get that. But sometimes we stumble over that concept when it comes to things regarding the spirit world. This may be because experiencers will sometimes say things like, "I think I was shown this in order to make me more comfortable, because I was so used to seeing things like this on the earth plain."

Sometimes when people speak of being on a beautiful landscape, and then later going on to stand in the glorious presence of God, they say that they think they were first shown the landscape so they wouldn't feel so out of place by going straight into the presence of God. If someone reads this experience without further context, they may assume that in the spirit world, there are not actually *any* landscapes at all—that these are just illusions shown to us to make us more comfortable during our transition into the spirit world.

And while it makes sense to understand it this way, or seem like a logical conclusion from the wording given by the experiencer, it appears that such a conclusion offers a severely limited view of the spirit world.

From everything I've read, heard, or learned from

individuals who have visited the other side, the spirit world is vastly dynamic, with so many levels and dimensions and with such diversity that I consider it much more likely that *every* place, and *every* being a person comes across in the spirit world is absolutely real. That incredible diversity simply lends itself well to the use of metaphor and symbolism.

A spirit may find herself in the midst of a pasture with sheep, and the shepherd is God. Just because God probably doesn't spend the majority of His time raising sheep doesn't mean the sheep she saw weren't real, or that God isn't the ultimate shepherd, or that the landscape she encountered wasn't a real, actual location in the spirit world.

I am of the opinion that while we on earth tend to place a thick division between what is *real* and what is *metaphor*, in the spirit world, the two are one and the same. Or, put another way, the need of metaphor is a beautiful way to introduce a person to the places, elements, and experiences available in the spirit world.

Another way of looking at this is to bring us back to this world again. I could invent a story to illustrate a point. Let's say my life is a mess, and I'm trying to find my way through. I could say that my life is like the aftermath of a forest fire—trees burned down and the grass blackened. Then from those ashes, new growth appears, providing a new opportunity for new life, new potential, and new experiences.

That would be an example of taking a "not real" thing and using it for a metaphor.

Now say I look out my window, and see the path up to my house, and I say to myself, "That path is a great metaphor for how I should spend more time at home— that I should follow that path that leads me to what matters most to me."

In the first example, I'm taking a real idea and using a made-up situation to illustrate it. In the second example, I'm taking a real-life situation to come to the understanding of an idea I may not have otherwise had.

My suggestion is that while on earth, these may be two separate things, in the spirit world, they may show themselves identically. Perhaps "inventing" a situation may simply bring the individual to an actual place where that situation is occurring. Remember, for spirits in the spirit world, time and location are non-issues.

The whole point I'm trying to make here is that just because someone sees something in their near-death experience that they consider to be a metaphor, or perhaps a situation "manipulated" for that individual for their situation, doesn't mean the place or scenario can't be literally and absolutely real.

Conclusion

I feel funny calling this end part a "conclusion," since the only way I've been able to bend my mind enough to understand what little I have about the spirit world is by not allowing myself to draw any final conclusions from the things I read or hear. But I don't know a better word for, "The last part of the book where I talk about some of my thoughts regarding everything in this book," so I'll just go with *Conclusion*.

I've long believed in the afterlife, but my knowledge of it's details was limited. In fact, having studied what I have, I now sense that the little tip of the iceberg I now see is attached to a much bigger iceberg than I could have ever previously imagined. Clearly there are open realms of darkness, light, water, air, clouds, stars, landscapes, mountains, cities, homes, people, children, family, food, fun, love, joy, knowledge, glory, and an Eternal Father that loves us more than we can possibly imagine—and each of these are more accessible to the common spirit than I ever thought possible previously.

Sometimes people will ask me questions regarding the spirit world, or life after death, which are structured something like this, "So, in the spirit world, does X happen, or does Y happen?"

And in nearly every case, the answer seems to begin with either "Both, and…" or "Oh, there's so much more to it than that!"

From all I've read, heard, studied, pondered, and researched, I'm led to believe that the spirit world is so vastly diverse and eclectic that even the earth, with all it's complexity and uniquely diverse biomes, structures, and natural laws, scarcely even makes a good metaphor for the incredible breadth and depth of all that can be found in the spirit world.

In fact, calling it the *spirit world* even seems to downplay it's vastness. Even if we were to call it the *spirit universe*, it leads one to assume that there is only one, and that it's a single parallel to our physical universe. I guess you could refer to it/them as *spirit multiverses*, but at that point you're getting really out there, and people won't have any idea what you're talking about.

I guess the problem we run into is that we're trying to take something infinite and eternal, and measure it with physical barriers and dimensions, which both limits our understanding of it and fails to quantify it anyway. But what else can we do? We live in a start/stop, beginning/end, birth/death world. It just can't be measured with the minds and tools we have here.

Does that mean we shouldn't try? I don't think so. I think we just need to do the best we can, adapt and evolve our tools and minds to better understand as we go along. When language fails us, we should (and yes, this takes time, effort, and patience) adapt our language. When comparisons to what we know fails us, we should expand what we know, and learn to visualize and conceptualize in new and original ways. When we can find no metaphor for what we experience, we may have to study more fields of knowledge to wrap our minds around new ideas and concepts that will one day provide a framework to begin to explain by apperception what we experienced.

But with all that, the ultimate message of both the near-death experience, the life-review, and the spirit world itself seems to be one of love. God is love, we are love, our lives are about love, the spirit world is filled with love, and the eternal nature of our existence is love. But are we talking about love for God? Love of self? Love of others? God's love for us? God's love for others? Yes, yes, yes, yes, and yes! All of the above! The ultimate message seems to be that showing love expands the server, the served, God, and the entirety of the universe.

So how then, exactly, do we do that? How do we really, truly, show love? Well... that might take another book.

Appendix

Spirit World Evidence

I think we would all love it if there was verifiable scientific proof of an afterlife. This doesn't seem to be the case. However what we do have mountains of strong anecdotal evidence of it.

I think one of the most interesting ways to consider the evidence of an afterlife is to consider the explanations necessary in order to *disprove* the existence of an afterlife.

While many, seeking to disprove the validity of near-death experiences, may show a plethora of physical conditions that can surround the death of an individual to seemingly account for miraculous sensations, visions, and light, all of which are common to near-death experiences, science is hard-pressed to give explanations for the evidences provided in individual experiences. From what I can figure, other than the potential for an actual afterlife, there are only a few possibilities that could account for the many, *many* evidences that come out of near-death experiences.

First, one *could* conclude that humans actually have remarkable empathic, telepathic, and psychic abilities that are only occasionally activated by the few who have near-death experiences. Hence they would be able to describe the incidents taking place around their body after their death but prior to their return, as well as those of many of their friends, family, and strangers who may not have even been anywhere near the location of the experiencer's body.

Second (or in addition, since the second is required in many cases to account for the first), the human brain, at the moment of its potential demise, speeds up comprehension to the point where time virtually stands still, allowing practically infinite time to ponder, consider, and calculate the events taking place around the experiencer. During this "infinite" time, the experiencer would have the time to rethink his/her entire life philosophy, change his/her heart as profoundly as Ebenezer Scrooge, and come up with dozens of scientific theories and spiritual ideas concerning life, the universe, and... yes, everything. In fact, the progress of thinking would have to be so profound as to allow a person to manipulate their own dying brain as to create what appear to be hyper-realistic places, people, landscapes, and situations. This could perhaps allow for the deluge of insights and experiences gained by those who have NDEs.

Third, that there is extraterrestrial technology or creatures of supernatural power in play during the moments approaching the death of a person. Basically, that it's aliens from space causing the NDE.

Fourth, that there is something of a consciousness that is separate from the body that is capable, when the body is under exceptional stress or at the point of death, to leave the body and wander—basically, that there is a spirit in the dying individual that separates just prior to death, and, as in the second possibility (timelessness), can experience virtual unlimited time passing in the moments just prior to death, when said soul will actually cease to exist.

Beyond these, I can't find a way to account for the near-death experience. Whatever rush of brain activity, sensory illusions, or hallucinogenic properties can take place at the final moments of human life, one of the above explanations must still be in place to account for what people are experiencing in near-death experiences.

Personally, I find all of the above possibilities at least as difficult (if not more so) to accept as the explanation that there is actually an afterlife, and our consciousness continues after our bodies die.

And we should take into serious consideration how common these experiences are, and the diversity of the kinds of people who have them. David San Falippo, PHD, of National-Louis University said,

"According to a 1991 Gallup Poll estimate, 13 million Americans, 5% of the population, have reported that they have had a near-death experience. Research has demonstrated that near-death experiences are no more likely to affect the devoutly religious than the agnostic or atheist.

"Near-death experiences can be experienced by anyone. According to Talbot (1991), near-death experiences appear to have no relationship to 'a person's age, sex, marital status, race, religion and/or spiritual beliefs, social class, educational level, income, frequency of church attendance, size of home community, or area of residence.' (p. 240)." [209]

Whether you want to say that near-death experiences are what experiencers claim them to be, or want to find some other explanation, it would prove ridiculous to try to say that *all* these people are lying, exaggerating, or following some kind of agenda.

True, from a strictly scientific point-of-view, we can't call near-death experiences proof of an afterlife. But I do see them as a clear indication that the idea of an afterlife is

---

209   Filippo, David San, *An Overview of the Near-Death Experience Phenomenon*, National-Louis University, https://digitalcommons.nl.edu/cgi/viewcontent.cgi?article=1026&context=faculty_publications, pp. 5-6

the best explanation we have so far to account for the experiences of the over seven hundred daily reports from United States citizens having a near-death experience.[210] And there are likely far more outside the United States, since the US population only accounts for 4.4% of the world's entire population. After all, in the United States, we only have the resources to track and record the experiences of those in our own country. We do, however, have accounts from many experiences outside our country. What we lack in statistical regularity is far made up for in the sheer numbers of anecdotal accounts gathered from those outside the United States.

So, while providing a comprehensive list of near-death experiences that show evidence of an afterlife is neither practical nor my intent, I will share a couple, in order to provide a taste of the kinds of evidences often provided by such experiences.

Brian was in a car accident, and had just returned from a near-death experience. While riding in an ambulance,

> "I kept lapsing into and out of consciousness. Many times, I could hear people talking but couldn't seem to react. At least three times that I recall, people felt my neck and said, 'This one's gone'.

---

210   This number of 774 Americans having near-death experiences per day comes from a 1993 Gallup poll published in the book, *Adventures in Immortality*, by George Gallup Jr. and William Proctor, and recorded on the Near-Death Experience Research Foundation website.
https://www.nderf.org/NDERF/Research/number_nde_usa.htm

"When I finally raised my head and made a statement to a state trooper who was bent over at the driver's door of my car copying my V.I.N. number off my dash, he leapt back and yelled, 'Hey, this one's alive, get over here!'

"I remember an emergency medical technician in my car and vibration from extraction equipment. I remember a television camera and stating, 'Get that @#$%$%$ camera out of my face'.

"I remember being in an ambulance and a woman emergency medical technician sitting on a bench next to me. I remember asking her, 'Where exactly are we?'

"She said, 'You're in an ambulance'.

"I said, 'No, where exactly on the ROAD are we, how far from the city?'

"She said, 'I'm afraid I have no way of knowing, there's only a little window.'

"I remember saying, 'That's all right; I'll go out and look.' I recall passing through the side of the ambulance and seeing a rock quarry that I always used as a landmark and noting that we were almost to it. I went back through the side of the ambulance and told her, 'We're almost to the rock quarry, good, we're getting close.'

"The emergency medical technician got up, went to a small window on the side of the ambulance, and said, 'Oh, I see it, yes, but how...' She didn't finish that sentence, nor did she say anything else other than, 'You just lay quiet, we're almost there,' when she sat back down." [211]

While there may be other explanations of how Brian could have known that they were passing the query, the most logical explanation is that his consciousness did indeed leave his body and "go and check." Since the EMT was there, and saw that he had no way of knowing their location, or how long he'd been in the ambulance (remember, he'd been fading in and out of consciousness), this could be considered anecdotal evidence.

Might he have made up the whole things and been guessing? Sure, it's possible. But people tend not to be wrong in these situations, so the evidence does suggest that he left his body and returned. This level of anecdotal evidence is extremely common.

Paul had a beautiful experience that not only provides evidence of an afterlife, but demonstrates the power of love on both sides of the veil.

"In 1970, I was hopelessly caught up in the tragedy and horror of the Vietnam war. My wife, Sue, was just two months pregnant when I received the dreaded induction notice.

"On April 30, 1970, President Richard Nixon announced that U.S. Troops had begun a ground offensive against the Communist strongholds in Cambodia. I was shipped out and participated along with over forty thousand troops with this maneuver in the

---

Army's Tenth Combat Division. On October first, my
platoon was moving west when we were hit hard by a
sniper attack. I was trying to retreat to safety when I
heard a blood-chilling scream. I turned in time to see my
buddy Pete go down in a hail of bullets from enemy fire.
Every instinct told me to save myself and keep on
running . I only had to hear his desperate cries to realize
that I could not abandon a man who had gone out of his
way to show a green recruit the ropes and given me hours
of badly needed escape from our mutual war trauma and
suffering by really showing an interest in my life and my
hopes to rejoin my wife and new baby when the
nightmare of war was finally over. I shared his dream of
finding the right lady some day and starting a family of
his own. He dreamed of becoming a teacher with the help
of the G.I. bill for education. I turned around and went
back towards where he lay moaning, screaming for a
medic the entire time.

"I had crossed the fifty feet between us in what
seemed like seconds when I was shot down by machine
gun fire. Pain ripped through my legs and I fell forward.
The next thing I knew I was viewing the scene from
about sixteen feet above my body. I saw that my body had
been hit several times in the right leg and once in the left.
I was convinced that I was going to bleed to death and felt
tremendous sorrow that I'd never see my wife and our
unborn baby. My sadness was joined by a growing
confusion and curiosity. So, this is death? I thought. No
pain! No fear! How weird, I don't feel any different. I still
can think. I stared at my body and wondered what was

coming next.

"My buddy, Pete was lying next to my body. I was shocked to see a mist leave from his head, which instantly turned into an exact duplicate of his body. I noticed that his spirit or new body was whole and glowed a bit. (His physical body below was missing his hand and part of his forearm due to being hit by the same sniper.) Pete looked dazed and I called to him. He immediately flew to join me and we discussed what was going to happen from that point. We noticed that a young black medic had discovered our bodies. First he checked Pete and then me. He began working on my body and Pete commented that he guessed that meant he was dead, but that I probably still had a chance.

"He reached out and shook my hand and said, "I want to thank you for being a good friend and for trying to save my life. I don't know why, but I just get this sense that I am not staying here. I am going someplace I've been before. It feels like home. I know this sounds crazy, but I think it's not your time to go yet. I think I'll try to say goodbye to my mom now, but you go on and have a groovy life and if your kid is a boy name him after me. OK?" I said, "You got it Pete!" I reached over to give him a pat on the back, but he vanished in a blink of light. I watched several soldiers below help carry me away from the scene while the medic continued to work on me. I was filled with a yearning to be with my young wife and my unborn child. Suddenly, I was slammed back into my body, as if I fell from forty feet above.

"Due to my injuries, I was shipped home one month later. I had no opportunity to attend my pal's funeral, but I did research his family and called his Mom. His mother, Thelma, answered and I offered my heartfelt condolences to her and she said her son had come to see her on the night he was killed. She had a visit in a dream where he had stayed long enough to tell her he had passed over to the other side, but not to grieve for him as he was happy and he had a job to do. He held out his arms and a light appeared to come to him. A beautiful, radiant child formed next to him. He was a five or six year-old boy with auburn curls and hazel eyes. He had a sprinkling of freckles across his nose and cheeks. "Who's that?" His mom asked. "Why, this is little Pete. He wants to know about his Daddy, what his earthly life will be like and what he can expect. I'm showing him the ropes. Little Pete and I will be together for a long time, HE CAN COUNT ON IT!!" He picked up the child and hugged him.

"The image faded quickly. Pete's mom wanted to know all about her son, where he was at, but had no chance. The image of the adorable child stuck in her mind. Since Pete had been a bachelor, was this child an illegitimate child of his? Who is the mother? Where could she go to see her grandson? Was this child even born yet? What did Pete mean about teaching this child about "his earthly life"? Little Pete obviously was named after his dad. She even felt there was a family resemblance. How would she ever know? Where could she go for help?

"All those questions seemed to haunt her every waking moment and increased even more after she was told that her son Pete had indeed been killed in action on the same day as the dream. She was sad and hurt by her only son's death, but felt he had given her proof that he was fine and was alive on a different plane. The child he had called "little Pete" was still a mystery she knew she had to solve.

"I told her about my wife's pregnancy and the promise I made to Pete about naming a son after him. I suggested this might have been the child she was shown in the dream on October 1, 1971. I promised to stay in touch and send photos of my child when he or she was born in 4 to 5 weeks.

"My son Peter was born on October 31, 1971. He was practically bald, but had striking hazel eyes. On his second birthday, I mailed photos to Pete's mom in Colorado, and she called to say thanks. The photos resembled the little boy in her dream especially the mop of auburn curls. On Peter's sixth birthday, she flew in to meet our family and burst into tears when she saw him. There was no doubt at all. This was the same boy she saw her son Pete with that awful night he died. We adopted her as "Granny Thelma" right on the spot. We stayed in touch through the years by phone and letters. She treasured each detail and photo of Peter.

"She passed on recently; however Peter, his wife Karen, and their two sons visited her in the hospital the week before. She knew she'd soon be joining Pete and his

Dad who had died in world war two. She was anxious to
be reunited and thanked 'little Pete' (now 27) for being
the grandson she had wanted since her first vision of him.
Peter told her he had always suspected that Pete was
watching over him, especially when he was in the Desert
Storm conflict.

"The experience was vivid and real and gave me hope
that when we die, we really live on and can see all our
own departed relatives."[212]

Explanations for Reincarnation

If you read through hundreds of near-death experience
accounts, you may discover a precedent for the concept of
reincarnation. Some return from an NDE believing firmly
that they have lived many mortal lives. Others return
believing the opposite: that we only get one chance at this,
so we need to make it count.

One of the big challenges that people have with the
study of near-death experiences is the prevalence of the
idea of reincarnation. And while the majority of
experiences don't suggest the possibility of reincarnation,
some do—and this scares some people away, which is
unfortunate. It is for the sake of those who may be
troubled by the idea of reincarnation that I share these
alternative views on the subject. I should state up front
that these are not evidences against reincarnation, let

---

212   Paul H, http://www.nderf.org/Experiences/1paul_nde.html

alone proof that it's not real. Rather, these are alternative explanations that could account for the occurrence of what appears to be reincarnation in the near-death experiences where it comes up.

And while I must acknowledge that there is enough evidence for the idea of the possibility of reincarnation, I think it worthwhile to offer several ideas that suggest that there may be something else going on in the cases where it seems apparent.

First off, let me talk about what reincarnation is, as it relates to NDEs. Reincarnation is the idea that we, as spirits, may come to earth multiple times to experience multiple mortal lives—of course, with the idea of learning, growing, and developing as needed for our spiritual progress.

Generally it is understood that spirits reincarnate into human forms, though some suggest that other life forms are possible to reincarnate to as well. It is also generally understood that gender is not a factor in this process—meaning that a man can die, and later return as a baby girl, etc. There are many sub-ideas branching from this basic premise, but that's the basic concept of reincarnation.

What is it that people are experiencing that suggests to them that reincarnation is taking place? There are a few things. First, a person may see more than one life review—

their own, and then someone else's, sometimes from the past, sometimes from the present day. Sometimes they will even see many life-reviews. They often conclude from this that the reviews that were not from their present life were previous or simultaneous lives.

Some get the idea of reincarnation from the spirits they interact with on the other side. These spirits may suggest that the experiences they had in this life were a means of sorting out or balancing experiences from previous lives. Often the concept of karma comes up here, that unfinished or incomplete lessons need to be completed or learned in a next life.

Memories from other lives, sometimes many lives, will fill the mind of the experiencer, suggesting that they have been to earth many times before this life they are now dying from.

Another thing that points people to belief in reincarnation is the past-life regression (PLR). A PLR means having conscious memories from a life that is not part of the one you are now living. This is most often accomplished by a trained hypnotist working with the individual in a hypnotic state to help them remember memories first from a young age, then as a baby, and then before. The idea is to push the memory back so far that it pushes into lives previous to this one. When successful, the individual usually experiences at least one powerful memory from another lifetime. And these memories are as vivid (or more so) as if the person were experiencing the event of the memory in real-time—much like a life review. Sometimes in this effort, the person will experience many such memories—usually strong, emotionally charged memories. And while hypnosis is the most common method of having a PLR, meditation has also sometimes been used to ignite such an experience. From my research, it appears that many who have such experiences are not inventing or making up the experience. They are absolutely experiencing something, and the effect can be profound.

The obvious explanation for PLRs is reincarnation.

So that's the basic idea. As I mentioned, there are many variations on the experiences that suggest reincarnation, but in my research, these are the most common evidences of reincarnation.

So if we are to consider the possibility that reincarnation is *not* what is taking place, how else might we account for what people are experiencing?

Reincarnation Explanation 1: Experiencing Another's Life Review

Some people, while in the void, passing through the tunnel, or in the light, find themselves in the presence of other people whom they may or may not see, but with whom they seem to be able to converse if they choose.

Some people experience their life review in the presence of others, and they sense that everyone around can see/hear what they are seeing and hearing.

It seems possible that while in the presence of others who are experiencing their own life reviews, the dying individual may also experience the other people's life reviews. If this is so, I'm sure it would be easy to confuse the life-reviews of others with one's own, suggesting to the dying person that it is a previous life of his/her own. In the presence of many such individuals, it may be possible to experience many life reviews. And since time is not the same factor it is here, it may also not be unreasonable to think that someone may be in the same tunnel who lived on earth in the middle ages, or some other distant past. Whether the spirit from the middle ages lingered on earth until now, or time just breaks down that much, there's no reason to assume that everyone in the tunnel with you must have died at the same time.

Some people, after first leaving their body, find that they can not only hear the thoughts and feelings of those around them, but they can see the context of their entire life—memories, etc. Some have even experienced something akin to the life reviews of other people on earth, including random strangers.

Rich Kelley gave an account of his near-death experience, where he found himself leaving the earth, being in space, floating over the earth, and looking down at it. After describing a life review, he says,

> "And what was so strange about looking at the earth like that was that at that moment, you could have asked me any given moment in my life (because I'd just relived it), but you could have asked me any given moment in any person's life on that planet, and I could have told you.

> "All that information was right there. It was available. And not just any person living there now; any person that had ever lived there or ever would live there. All of that information is all available, it's right there.

> "And what kept going through my mind at this point was: *Oh, of course!*

> "I was, if you will, remembering what I had forgotten very intentionally in order to be on this planet; which is what we all do." [213]

Another describes seeing into the souls of everyone on the planet, and feeling connected to them.

> "I was taught a lot of things, and was able to, for want of a better phrase, 'see into people's souls' and understood in an instant all the ramifications of all our actions on each other, that anger is borne of pain or fear, and many other teachings about what I now think of as the human condition. Then I saw everyone on the planet interconnected on these lines, and a feeling of such overwhelming love and empathy went through me I felt

213   Rich Kelley, *Rich Kelley near death experience*, from Karen Kelley's Youtube channel, https://www.youtube.com/watch?time_continue=337&v=v2NLEYHjG1g

like my heart was going to explode." [214]

If this is an ability shared by all, no wonder some people might confuse others' lives for his/her own past lives.

Reincarnation Explanation 2: Merging

Earlier in the book we discussed merging: it's the idea that a spirit can "merge" with another spirit and share feelings, thoughts, history, memories, experiences, etc. The most common merging that seems to take place is merging with the light, where a person enters into the light of God and finds themselves completely engulfed in everything—the universe, God, and all. In this state, there is a reduction in the sense of self, and the person feels part of everything.

When two individual spirits merge, a similar thing happens, but instead of becoming one with everything, the person becomes one with that person—their history, memories, emotions, thoughts, etc. It's a very intimate and deeply empowering experience for those who participate in it. During a merge, life reviews are often shared, where the person who has just died may see the entire life of the spirit with which they are merging. This shared life review can be selective, or it can be complete. Either way, the memories are so thorough, with the full-spectrum view of the results of every act ever done, that it would be easy for

---

214 Anthony N, https://www.nderf.org/Experiences/1anthony.n.nde.html

a person, after merging with another spirit, to confuse the life and memories of the other spirit with their own.

One possible alternative explanation for the idea of reincarnation is that the departing individual either revisits the memories of a spirit they once merged with, or that they merge with a spirit during their NDE and forget (or don't fully draw the connection with) the context that led to the foreign memories.

Reincarnation Explanation 3: Pre-mortal Preparation Merging

I don't know if merging is unique to post-mortal spirits, but I've not heard this to be the case. If merging with other spirits was common in our pre-mortal life, we may come to this earth with a plethora of shared (merged) memories that were instrumental in our preparatory instruction. I would imagine experiencing the memories of someone else who went through the same kind of lessons I would need to learn would be beneficial. If that were the case, I can imagine running through many memories of many people who experienced the kinds of things I would one day experience in order to prepare me to learn the lessons I needed to learn.

These memories, like movies that we see on earth and relate deeply to, may come to mind at moments when the applicable lessons come up.

If this is so (and again, this is all conjecture) it could explain those who remember a previous life where they faced the same challenge, or where they felt like they were working on the same "karma" they are working on in this life. They may even remember many lives, facing up against the same emotional/psychological predicaments, and may understandably conclude that they have faced this same problem through many lifetimes. But in reality, they are remembering the lives they reviewed prior to coming to earth in order to prepare them for their own life on earth

Reincarnation Explanation 4: Oneness with All

As mentioned previously, many people experience a deep oneness with the universe, sometimes to the extent that they feel they can see, hear, understand, and even experience the lives of anyone throughout history. This oneness can be so compete that some people, upon returning, have a difficult time time separating their own identities with those with whom they came in contact during their NDE. They'll talk about a friend or family member they were with, but may say things like, "But it may have just been an alternate form of my own self—a higher version of myself."

Whether conversing with one's own self is possible or not, I can't say (I haven't come across enough accounts of this even to make a fair conjecture), but what does seem consistent is that the oneness a person feels with other people in the spirit world is so powerful and complete that it makes sense to me that to experience the memories of another person probably feels like experiencing a previous "incarnation" of ones' own life.

In fact, if we are all truly "One;" if we are all part of some great perfect eternal "Self", and the separation between us is as much an illusion as mortality itself, then might one conjecture that *every* life lived is a past (or future) life? If you and I are so deeply connected that it might be said that we are two sides of the same coin (or one side of an infinite-sided coin), then isn't each of our lives another rendition of the same being?

If that is the case, then the little thing called agency that separates us into individual, independent beings may be the only thing making us different lives anyway. I'm not suggesting that I believe this to be the case (I'm not ready to go that far), but it does offer an alternative view of reincarnation.

Reincarnation Explanation 5: Spirit Possession

This is possibly one of the more disturbing alternative explanations for the experience of reincarnation, and it relates directly to the past-life regression. As mentioned previously, past-life regression is usually done through hypnosis at the hand of a professional or experienced hypnotist.

I don't know much about the phenomenon of spirits who remain on the earth-plane, whether they remain here as spirits who have never been alive, or they choose not to leave the earth-plane at the time of death, but it does appear that it happens. Some choose to stay on earth and NOT go to the light. Some are never born on earth, but remain on the earth-plane anyway. I don't know the reasons for their tarrying here, but it appears that many have great interest in the lives of mortal people, seeking to make connection with mortals. Likely their motives vary, but some with less-than-pure motives may even try to visit, inhabit, or even take over a mortal person. This is the best explanation I know of for "demonic possession," where a person loses control of their own faculties and have to have a spirit "cast out" of their body before they can regain full control of themselves.

This is the point where what we know and what I've already conjectured come together in a way that may be either enlightening or slightly disturbing. I don't know if merging is a form of voluntary possession—or better said, if possession is a form of involuntary merging, but it may be possible that the difference between merging and spirit possession is the same difference between sexual intimacy and rape. One is a voluntary act of spiritual intimacy, and the other is an unasked-for act of spiritual violence.

It's possible that during the hypnosis required for past-life regression, post-mortal spirits who have chosen to remain on the earth-plane merge with the person sufficient to open their mind to the memories and life of the departed spirit. If so, it may be fair to suspect that not all of these post-mortal spirits have ill intent, or choose to try to take full advantage of the individual doing the PLR. If post-mortal spirits are remaining on earth in an effort to make connection with mortal people, they may congregate around someone with the ability to perform PLR hypnosis in order to make the desired connection.

If this is the case, then the person experiencing the PLR may see and even experience vivid memories, along with the emotions, thoughts, and full-context of the spirits who have come to merge with them.

This is also one reason that people (like myself) who do believe in near-death experiences and the incredible abilities that we all have as spirits may yet withhold from such practices as past-life regressions, seances, or other meetings with psychic mediums, etc. Though the medium or hypnotist may be exceptionally gifted and accurate in his/her findings, it's sometimes the integrity of the connecting spirits that could be in question. Since spirits can take on other forms (including the forms of known loved ones), and may even have some ability to read the thoughts and/or memories of the person being "read," it's tricky to know when one might be being deceived or misled. Again, even when the intent of the visiting spirits may not be malicious, if the result is a mistaken belief in a previous life that wasn't actually the person's own, perhaps it would be wise to maintain a level of skepticism regarding the assumptions made from experiences that take place in such readings.

Reincarnation Explanation 6: The Practice Run

During her near-death experience, Diane remembered her pre-earth life, and gained insight into the struggles we might experience on earth:

> "I instantly knew that we were before we came here to earth, and understood why we come to earth. We come but once, we do not reincarnate, but might remember a test phase before our final decision on the time frame of our life. We do get to check out the role we pick before we come and we basically know how it will go. We can even decide to come during the same time frame as others we knew very well in Heaven and try to meet while here. We do pick our families, and we do pick our race, color and creed. That's part of the test. And I will explain why the test, why some are deformed, why there is good and evil as well. It was enlightened to me while there. And something almost like wait, wait, it is not yet time to reveal this information. There is logic to all of this as well.

> "I understood death was really a transitional birth. As a baby is born from the mother's womb, it actually has

died to its previous life in her womb—the life of water into the life of air. When we die to earth, we are born again, this time into the life of life from whence we originally came. It is full circle but must be done to pass the test."[215]

If I understand Diane correctly, she's saying that in our premortal life, as we prepared to come into the mortal world, we were given some choice about when and where we would come. We may have even been given a life *preview* of what our life would be if we chose to be born during different eras, having different contexts to be striving to learn the lessons we came to learn. If that preview was potent enough, it may account for some of the past-life memories people experience.

Reincarnation Explanation 7: Cellular Memory

This explanation is given by Bettie J. Eadie, who, during her near-death experience, learned about this very subject:

"As I understood this, I saw again the spirits who had not yet come to earth, and I saw some of them hovering over people in mortality. I saw one male spirit trying to get a mortal man and woman together on earth—his future parents. He was playing cupid and was having a very difficult time. The man and woman seemed to want to go in opposite directions and were unwittingly very uncooperative. This male spirit was coaching them,

215   Diane, https://www.nderf.org/Experiences/1diane_c_nde.html

speaking to them, trying to persuade them to get together. Other spirits became concerned as they saw his difficulty, and they took up the cause, several of them trying to 'corral' these two young people.

"I was told that we had bonded together in the spirit world with certain spirit brothers and sisters—those we felt especially close to. My escorts explained that we covenanted with these spirits to come to earth as family or friends. This spiritual bonding was a result of the love we developed for each other over an eternity of being together. We also chose to come to earth with certain others because of the work we would do together. Some of us wanted to unite in a cause to change certain things on earth, and we could best do it with certain circumstances brought about by selected parents or others. Some of us simply wanted to strengthen a course already set and to pave the way for those who follow. We understood the influences we would have upon each other in this life and the physical and behavioral attributes we would receive from our families. We were aware of the genetic coding of mortal bodies and the particular physical features we would have. We wanted and needed these.

"We understood that memories would be contained in the cells of our new bodies. This was an idea that was completely new to me. I learned that all thoughts and experiences in our lives are recorded in our subconscious minds. They are also recorded in our cells, so that, not only is each cell imprinted with a genetic coding, it is also imprinted with every experience we have ever had.

"Further, I understood that these memories are passed down through the genetic coding to our children. These memories then account for many of the passed on traits in families, such as addictive tendencies, fears, strengths, and so on. I also learned that we do not have repeated lives on this earth; when we seem to "remember" a past life, we are actually recalling memories contained in the cells.

"I saw that we understood all the challenges of our complicated physical makeup, and we were confident in accepting these circumstances."[216]

Reincarnation Explanation 8: Guardian Angel Memories

Kim Rives, during her near-death experience, dealt with the question of reincarnation. She says,

"What I saw was that we have a pre-existence, and then we come down here to mortality to get a body, and then we return into spirit form and eventually be resurrected with our bodies. That was my understanding. But this is my interpretation, and I think whether or not you agree with me, I'm not here to offend anyone—I'll just tell you my point of view.

"I felt that in the pre-existence, we could be angels and guardian angels, and help those who are down in mortality. For example, my son was totally into the Titanic for many years—he couldn't get enough about the

---

216   *Bettie Eadie, Embraced by the Light, (Gold Leaf Press: Carson City, Nevada, 1992).*

Titanic. I honestly believe that he probably was a guardian angel that was to help the people on the Titanic when they were dying. Before he came to earth, he was probably one of their ministering angels, and people that say they've had other lives, I feel like they're probably really literally remembering when they helped someone while in spirit form. That's my take on it."[217]

Reincarnation Explanation 9: Multiple Afterlife Philosophies

This explanation is primarily in response to a particularly rare type of experience where some kind of light-being in the spirit world *tells* the experiencer that reincarnation is a thing. In my studies, it's the least common reason for the idea of reincarnation, but certainly worth addressing. Basically, the experiencer is in the spirit world, and their guide (or some other being) explains to them that they have experienced many mortal lives, and/or will experience more later.

I can only think of one or two experiences in my studies where this has taken place, and while one *may* try to argue that true reincarnation is not what they were referring to, *or* that the "guide" was not as benevolent as the experiencer thought, I think it's only fair to assume for the sake of our discussion that the message was communicated honestly and clearly by a spirit being who

---

genuinely meant well.

So how do we explain away reincarnation if a spirit on the other side said it's really a thing?

The best way I can think to do this is to consider that when a person has a near-death experience, they tend to assume that any being they encounter (that is not malevolent, of course) will communicate words and ideas to them that are statements of pure fact. It is assumed that if a spirit is good, carries no feeling but absolute love, and the landscape or situation clearly indicates that the location of the conversation is heaven, that said spirit can only speak absolute truth.

I'm not suggesting that such a spirit would be trying to deceive, or that they would be lying to the experiencer. What I am suggesting is that the spirit may be innocently mistaken in their understanding of what is happening.

That may seem a tough idea to swallow, but consider for a moment: is every good and decent person who dies and goes to heaven going to have perfect agreement in all matters relating to everything? Obviously there won't be arguments and fighting about ideas, but is it possible that people think differently about reality? Is it possible that spirits on the other side have different goals, and thus different philosophies about how eternal life progresses?

Is it possible that even with shared love and acceptance, good and pure spirits may still have some differing ideas about the whole plan of God?

True, those who ask God will likely find answers there. True, those who find answers will form their opinions, philosophies, and understandings based on truth they receive from God, but isn't it also possible that in considering all of the answers people get on the other side, that there's always more to learn—leaving just enough room for people to have differing beliefs?

It makes sense to me that though we may see the unity, love, and cooperation on the other side as evidence that everyone believes the same, it might not be so. It could be that there are differing ideas in the spirit world concerning how growth best happens, or what we will be doing in the eons to come, or how it will all play out.

What I'm suggesting is that there may be different schools of thought in the spirit world about how things work, and with all of the incredible insights and abilities we know are possible from what we've already studied, it's no wonder some good, benevolent spirits might conclude that reincarnation is a fact. And if they believe that of themselves, why would they not teach it to those coming for a quick visit?

And though I haven't heard of a case where God himself stated in an NDE that reincarnation is real, I have heard of a case where an experiencer spoke with God (as he assumed at the time), but long after returning to his body, found a picture of his ancestor that was the spitting image of the "God" he'd seen. Thus when he thought he was talking to God, he'd actually been talking to a great grandfather. Maybe I'm grasping at straws, but if someone did hear from "God" that reincarnation is real, I'd still want to know for sure that it was actually God that said it.

Which, at the risk of going off on a tangent, raises an interesting question—one that I've wondered a lot about. There are many who experience who they think is God, but later in the experience discover that it was someone else. Usually (unlike the experience cited above) they find out before the end of the experience who they were really talking to—that it wasn't really God. But the person they mistook for God must have recognized the misconception, so why didn't they clarify at the time? Did it just not seem pertinent to what they needed to communicate? It seems to me that most people, if they were mistaken for God, would *immediately* correct the assumption. But it appears that in the spirit world, they rarely do.

But I digress...

Reincarnation Explanation 10: There's More to It Than We Think

Regardless of whether or not any or many of the previous explanations are true, I suspect this one is also true. This life is apparently exceptionally important to us as spirits, but we have and will exist for eternity. You can bet there are many things to do before and after this life. Whatever kinds of adventures we have—whatever work we do, places we visit, missions we set out on, experiments we try, tests we put ourselves through, education we seek, services we render, and things we create, all we do is part of life. Just as my elementary school years seem like a completely different lifetime than the one I have now, so I am sure our different experiences throughout eternity can be described as different lifetimes.

Christian Andreason had a near-death experience, and mentions something of the mystery of lifetimes before.

> "It was through this method that I was shown my life review. (Or rather I should say my LIVES IN REVIEW!) Without ever having to turn my head, I saw my past, my present, my future and there was even a screen that displayed a tremendous amount of scientific data, numbers and universal codes. I saw the beginning of my known existence as a Soul and saw that I had existed Spiritually long before this incarnation—where I am now a male human known as Christian Andréason! In Heaven, I undeniably saw that I had lived an innumerable amount of lives. Yet, what I saw went way beyond our comprehension of what we think reincarnation is. So, I am not exactly speaking of being born again and again on this planet alone. I saw that it is a big Universe out there and God has it all organized perfectly. Each of us is sent where we can obtain the best growth according to our

Divine purpose."[218]

If I'm understanding Christian right, he's saying that there *is something* to the idea of reincarnation, but it's not what we thought.

I think that's probably the case with everything we know about the spirit world. There is more about it than we can possibly understand here, and though we can expect *NOT* to get it all while we're here, the pursuit is so enlightening that we're doing ourselves a disservice if we reject its study outright because we don't have all the answers.

Keeping an open mind doesn't mean we accept everything that comes into it. It means we place everything we learn on a shelf to be reexamined later. As new information becomes available, we have new and old bits to work with. Like a puzzle piece that doesn't fit any of the clumps of pieces we've fit together so far, as new pieces fit in, eventually every piece finds it's way onto the puzzle. Eternity is a long time. We're infinite beings. Clearly there is more going on than we can yet comprehend, and what an exciting adventure it is to be in a situation where we *can't* fully understand what's going on. Clearly, as spirits, we wanted to come to a place where we'd have confusion, mistaken ideas, and limited access to real, clear, complete answers. Whether we saw it as a school or a grand adventure (or more likely, both), here we are.

---

218   Christian Andreason, https://www.near-death.com/experiences/notable/christian-andreason.html

Let's make it the greatest adventure of eternity. And how do we do that? From everything I read, it appears that the best way—if not the only way, is love.

Glossary

Distressing Near-Death Experience: A near-death experience that includes unpleasant, frightening, or hellish experiences.

Life Review: An experience where one sees or experiences either part, or the entirety of his/her life in a short period of time during a near-death experience.

NDE: Abbreviation of *near-death experience*.

Near-Death Experience: An experience where a person approaching death (or in an event that has a similar disembodying effect to death) has a conscious experience that extends beyond the limitations of their mortal body.

OBE: Abbreviation of *out-of-body experience*.

Out-of-Body Experience: The experience of leaving one's body (either as a spirit or disembodied consciousness) and traveling beyond it's confines.

Past-Life Regression: Having conscious memories of a life that is not part of the one you are now living.

PLR: Abbreviation of *past-life regression*.

Index

Abilities.. 217

Age...121, 122-124, 165, 176, 178, 180, 284

Agency..60, 61, 100, 197

Ancestors..82, 253, 256

Angels.. 61

Animals...174, 194, 270, 271, 277, 279-284

Answers...44, 130, 161, 212-214, 230, 231, 233, 325, 328

Art...188, 189, 193, 194, 207

Atheism.. 8, 24, 299

Attention...174, 239

Auditorium...154, 155

Book of Life.. 204

Books...151, 154, 159, 161, 189, 200, 204, 206, 209, 210, 216

Buddhism..8, 48, 75

Buildings.......................72, 127, 151, 152, 156-158, 161, 163, 164, 173, 187, 194, 204, 205, 210, 211

Children...144, 151, 154, 262

Christianity...8, 197, 327, 328

Cities....107, 109, 122, 127, 134, 138, 141, 150-152, 154-161, 163, 182, 183, 192, 201, 204, 219, 292, 301

Clothing...244, 245, 246

Colors......35, 94, 113, 119, 120, 140, 141, 144, 150, 155, 157, 162, 168, 170, 174-176, 184, 190, 198, 204, 210, 221, 270-272, 278, 281-283

Communication...9, 17, 19, 20, 67, 80, 87, 106, 123, 126, 129-131, 168, 176, 179, 225, 245, 258,

275, 279, 281, 282, 284, 323, 324, 326

Computers..196, 208

Countryside..148, 163, 277

Dance...207

Death...14

Deception...7, 318

Deliverance...81, 84, 87, 88

Desert...125, 145, 163, 279

Distressing Near-Death Experience..80, 84, 88, 97

Education...195, 197, 200, 201, 204, 206, 213

Evidence..296, 297-302

Expanded Awareness...17, 218, 220, 223-226, 229-231, 239

Family. 29, 41, 52, 66, 67, 98, 99, 121-123, 141, 143, 180, 182, 194, 219, 246, 252-256, 259, 260, 275, 326

Fields...................................10, 67, 125, 137, 140, 146, 149, 150, 159, 255, 281, 294

Flying...26, 83, 118, 147, 175, 196, 210, 219, 220, 271, 278

Food...127, 165, 183, 184-186

Forest..75, 136, 147-149, 173, 255, 280, 290

Frequency...227

Future...53

Gender...165

Goals...264

God...12, 68, 70, 72-74, 155

Grass. 45, 102, 112, 113, 115, 116, 124, 130, 136, 138, 140-142, 144, 146, 147, 150, 152, 154, 158, 162, 250, 251, 255, 275, 277, 278, 280-283

Hearing...31, 222

Hell...25, 80-84, 85-87, 89, 94, 170

Homes...189, 190, 198

House of Learning...157, 161, 194, 203, 204-206, 209-211, 212, 213-215

Houses...149, 160, 187, 220

IANDS...11

Intelligent Consciousness...169-171, 172, 173-177, 179

Jesus Christ...4, 12, 48, 68-70, 75-78, 81, 88, 154, 231

Judgment...38, 48, 49, 51, 54, 232

Kindness...56

Knowledge............................36, 126, 131, 133, 203, 213-215, 217, 218, 228-231, 233, 234, 238, 239

Landscapes...138, 139-143, 144, 145, 146, 150, 163, 173, 292, 298

Laughter...204

Levels..98, 99-101, 103, 104, 265-268

Life...112, 142, 283

Life Contracts..53

Life Purpose...54

Life review..............37-40, 42, 44, 46, 48, 53-56, 60, 62-64, 81, 197, 203, 211, 308, 310-313, 327

Light..35, 37, 42, 112

Location...16

Love..54, 74, 294

Mathematics..15, 130, 228, 230, 234

Meadows..138-140, 144, 149, 162, 231, 284

Memory...10, 37, 192, 312

Merging...20, 69, 172, 173, 273, 313, 314, 317

Metaphor...287, 290

Mountains..........................112-114, 136, 143, 144, 146, 158, 162, 194, 255, 283, 292, 296

Music 96, 142, 143, 145, 146, 159, 161, 194, 201, 202, 204-207, 220, 230, 248-251, 266, 273-275, 278

Nature..39, 118, 138, 140, 141

NDERF...11

Oneness..132, 133, 135-137, 172, 173, 315, 316

Out-of-Body Experience..17

Pain..79

Pets..283-285

Piano..209, 251

Plants..39, 112, 138, 141, 142, 162, 174, 175, 185, 194, 270, 271-282

Premortal Spirits...261, 262

Reincarnation..............................63, 64, 307, 308-310, 313-316, 319, 320, 322-328

Repentance...57, 63

Robes..211

Romantic Relationships..257, 261

Schools..151, 154, 210

Senses...18, 173, 176, 222, 235, 237

Sleep...181, 182

Sound 22, 23, 69, 82, 96, 142, 145, 147, 157, 168, 173, 201, 204, 207, 221, 222, 249-251, 264, 271, 273

Space...105, 108, 110, 111, 124, 125-127, 155, 175, 266, 267

Spirit Bodies..165

Spirit Body..108, 165-168, 172-178, 183

Spirit Possession...20, 317

Suicide..83, 89, 90, 91, 92-95, 96, 97, 241

Symbolism..287

Talents..194, 207

Technology..191, 195-199, 201, 208

Telepathy..18, 69, 131, 236, 238

Temples..152

The Church of Jesus Christ of Latter-day Saints..4

Throne of God..153, 155

Time..III, 112, 113, 115-117, 119, 121

Tools..189, 199

Travel..16, 105, 106-109

Tunnel 28, 29-37, 44, 79, 80, 82, 83, 88, 94, 97, 102, 116, 122, 125, 126, 140, 149, 169, 174, 194,
204, 221, 254, 255, 284, 310, 311

Veil..5, 9, 66, 195, 246, 258, 270, 281, 302

Vibration..104, 162, 194, 227, 250, 251, 278, 301

Vision..15, 176

Void..22, 24-26, 28, 88, 170, 279, 310

Water..21, 39, 72, 75, 80, 103, 124, 140-143, 145, 147, 149, 151, 154, 160, 163, 164, 190, 194, 229,
233, 234, 250, 273, 276, 278, 279, 281, 282, 292, 320

Work..191, 192, 193, 195, 196, 205, 209

Writing..195, 216

Made in the USA
Coppell, TX
20 September 2020